REFORMING EUROPEAN WELFARE STATES

Reforming European Welfare States

Germany and the United Kingdom Compared

JOCHEN CLASEN

OXFORD
UNIVERSITY PRESS

OXFORD

UNIVERSITY PRESS

Great Clarendon Street, Oxford OX2 6DP
United Kingdom

Oxford University Press is a department of the University of Oxford.
It furthers the University's objective of excellence in research, scholarship,
and education by publishing worldwide. Oxford is a registered trade mark of
Oxford University Press in the UK and in certain other countries

Published in the United States of America by Oxford University Press
198 Madison Avenue, New York, NY 10016, United States of America

British Library Cataloguing in Publication Data
Data available

Library of Congress Cataloging in Publication Data
Data available

ISBN 978-0-19-927071-2

ACKNOWLEDGEMENTS

There are a number of people I would like to thank for helping me in different ways with the completion of this book. First, there is my family who agreed to move to Germany for a year, thereby allowing me to gather data and to spend a great deal of my time working on the book. Little did they know that after our return to Stirling the ordeal would not quite be over, and in addition, on the condition of a 'big present', Fiona read the entire manuscript for which I am extremely grateful.

Second, I owe major thanks to Jacqueline Davidson for not getting tired of my frequent requests for literature to be sent from Scotland to southern Germany and for her help with the identification of relevant data and preparation of graphics. Daniel Clegg, Jacqueline Davidson, Karl Hinrichs, Sven Jochem, Traute Meyer, Lisa Warth, and Reimut Zohlnhöfer all read and commented expertly on draft chapters. Many others helped with clarifications, locating data and literature, or providing me with texts often in pre-publication stage. They include Jens Alber, Karen Anderson, Andreas Aust, Fran Bennett, Giuliano Bonoli, Milena Büchs, Mary Daly, Carl Emmerson, Martin Evans, Heiner Ganßmann, Irene Gerlach, Jay Ginn, Linda Hantrais, Karl Hinrichs, Tine Pernille Larsen, Stephan Lessenich, Jane Lewis, Ruth Lister, Tony Maltby, Traute Meyer, Jane Millar, Mick Moran, Ursula Münch, Ilona Ostner, Gillian Pascall, Winfried Schmähl, Isabelle Schulze, Martin Seeleib-Kaiser, Nico Siegel, Peter Taylor-Gooby, Alan Walker, and Dorian Woods.

I am grateful to the University of Tübingen, and to Josef Schmid in particular, for inviting me to join the Institute of Political Science for a year, for making me feel extremely welcome, and for providing a congenial working environment. For the same reasons I owe thanks to Christian Steffen, Christian Roth, and Ute Hörrmann. Two *Hauptseminar* courses allowed me to present some of the ideas which influenced the book to students at Tübingen University. Participants at seminars where I presented parts of the project at the universities of Bath, Bremen, Darmstadt, and Tübingen provided useful advice and comments.

I owe thanks to the University of Stirling for allowing me to spend a year on study leave at the University of Tübingen, and to my colleagues in the Department of Applied Social Science for taking over some of my responsibilities during that time. Financial support for leave and the stay at Tübingen was provided by the Carnegie Trust for the Universities of Scotland and the DAAD. Finally, some of the data presented in the book were drawn from two research projects which I conducted jointly with Daniel Clegg (ESRC; R000223983), and with Heiner Ganßmann, Jacqueline Davidson, and Andreas Mauer (Anglo-German Foundation, project 1401, and the Department for Work and Pensions). I would like to thank my colleagues for allowing me to exploit some of our results in this way. Of course, they or anybody else mentioned earlier are in no way responsible for factual errors or interpretations put forward in this book.

JOCHEN CLASEN
University of Stirling
December 2004

CONTENTS

LIST OF FIGURES

LIST OF TABLES

LIST OF APPENDICES

1

Introduction

For more than a quarter of a century now, mature welfare states have been considered to be in crisis. In the wake of the second major post-war economic recession in the early 1980s, European welfare states in particular began to be criticized as having become too large, too expensive, and too bureaucratic. Within a fairly short period of time publicly provided benefits and services were no longer regarded as measures which effectively addressed market failures but were seen rather as impeding economic growth and undermining individual and communal self-reliance. However, cross-national research suggested that even governments vigorously subscribing to such notions found it difficult to scale down and refashion public provision (Pierson 1994). Large welfare states appeared to be resistant to restructuring and retrenchment. This image began to change only in the late 1990s and now European welfare states are considered to be in the midst of rearranging and reconstructing traditional social policy arrangements (Ferrera and Rhodes 2000; Kautto et al. 2001; Taylor-Gooby 2001, 2004; Huber and Stephens 2001).

One of the reasons why the image of welfare state resilience and stability has given way to notions of restructuring might simply be time. The effects of welfare state reform twenty years ago might have become more clearly visible, and measurable, only years or even decades after policy implementation. Another reason might be the research perspective adopted. Cross-national comparisons across mature welfare states tend to rely on expenditure data as the major, or sole, indicator of change. Even if disaggregated by policy domains, trends in social spending indicate stability or growth rather than dynamics or retrenchment (Castles 2004). And yet, underneath the surface of public resources devoted to welfare state programmes, significant restructuring has occurred in many countries. Eligibility and entitlement criteria have been altered, universal or citizenship-based programmes have been replaced or supplemented with means-tested schemes, and the balance between intra- and interpersonal types of redistribution within social insurance, between reciprocity and solidarity, has altered significantly in some countries. In short, employing legal or 'social rights' indicators might suggest more dynamics than spending parameters.

Systematic observations over relatively long periods seem best suited to capture such changes and their effects. Moreover, because actors and institutional structures vary across welfare state programmes, analyses of separate policy domains, such as pension systems, unemployment support, and health care, seem more appropriate than broad comparisons of welfare states per se. However, applying robust indicators and analysing reform processes and outcomes across different welfare state programmes require considerable efforts. This might be one of the reasons why such studies are thin on the ground and tend to cover no more than a few countries. And yet studies which systematically compare and contextualize reform processes are immensely valuable for an empirically grounded identification and causal analysis of contemporary welfare state reform. This has recently been demonstrated in Green-Pedersen's (2002) study of welfare retrenchment in Denmark and the Netherlands in the 1980s and 1990s.

Adopting a similar perspective, this book compares welfare state reforms in the UK and Germany over the past twenty-five years or so. Of course, covering two countries does not allow inferences about European welfare reforms per se, or changes in the diverse social policy landscapes within the twenty-five countries of the European Union (EU). At the same time, British and German welfare state arrangements affect almost a third of the EU population. Moreover, both countries are often portrayed as paradigmatically representing two distinctive models or types of European welfare states, embedded in different national political economies. Characteristic for the UK, at least in the field of monetary transfers, are liberal and residual social programmes with an emphasis on poverty alleviation, largely deregulated and flexible labour markets, and a strong reliance on market coordination. Within the German welfare state, earnings-related social insurance transfers aimed at preserving status or accustomed living standards are dominant, the labour market is much more heavily regulated, and corporatist negotiations and coordination complement market relations (Wood 2001*b*). In the comparative welfare state and labour market literature, from Esping-Andersen's three worlds of welfare capitalism (1990), to Hollingsworth and Boyer's 'social systems of production' (1998), or Hall and Soskice's 'comparative institutional advantages' (2001*a*), the UK and Germany have not only consistently ended up in different typological boxes, but been regarded as paradigmatic representatives of distinct European models.

Within the analysis of contemporary welfare state reform and its political management (e.g. Pierson 2001*a*) the two countries tend to be associated with different paradigms. In accordance with the notion of 'frozen welfare landscapes' (Esping-Andersen 1996*b*), Germany, as the prototypical conservative welfare state, arguably suffers from institutional sclerosis and an inability to change. Rigid employment structures and public welfare provision favour a shrinking core of 'insiders', such as male full-time workers, and are thus widely perceived to be in need of reform. However, pensions or employment policy seem extremely difficult to restructure not least due to a form of governance which favours dispersed vested interests. As a result, German social policy has 'adjusted badly' (Manow and Seils 2000) to a more economically globalized and politically Europeanized context.

By contrast, British social policy over the past twenty-five years is often portrayed as having undergone radical overhaul. Moreover, hitherto criticized on the grounds of fostering distributive injustice and increasing poverty and inequality, more recent changes have attracted considerable attention and been held up within other EU member states as an example of progressive modernization. Once a reticent participant on the EU scene, recent domestic British social policy reform has even positively influenced the EU policy agenda. This is perhaps most evident in employment policy, where a considerable congruence between some (but not all) aspects of the European Employment Strategy and the British New Deal programmes can be identified (Büchs and Friedrich 2005). More broadly, the somewhat vaguely defined 'third way' agenda (White 2001) has played a role in reform debates, particularly in EU member states governed by centre–left parties in the late 1990s. One reason for the apparent new appeal of British social policy is its supposed compatibility with economic internationalization and flexibilization of labour markets and social protection systems, as well as the combination of public safety nets with non-statutory forms of social protection.

While this picture of the current state of German and British social policy certainly needs qualification, the suggestion of diverging policy paths and role reversal during the past twenty years or so seems difficult to dismiss. Back in the 1980s the German welfare state appeared to be part and parcel of a successful societal arrangement, measured by indicators such as economic growth, productivity, unemployment, poverty, inequality, and stable industrial relations. Social spending was incrementally but successfully consolidated (Alber 1998). Compared with its coordinated political economy (Hall and Soskice 2001*a*), British shareholder capitalism based on short-term investment strategies and labour market deregulation (Hutton 1995) seemed economically and socially inferior, provoking industrial conflict and reinforcing problems such as social exclusion and labour market marginalization. Some twenty years later, Germany is facing sluggish economic growth, chronic levels of fiscal deficits, and persistent mass unemployment with apparently little prospect of improvement (Kitschelt and Streek 2003). Once the economic 'locomotive' in Europe, German GDP and per capita dropped to below the average across the EU for the first time in 2003. The recently published second government 'poverty report' indicates that inequality and poverty, and child poverty in particular, have risen markedly under the red–green government (*Der Spiegel*, 29 November 2004). Meanwhile, in the UK a much more favourable economic backdrop since 1993 helped unemployment to decline steadily and new jobs to emerge. Poverty rates and inequality remain high, but trends have been downwards in recent years, with improvements for some groups in particular, such as children and older people (Hills 2004; Brewer et al. 2002). In short, over the past twenty-five years or so the economic and social positions of Germany and the UK within Europe seem to have been reversed. While the appeal of Germany as a role model of welfare capitalism seems to be waning fast, the UK might be on its way to gaining such a position.

In addition to these trends, what makes a comparison between the two countries since the early 1980s intriguing are political parallels. Four legislative periods of conservative governments in the 1980s and 1990s were followed by centre–left administrations from 1997 (UK) and 1998 (Germany). Whereas similar trends in electoral fortunes for social democratic parties during the 1990s proved short-lived in many other European countries, Tony Blair's New Labour and Gerhard Schröder's red–green coalition government were re-elected in 2001 and 2002 respectively and are now nearing the end of their second terms in office. Potentially therefore the two countries represented opportunities for modern social democratic parties to make an imprint on welfare state structures. Moreover, while the magnitude of social, economic, and demographic pressures might have differed in the two countries, there were signs of a broad understanding regarding the overall direction of welfare state reform, as indicated in the much discussed Blair/Schröder paper from 1999—notwithstanding contextual differences for respective 'third way' modernizers in each country (Clasen and Clegg 2004). Even administrative reorganizations and semantics illustrated some remarkable similarities; for example, following their second election victory both governments abolished traditional government ministries for social security, replacing them with ministries for 'Work and Pensions' (DWP) in the UK and 'Work and Economy' in Germany, thereby symbolizing the new path of linking social protection more explicitly to labour market and economic aspects.

Finally, the transformation of the term 'reform', and welfare state reform in particular, indicates a new political readiness for structural change in both countries. As one of its core electoral strategies, the Labour Party portrayed itself as the party of 'welfare reform' and after having won the

1997 general election installed a minister with the same title. Indicating a political risk involved in embarking on far-reaching change, German social policy legislation was only sparingly declared as 'reform'. Nevertheless, after the mid-1990s the 'half-life period' of such reforms shortened markedly and the willingness to restructure the welfare state has recently become a political matter of course. In fact, after decades of mainly technical and incremental change, the current domestic policy agenda is dominated by welfare state reform. Political talk shows devoted to the need for a fundamental overhaul in pensions, health care, labour market, and family policy have become ubiquitous. Politicians from all major parties agree on the need for structural change, putting into question existing arrangements. Even social insurance, hallmark of the German welfare state, appears to have lost much of its appeal and its funding structure is regarded as economically counterproductive because of its impact as a payroll tax, and socially inadequate because of its arguably 'insider-oriented' character. In short, Germany might finally be ready to remodel its welfare state. And yet, some commentators have argued that not only the British but also the German welfare state has already changed 'radically' (Hassel and Williamson 2004). One aim of this book is to investigate this claim empirically.

THE AIMS AND THE STRUCTURE OF THE BOOK

Embedded within the context of comparative welfare state research, and contemporary European welfare state reform in particular, this book analyses the development of British and German social policy since the early 1980s. More precisely, the starting point for the observation is 1979 in the UK and 1982 in Germany, that is, the years in which conservative governments took over political power. The end points are developments in 2003 and 2004, as far as data were available or significant reforms were implemented or decided upon. General questions underlying the analysis include those of convergence and divergence. Have national social policy arrangements become more or less similar over time? Equally, have the contours of social policy reforms changed once centre–left parties took over political power from conservative administrations, and if so in what ways? Is the image of a 'frozen landscape' and policy inertia in Germany empirically justified, and how much structural reform has the UK undergone? More generally, with the help of systematic and contextualized comparison the book aims to explain policy processes and trajectories.

The book is located within the current debate on welfare state retrenchment and restructuring. However, for theoretical and empirical reasons (outlined in Chapter 2 and 3), the analytical perspective is not the welfare state per se but particular policy domains or programmes designed to deal with the same risk or same social contingency. The aim is to identify historically contingent reform paths in the fields of unemployment support, public pensions, and family policy. Of course, other policy domains could have been included. Health care policy is certainly an area which has undergone reform in both countries (Freeman 2000; Wendt 2003) and major parties in Germany are currently contemplating far-reaching changes. Other services, such as education or social work, are relevant components of national welfare states in both countries. However, for reasons of manageability and comparability, programmes were chosen which regulate access to transfers (cash or credits) and rights (e.g. leave entitlements) but not the provision of services (with the exception of child care, which until recently played a relatively minor role in family policy reform; see Chapter 6). Such a restriction limits the range of potentially relevant actors by excluding those engaged in the provision of welfare state services such as medical staff or teachers.

The book does not aim to be all-encompassing, covering German and British welfare states as a whole (however defined), but to analyse processes in core policy domains which have been at the centre of political reform debates and activities for some time. This applies to pensions and unemployment support policy both at national and supra-national level. In the early 1980s unemployment rose steeply in both the UK and Germany, exerting fiscal pressure on public finance with governments arguably failing to offer benefit claimants pathways back into work. Persistent mass unemployment also in other mature welfare states led the OECD (1994) and the EU (European Commission 1997) to emphasize the need for structural social policy reform, promoting 'active' measures of employment integration at the expense of arguably 'passive' benefits (critically, see Sinfield 1993, 1997). Similarly, demographic ageing and the impact of past commitments inherent in large public sector pension programmes have contributed to national and international advocacy in favour of enhancement of non-statutory provision at the expense of the scope of public pensions (Hinrichs 2002).

In short, unemployment support and public pensions are potential prime candidates for investigations into processes of retrenchment, a concept which has dominated comparative analyses of welfare state reform for some time. However, while curbing welfare spending and social entitlements have been prominent themes also in the UK and Germany, subsequent chapters will identify instances of expansion in both policy domains. Moreover, some recent welfare state reforms (such as benefit activation or part-privatization of pensions) are inadequately captured by the notion of retrenchment. Finally, there is a social policy field which, looking back over the entire period under investigation here, has expanded rather than contracted in both countries. Compared to the early 1980s, state support for families has certainly become more generous and government policy more interventionist, bringing about some innovation in line with shifting priorities within government parties in both countries. The inclusion of family policy as a third domain for investigation seemed therefore appropriate as a reminder that contemporary welfare state reform cannot be reduced to retrenchment but involves both expansion and restructuring.

Identifying and assessing the direction and nature of welfare state change are two central aims of the book. Chapter 2 thus elaborates on the ways in which the concepts of retrenchment, expansion, and restructuring have been employed in subsequent empirical chapters. In addition, the chapter introduces the notions of policy direction and policy profile as core 'dependent variables' characterizing variations of welfare state reform. However, the analysis is also concerned with 'explanation and the identification of causal configurations that produce major outcomes of interest' (Mahoney and Rueschemeyer 2003: 11). This, and the aim of engaging in systematic and contextualized comparisons of temporal processes, associates this book with a research tradition that has been defined as 'comparative historical analysis' (Mahoney and Rueschemeyer 2003), even though the time frame here spans merely twenty-five years or so.

Chapter 3 discusses the framework for the causal analysis of reform paths presented in subsequent chapters. It introduces three sets of core explanatory variables: actors and their preferences, contingent or contextual conditions, and institutional frameworks in which actors operate. First, in both countries government parties represent the driving force for reform, albeit not the only one. However, covering a relatively long period of reform processes helps to show that party priorities have altered over time, partly brought about by shifting power relations within governments and also by changes in policy preferences against the backdrop of dynamic contextual conditions. Second, often ignored or neglected in comparative analyses, subsequent chapters show that major contextual changes can have a considerable medium-term impact on policy preferences and policy formation. German reunification is a prime example. Other secular and gradual changes (such as employment patterns), or unexpected short-lived events (such as public scandals) can facilitate or constrain, delay, or add impetus to reform initiatives. Third, three levels of institutional parameters help explain cross-national variations in policy outcomes: formal rules of policy-making, programme-specific characteristics, and the linkages between social policy programmes and other aspects of national political economies. Chapter 3 outlines the relevance of these three institutional aspects.

Chapters 4–6 empirically investigate reform paths in respective policy domains. In order to gain a first glimpse of the magnitude and patterns of change, each chapter begins with a diachronic comparison, contrasting salient programme characteristics as they existed in the late 1970s or early 1980s with current parameters. Equally, using quantitative and qualitative indicators, the scale and type of change for each policy programme is sketched out before reform trajectories are discussed. Changes in political contexts made possible a division of reform paths into three subsections, covering the period before 1990 (i.e. until the German reunification and the stepping down of Margaret Thatcher as Prime Minister, respectively), conservative government rule until 1997 in the UK and 1998 in Germany, and the period under centre–left administrations since then. Appendices A–F provide readers with more detailed information on major pieces of legislation over the entire period under investigation.

Chapter 4 identifies a common general policy direction of retrenchment in unemployment support, although interspersed by instances of selective expansion during the 1980s in Germany. However, distinct national policy profiles can be observed. A significant shift in the balance of principles of distributive justice, encompassing activation and global benefit curtailment, are characteristic for the UK. By contrast, unemployment support in Germany has remained more heterogeneous, albeit characterized by a growing periphery of less protected and a shrinking core of relatively well protected clientele, a process exacerbated by recent structural reform. This chapter illustrates the relevance of programme-specific institutional settings and their link with national political economy structures as important influences on variations of policy paths and profiles.

Chapter 5 identifies processes of retrenchment in public pension programmes in both countries, but also cross-national differences in the scale and profile of retrenchment. Confirming earlier comparative studies (e.g. Myles and Pierson 2001), the analysis points to institutional characteristics (policy legacies) and the relative balance between public and private pensions within respective countries as factors with a strong impact on reform outcomes. Arguments of 'path dependence' seem more easily applicable to pension policy than to either unemployment support or family policy. Programme-specific features provide different opportunities for and suggest different paths of policy reforms. Differences in structure and scope of public pension systems, for example, impact on different degrees of pressure exerted by demographic or labour market developments. Moreover, the chapter shows that reform outcomes can have a strong impact on subsequent rounds of policymaking. A case in point is the impact of reforms in the 1980s on the British pension landscape, contributing significantly to the processes of policy reorientation within the Labour Party in the first half of the 1990s.

Examples of policy self-reinforcement can also be found within family policy. However, in contrast to unemployment or pension provision, pro-gramme-specific policy legacies proved less important, which is not sur-prising both since family policy is less institutionally entrenched and since public provision has expanded over time, partly through innovation.

Chapter 6 discusses variation in the timing and profile of expansion, as well as diverse causal factors. For example, the German Constitutional Court influenced not only the speed and timing of reform but at times also policy profiles. In both countries, institutional aspects were generally less relevant than contextual changes. Altering employment patterns and household structures in particular influenced the dynamics of policy pref-erences within government parties and shifted traditional priorities in favour of employment-oriented family support, in Germany and in the UK, partly superseding more generous transfers targeted at families with children.

Finally, Chapter 7 summarizes answers to questions posed earlier in this chapter; for example, if and to what extent German and British welfare states have diverged or converged since the early 1980s. Tapping into some of the results of the empirical chapters, it emphasizes the three major concerns which guided this book: (*a*) the relevance of investigation reform processes over longer periods of time, (*b*) the need for contextualized comparative analyses, and (*c*) the appropriateness of studying welfare state reform at the programme level.

2

Welfare state reform and restructuring

Three sets of interrelated research interests have been at the centre of an burgeoning body of literature on the comparative analysis of welfare state development. First, what is the nature of change in contemporary welfare states and how can it be captured? Second, what is the magnitude or scope of change and how can it be measured? Finally, what are the causes of welfare state transitions? One point of departure seems fairly uncontested across all three areas of analytical concern. Mature welfare states are faced with more challenges which exert greater pressure for reform than a decade or two ago. As a response, more than incremental change has already been introduced in some countries and across some programmes. Elsewhere, the need for restructuring has become more widely accepted than in the past. Beyond this, however, there is little common ground.

As for the debate on causes for change, structural socio-economic forces, political actors and party competition, the influence of political institutions, policy legacies, and national political economies have been identified as principal influences on welfare state transitions (for recent overviews, see Myles and Quadagno 2002; Amenta 2003). Some authors point to external pressures as major influences for change, such as growing economic interdependence (globalization) or supra-national political developments (e.g. European integration) which arguably undermine the capacity of national economies and limit governments' sovereignty for providing services and transfers at the same scale or in the same fashion as in previous decades. Others emphasize internal transitions, such as changed employment patterns, the decline of industrial and the growth of service sectors, population ageing, and commitments attached to existing welfare state schemes (public pensions in particular). Irrespective of economic globalization these factors represent 'irresistible forces' (Pierson 1998) which simultaneously increase demands on and squeeze resources for the funding of traditional social policy programmes.

For a third set of authors, the debate about the relevance of external versus internal factors pushing welfare state change seems largely irrelevant because it tends to 'partial out' and artificially create competing explanations of what are regarded as parts of a 'phase shift in capitalism from industrial to postindustrial' (Byrne 2003: 204). Analytically such an approach is located at a higher level of abstraction, and thus more interested in analysing common forces affecting welfare states generally rather than comparing and explaining variations of national, or regime-specific, welfare state transitions. This is analogous to different research foci within political economy, that is, concerns over the general nature of transformations of capitalism (e.g. Strange 1997) versus the study of 'varieties' of capitalism and diverse national responses to common challenges (e.g. Scharpf and Schmidt 2000). Authors with a closer interest in social policy formation tend to focus on variations of national reform processes, on processes for and causes of divergence or convergence, and on factors which lead to national or regime-specific reform paths (Esping-Andersen 1996a; Pierson 2001a; Huber and Stephens 2001). For example, within a common general context of curbing welfare state efforts, Seeleib-Kaiser (2001) identified distinct national trajectories of restructuring, or processes of 'divergent convergence'.

However, at times this debate suffers from a lack of specification regarding the area of interest. Broadly defined, the 'welfare state' includes all mechanisms which provide social protection and redistribution, that is, not only transfers and services but also tax expenditures, minimum wages, regulation of labour markets, forms of collective bargaining, and so on, all of which are instruments which 'disconnect or buffer income streams from market outcomes' (Schwartz 2003). More conventionally, the welfare state tends to be more narrowly conceived as the provision of statutory transfers and services, generally leaving aside education. The decision in favour of a wider or a more narrow definition is not merely a matter of perspective but determines the level of analytical abstraction and thus influences whether different theoretical accounts of welfare state change can or cannot be assessed against each other. Dependent on the analytical interest, the welfare states as a whole might be an inappropriate concept for analysing change if individual components (transfer programmes, services) vary strongly in terms of structural design, actor constellations, interdependencies with other policy fields, and embeddedness within national political economies. In short, in order to be able more adequately to capture variation both in terms of policy outcome (Huber and Stephens 2001) as well as processes of reform (e.g. Ferrera and Rhodes 2000), comparative analyses of welfare states might be more instructive if disaggregated into investigations of particular policy domains and the ways in which they develop over time.

As outlined in Chapter 1, this was also one starting point for the analysis of welfare state reform in Germany and the United Kingdom. Another was the assumption that, by observing programme-specific changes over a relatively long period of time, the relevance of multicausal explanations will become obvious for an understanding of reform trajectories. Rather than searching for a limited set of causal mechanisms or even proposing a single 'key independent variable' (Siegel 2003), subsequent chapters aim to show that it is the interaction of several factors which drive the direction and shape of welfare reform. Analytically, three types of influences might be distinguished: (*a*) actors and the dynamics of their relative power positions, interests, and preferences; (*b*) three sets of institutional settings within which actors operate; and (*c*) contingencies and changes in contextual conditions. Often the latter tend to be neglected and yet can leave a strong imprint on the timing of policy implementation and, at times, on policy design. The analytical framework above will be outlined in more detail in Chapter 3. This chapter meanwhile concentrates on two aspects which relate to the 'dependent' rather than the 'independent' variable of comparative welfare state analysis: how to characterize the nature of reforms, and how to measure their scale and scope.

2.1 RETRENCHMENT AND RESTRUCTURING

Recently, Sainsbury (2001: 264) emphasized the need for a 'clearer specification of the concepts of retrenchment and restructuring since they often form the dependent variable of our analysis'. Indeed, much contemporary welfare state research rests on the assumption that, if not dismantling, governments in mature welfare states are primarily driven by the motive of welfare retrenchment, that is, cutting back social spending, reining in entitlements, and making benefits less generous. With justification, Hinrichs and Kangas (2003) have identified Pierson (1994) as the initiator of this 'retrenchment business' in welfare state analysis: cross-national investigations into the causes for and the political management of scaling back welfare state programmes. In contrast to distributing gains during the era of expansion, over the past two decades politicians have largely been engaged in 'imposing losses'. A variety of strategies have thus been adopted in order to reduce the risk of political backlash in the face of unpopular cuts in welfare programmes (see Bonoli 2000 for pension policy). By implication, since the direction of policy has changed, previous theoretical propositions aimed at explaining welfare state expansion (see van Kersbergen 1995: ch. 2) would no longer be suitable for explaining retrenchment within what are regarded as the 'new politics of the welfare state' (Pierson 1996, 2001*a*).

Neither the suggestion of an exhaustion of traditional theoretical propositions nor the articulation of 'new' politics of the welfare state has remained uncontested (Korpi and Palme 2003; Scarborough 2000; Ross 2000*a*). Moreover, 'retrenchment' as the central concept of contemporary welfare reform has also been criticized (e.g. Palier 2002). Indeed, not only does the term ignore instances of welfare state expansion (see below), other types of transitions across mature welfare states and within different social policy programmes can only be partially or even inappropriately character- ized as retrenchment. Also, the theoretical interest in ways in which decision makers are able to 'avoid blame' (Weaver 1986) for cutbacks has rarely been matched by reflections as to how to empirically measure retrenchment within or across welfare state programmes (Alber 1996).

While much of the current welfare state agenda might be regarded as informed by motives of retrenchment, alternative or complementary con- cepts seem necessary in order more adequately to capture the nature of some major forms of welfare state transitions. Pierson (2001*b*: 419) himself has pointed out that many contemporary reforms are multidimensional in character, with some policies aimed at 're-commodification', that is, 'dis- mantling those aspects of the welfare state that shelter workers from market pressures' (Pierson 2001*b*: 422), others at 'cost-containment', and others still at 'recalibration'. The latter concept has been disaggregated into 'rationalization' and 'updating' (i.e. responding to 'changing societal de- mands and norms'). Arguably, some concepts are more suitable for par- ticular social policy domains than for others. For example, Pierson (2001*b*) suggests that reforms in labour market policy have largely been aimed at both 're-commodification' and 'recalibration', that is, making social policy programmes 'more consistent with contemporary goals and demands for social provision' (ibid.: 425). By contrast, much of pension policy has arguably been driven by motives of cost-containment. What is more, the salience of the different types of transitions within the configuration of reform tend to vary across welfare regimes, with 're-commodification' as a dominant factor in liberal welfare states and 'recalibration' and 'cost- containment' as the more relevant driving forces in continental European welfare states.

The attempt to capture what contemporary welfare state restructuring involves in a more multidimensional fashion seems more appropriate than a reliance on a single indicator which tends to imply changes along a con- tinuum of more or less cutback or expansion. However, a greater degree of complexity creates the problem of delineating clearly between different dimensions of reform. As Pierson (2001*b*: 425) acknowledges, empirically it can be difficult to distinguish between 'recalibration' and 'simple cutbacks'. More theoretically, the ways in which dimensions of reforms relate to each other is difficult to envisage (Sainsbury 2001: 260), while particular con- cepts have been criticized as ambiguous in their consequence. This applies to 're-commodification' in particular, which presupposes 'commodification' and 'de-commodification' in the first place and thereby ignores gender differences. It also neglects historical examples of the active role played by social policies in the creation of barriers for commodification for some social groups (Knijn and Ostner 2002). Some authors have therefore employed concepts such as 'de-familialization' (McLaughlin and Glendinning 1994) or 'individualization' (Ostner 2003) as alternative or complementary dimensions for assessing welfare state transitions. More broadly, Lewis (2002) advocates a 'gender-centred approach' to welfare state change with a focus on the modification of the relationship between work and welfare across different countries and its implications for women.

To some extent the above concepts are not mutually exclusive but represent different analytical perspectives. Some analyses are interested in capturing the essence of policy processes, others in policy outputs or the nature and impact of change. Some are driven by normative concerns either at the level of policy instruments (e.g. distinguishing between positive and negative forms of benefit activation) or of policy outcomes, which can often be ambivalent. For example, Leitner et al. (2004) illustrate that a single type of policy change (e.g. new entitlements for child care leave) can imply re-commodification (and de-familialization; i.e. weakening the dependence on intra-family transfers) for some social groups but re-familialization for others. Nevertheless, the debate on capturing the nature of welfare state restructuring seems to be at the risk of conceptual overload. Recently Powell (2004) thus suggested 'residualization' as an overarching and parsimonious concept for capturing the outcome of major reform trends across countries. However, any approach that aims at reducing the multifaceted reality of welfare state changes to one dominant concept of change pays a high price: it runs the risk of oversimplifying patterns and contents of change.

This also applies to the concept of retrenchment, which has been employed here (see below), but not as a sole indicator of change. In all of the three policy domains covered in this book, many reforms introduced can be regarded as retrenchment and yet, on its own, retrenchment seems to be an unduly narrow concept. As subsequent chapters will show, there have been instances where the level of transfers for unemployed groups, retired people, or families were either cut or nominal values left unaltered, implying a loss in benefits' purchasing power. Similarly, shortening entitlement periods or increasing the retirement age for pension eligibility might be seen as straightforward examples of retrenchment. However, contemporary welfare reforms have generally been more complex. In the field of family policy, for example, the overall direction of public provision in both countries since the 1980s was expansion rather than contraction. In the other two fields, some reform packages included retrenchment for some groups, but expansion for others. Some cuts for state provision were mitigated or even compensated by simultaneous improvements of tax breaks. Moreover, the overall impact and incidence of a policy change is sometimes difficult to assess as a clear-cut case of retrenchment, particularly if long-term horizons are involved, as in pensions policy.

Finally, much of contemporary welfare state reform is about changes in the balance and the introduction of new forms of conditionality (Clasen et al. 2001; Clegg and Clasen 2003). Public support for unemployed people is a good case in point. To a differing degree, the receipt of unemployment benefits has always been linked to conditions aimed at fostering the return to paid work, such as work tests, job search requirements, fulfilling suitability and mobility criteria regarding prospective employment or the participation in labour market programmes. There is ample evidence that these conditionality criteria have become stricter since the early 1990s within a process which has become widely known as 'activation' (e.g. Gilbert and van Voorhis 2001). For some commentators this trend has marked a qualitative shift from welfare to 'workfare' (Lødemel and Trickey 2001), and thus may be considered as a form of retrenchment of social rights. And yet, activation programmes are generally more expensive than simply paying out benefits, rendering public expenditure as a parameter for retrenchment meaningless. Furthermore, from a perspective of policy outcomes, and depending on individual circumstances and possible wider impacts on employment levels, activation policies might include labour market training which increases skills and thus the probability of a return to paid and sustained employment. Given that the latter is the ultimate aim of unemployment support, it seems difficult to equate activation per se with welfare retrenchment. Instead, activation epitomizes a type of reform which could be more generally characterized as restructuring. From a perspective of policy outcomes, it might also be a form of retrenchment, but this would require empirical research and evaluation.

As subsequent chapters demonstrate, even in conceptually more easily discernible cases, relying on retrenchment as a single parameter of welfare state change would imply losing track of examples of restructuring which potentially alter the 'architecture' (Hinrichs and Kangas 2003) of traditional social policy arrangements in significant ways. In short, subsequent chapters aim to capture two dimensions of welfare state reform: retrenchment and restructuring. Moreover, these concepts have been employed in order to be able to assess shifts in both 'policy direction' and 'policy profiles'. Before outlining these core concepts in more detail later, the next section discusses the problem of operationalizing retrenchment and restructuring.

2.2 PARAMETERS OF CHANGE: SOCIAL SPENDING AND SOCIAL RIGHTS

Representing a relevant but incomplete dimension of contemporary social policy reform, the concept of retrenchment epitomizes yet another difficulty for emprical comparative welfare state analysis. Basically, as long as there is no common yardstick, even sophisticated analyses tend to 'talk past each other', methodological improvements remain meaningless, and theoretical propositions are not rigorously contestable (Alber 1996; Siegel 2003). In short, the problem of finding an appropriate concept for retrenchment, as a dependent variable, is linked to the question of identifying appropriate parameters for its operationalization and measurement (Green-Pedersen 2004).

One classic indicator for measuring change is social expenditure, which continues to figure prominently within analyses of the contemporary welfare state generally and is increasingly also used in studies of programme-specific changes (Castles 2002, 2004). Increasingly sophisticated techniques of statistical analyses have been applied (e.g. Kittel and Obinger 2003) and attempts have been made to control for demographic changes and variations in claimant numbers, thus allowing for comparisons of 'standardized' or 'adjusted' social expenditure (Siegel 2002). Yet, problems remain. For example, the extent to which people who are not in employment are able to make claims against unemployment compensation or other (functionally equivalent) transfer programmes varies considerably across countries (Ganßmann 2000; Clasen et al. 2004). Rather than differences in the generosity of unemployment support, cross-national variations might thus simply reflect differences in programme design. Thus, even though needs-adjusted expenditure can avoid some of the classical misinterpretation of social expenditure, namely to take welfare state efforts as measures of welfare state generosity, it only partly bridges the gap between social expenditure and other, social rights–based, indicators.

Another reason is that social spending data on its own is unlikely to capture programmatic readjustments, even at the most disaggregated level of analysis. For example, with a few exceptions (Ireland and the Netherlands), aggregate data suggest that national levels of social expenditure moderately increased rather than decreased in mature welfare states between 1980 and the late 1990s. By contrast, programme-specific expenditure patterns reveal a considerable scope of internal 'structural transformation' (Castles 2002: 626). For example, the British social policy landscape seems to have undergone more change than anywhere in the EU. By contrast, Germany is often placed at the opposing end of the spectrum, displaying the apparently lowest degree of structural transformation. And yet, subsequent chapters will confirm earlier studies which have identified a considerable degree of change and restructuring even in the arguably sluggish countries of continental Europe (Palier 2000; Leitner and Lessenich 2003; Bleses and Seeleib-Kaiser 2004). Thus, if analyses of aggregate spending indicate no observable systematic retrenchment, this does not mean that either social rights or institutions remain unchanged. It was precisely in order to emphasize welfare state dynamics beyond the surface of volume changes that terms such as 'restructuring' or 'recasting' (Pierson 2001*b*; Ferrera and Rhodes 2000) have been employed. In short, the 'dependent variable problem' (Green-Pedersen 2004) cannot be solved by improved techniques of quantitative (or qualitative) analysis.

Siegel (2003) has recently suggested combining different research strategies and levels of analysis for 'poly-centred' perspectives on welfare state change. 'Bird's-eye' macro-analyses (e.g. total welfare expenditure) could be used for some basic descriptive and analytical purposes, he argues, and combined with 'worm's eye' analysis 'lower down the ladder of abstraction', for example, with programme-specific, case-oriented analyses which are able to 'accumulate substantial knowledge about the political logic of welfare state change' (Siegel 2003: 31). In some respects, the approach adopted here has attempted to follow this suggestion. Far from discarding social expenditure from the analysis, attempts have been made to gather spending data disaggregated at programme or even benefit level, and to take account of changes in claimant numbers as one indicator. However, in addition, social rights indicators (defining conditions of eligibility and entitlement) and other forms of restructuring have been employed to assess the level of transformation. In some respects, this aspect is similar to the one employed by a recent study on welfare state change in the Netherlands and Denmark (Green-Pedersen 2002), which employed 'retrenchment' as the central concept, defined as 'making a scheme less attractive to the (potential) claimants' (Green-Pedersen 2002: 58). 'Attractiveness' refers to 'quality' of benefits, indicated by the value of a benefit received, its duration, and attached eligibility criteria. Changes in these parameters have been translated into potential budgetary savings, thus allowing measurements along a continuum of 'more' or 'less' retrenchment inflicted.

This study on Germany and the UK also employs retrenchment. However, the concept is operationalized somewhat differently (see below) and is complemented by restructuring as a second dimension. The reason is that the analysis is concerned with both policy change along a continuum as well as identifying different patterns or profiles of change, both across countries and across social protection programmes. In other words, intent on capturing both policy direction and policy profile, Chapters 4–6 ask not only about the direction of reform (retrenchment or expansion) but also investigate variations and patterns of restructuring.

2.3 WELFARE REFORM: CAPTURING CHANGE IN POLICY DIRECTION AND POLICY PROFILE

Most welfare state analyses in recent times have been interested in changes in policy direction. Typically, the mid-1970s or early 1980s have been identified as 'turning points' for the development of welfare states as a whole, with the economic and labour market impacts of steep increases in the oil price as significant factors contributing to governments switching from expansion towards cutbacks. Other time periods have been identified for changes in the direction of policy development in particular programmes. What these studies have in common is a particular focus on change, that is, from expansion towards scaling back. For example, Bleses and Seeleib-Kaiser (2004) identify a turning point after which earlier policies of 'de-commodification' came to a halt in the former West Germany. Influenced by structural macro-economic changes (globalization), after the mid-1970s, relevant actors adopted a 'new interpretative pattern' of constraints and incentives and pursued policies of 're-commodification' instead (for other 'social constructivist' explanations of welfare state change, see Cox 2001; Schmidt 2002; and, critically, Lessenich 1999). Heinelt and Weck (1998) locate a transition from 'labour demand' to 'labour supply' strategies within German labour market policy in the first half of the 1990s. The change of direction is explained with reference to Sabatier's (1993) notion of 'core beliefs' and the relative strengths of 'advocacy coalitions' within and across relevant political parties.

These studies rely on careful programme-specific empirical investigations over relatively long time periods, thereby proving instructive for the analysis pursued here. However, there are two caveats. First, as subsequent chapters will show, within the general direction of retrenchment there have been instances of expansion, not only with respect to particular policy domains as a whole (e.g. family policy) but also within otherwise contracting fields, such as unemployment support and pension provision. In fact, as recent analyses have emphasized, the focus on retrenchment has somewhat ignored the emergence of 'new social risks' (Bonoli 2005) within mature welfare states and the ways in which governments have responded with extended rather than diminished levels of public provision. Problems such as reconciling employment with care responsibilities, long-term unemployment, or the exclusion from mainstream forms of social protection have led some governments to expand schemes such as parental benefit and leave programmes, child care, and innovative labour market programmes. Systematic cross-national empirical and theoretical investigations into causes for policy formation in these fields have only just begun (Taylor-Gooby 2004; Armingeon and Bonoli 2005).

Second, for comparative analyses of welfare state reform, investigations into changes of policy direction, tend to lose sight of patterns of restructuring. Two countries might have started scaling back social spending of a particular programme around the same time. In order to compare and assess the significance of this, however, more information would be needed both about the magnitude of restrictions imposed as well as about the particular pattern of retrenchment. The latter might consist of lowering benefit rates, alterations of eligibility conditions or entitlement criteria, the introduction or the tightening of a means-test, new configurations of benefit and tax benefits, and so on. In addition, the incidence of change might differ across countries. Restrictions might apply universally across a social category (unemployed, pensioners, parents) or affect only particular groups. Finally, there might be different patterns of restructuring across different policy domains within the same country. In short, apart from similarities and differences in policy direction (retrenchment/expansion), the identification of and explanations for particular national or programme-specific profiles (or patterns) of change seem highly relevant for comparative analyses.

Subsequent chapters aim to identify both changes in policy direction and national policy profiles (see Table 2.1). In order to assess the magnitude of retrenchment (or expansion) over time, volume indicators such as programme-specific expenditure, beneficiary rates, as well as legislative changes in social rights will be considered. The latter affect access, level, or the duration of benefit receipts. Both spending and social rights data can usually be expressed in quantitative terms. By comparison, instances of restructuring are less easily quantifiable (e.g. Goul Andersen 2002)—and not independent from retrenchment either—and yet highly significant. For example, the introduction of pension credits in return for looking after young children at home and the partial privatization of retirement provision represented social policy innovation in Germany. Within a common context of expansion of family policy during the 1990s, the respective profiles of expansion were different in the two countries; the social incidence of retrenchment in unemployment support during the 1980s were highly distinctive (see Chapter 4).

Table 2.1. Indicators of welfare reform

Policy direction	Retrenchment/expansion (scale, scope, pace)	More quantitative	Social spending Social rights (benefit value, eligibility, entitlement)
Policy profile	Restructuring	More qualitative	Examples • incidence of retrenchment • shift in public/private mix • activation • innovation • shifts in conditionality mix (need, reciprocity, universalism)

Changes in the conditionality attached to state support can represent other types of restructuring. An important aspect of conditionality refers to distributive principles upon which transfers and services are based. The distinction between means-tested, insurance-based, and universal provision is one that has been used widely (e.g. Atkinson 1989; Barr 1998; Rainwater et al. 1986). With respect to insurance-based benefits, the distinction between variants drawing on different degrees of the same principle (reciprocity) is captured ideal-typically in the contrast between 'Bismarckian' and 'Beveredgian' social insurance (e.g. Clasen and van Oorschot 2002). Both are social insurance types, but quite different in character. The insurance (reciprocity) notion tends to be weak in Beveridgean schemes (low contributory entry requirements, modest flat-rate or capped benefits, prominent role of crediting) and strong in Bismarckian schemes (tight link between contributions and benefits, earnings-related transfers, low level of crediting). Adjusting levers of conditionality, that is, contribution requirements, benefit formulae, degree of crediting, and so on, alters the character of a particular social insurance programme, making it more Beveridgean or Bismarckian, or more or less encompassing (Korpi and Palme 2003). But also means-tested benefits allow for a considerable adjustment of conditionality, because of differences in type (individual, partners, households, family), extent (narrow or wide definition of family obligation, types of income and wealth), and intensity (level of income and wealth disregarded, level of marginal tax applied).

Restructuring in terms of alterations in the mode of conditionality across and within welfare state programmes may involve a reconfiguration of traditional principles (need, reciprocity, citizenship), or the introduction of additional conditions, such as work-related activation elements.

Unemployment support in the UK is a good case in point. As discussed in Chapter 4, since the late 1970s there has been a considerable erosion of (reciprocity-based) social insurance and a growth of needs-based support, accompanied by the introduction of activation policies for working-age benefit claimants. Clearly, expressing such forms of restructuring in quantitative terms is problematic. How much of a transition from insurance-based to means-tested provision is required before a change becomes structural rather than incremental? There is no a priori answer to this. And yet, means-tested benefits confer a different type of social right than either contributory or universal benefits and over a longer time frame a shift from a system based largely on a social insurance principle towards one which is almost exclusively means-tested signifies structural change, even if benefit levels are left unaltered (Evans 1998: 286). In short, observing programme characteristics over a period of more than twenty years helps to identify the structural impact that particular forms of retrenchment have in the long run.

2.4 CONCLUSION

The purpose of this chapter was to locate following chapters within the current debate of welfare state reform and restructuring in Europe. Dominant since the early 1990s, the notion of retrenchment, that is, of cutting back social provision, has recently been complemented by several other concepts which are arguably able to (better) capture the nature of change within mature welfare states. However, these concepts have rarely been sufficiently conceptualized or operationalized in order to be employed in systematic empirical analyses. Subsequent chapters on developments in three welfare state domains employ retrenchment (and expansion) as one dimension of change which allows assessments of the respective scale and speed with regard to policy direction. In addition, aimed at identifying national or programme-specific patterns and manifestations of change, observations over a relatively long time period have been made so that not only the policy direction but also policy profiles can be assessed as a second dimension of transition in mature European welfare states. However, before embarking on this empirical journey, the next chapter will present the analytical framework which has informed the interpretation and explanation of both types of change.

3

Motives, means, and opportunities: analytical perspectives

Rather than welfare states as a whole, this book investigates reform processes between and across specific social policy domains. Different policy programmes involve different sets of actors within the same country. Equally, institutional contexts vary within the same welfare state domain across countries. At the same time, programme-specific policymaking is not independent from contextual changes, exerting pressures, presenting constraints, or facilitating opportunities for change, as well as influencing processes of policy reorientation. In short, the analytical perspective aims to take account of programme-specific institutional contexts within which specific sets of actors operate who are, in turn, exposed to political, economic, and social dynamics. As subsequent chapters illustrate, often a particular alignment of actors' preferences (*motives*), institutional capacities at their disposal (*means*), and contextual conditions (*opportunities*) impinges on the timing, but also the type and scope, of policy change (see also Clasen 2000).

There is a resemblance between this approach and Kingdon's (1995) notion of 'process streams', according to which only a particular constellation of problems (which need to be recognized as policy relevant), policy proposals (which need to be technically and politically feasible), and politics (e.g. change of government or of key policy participants) provides 'policy windows' for substantial policy change. However, the three components of the analytical framework discussed later differ from Kingdon's concept of process streams and are not regarded as independent from each other. On the contrary, political preferences, for example, are shaped by institutional settings and changes in economic conditions impinge on political struggles and party policy reorientation. This can make the interrogation of policy developments difficult and the explanation of welfare state reform often tricky. Before the empirical investigation of social policy trajectories (Chapters 4–6), it seems sensible therefore to introduce the three sets of influences in analytically separate sections.

3.1 ACTORS AND PREFERENCES

One of the intriguing facets of comparing welfare state development in the UK and Germany over the past twenty-five years or so are parallel trends in political power. In both countries conservative parties won four successive general elections with long reigns of individual prime ministers, namely, Margaret Thatcher (1979–90), followed by John Major (1990–97) in the UK and Helmut Kohl who remained German Chancellor during the entire period of Christian Democratic Union/Christian Social Union (CDU/CSU) dominated governments between 1982 and 1998. In 1997 under Tony Blair and 1998 under Gerhard Schröder respectively, social demo-cratic parties took over which, at the time of writing, were nearing the end of their second terms of power. Potentially long periods in office should have allowed ruling conservative parties to leave a strong imprint on the respective landscapes of welfare state provision. Moreover, similar policy directions could have been expected. Albeit different in actual policy formation and ideological fervour, conservative governments in both countries started off with similarly strong pro-market stances and critical notions towards existing welfare state structures which were portrayed as having become too large, too bureaucratic, and as undermining self-reliance and feeding attitudes of dependency. Helmut Kohl's plea that a 'U-turn' in public policy was needed and his call for a return to an incentive-oriented policy (*Leistung muss sich wieder lohnen*) was not so far from conservative governments' discourses on the adverse economic and moral consequences of welfare programmes in the UK. Beneath similarities in rhetoric however, the ideological commitment towards a neo-liberal macro-economic policy was much stronger within the British government, which can largely be attributed to differences in the make-up of the two conservative parties.

Before entering political power in 1979 the British Conservative Party was without clearly formulated social policy aims but had specific economic objectives, most of all tackling inflation while disregarding unemployment and reducing the level of government spending. Deakin (1994: 84) pointed out that these economic goals were 'themselves only means to still broader ends: and those ends were essentially political', such as reducing the level of public ownership, ending any collaboration between the government and social partners, and excluding the trade unions from any influence on political power in particular. The role of other political actors, such as local authorities, was heavily circumscribed in an attempt to locate the centre of decision making more firmly in Westminster, residing with the Prime Minister, the Chancellor of the Exchequer, and a small circle of like-minded ministers in particular.

The existing level of public expenditure was seen as a major barrier to stimulating private economic initiative and overcoming the traditional 'stop–go' macro-economic course. Lower levels of direct taxation and public borrowing were regarded as essential requirements for a more steady and sustainable economic framework (Hills 1998). As the principal driver of this policy, the Treasury gained considerable political weight during the 1980s and beyond. Once critical ministers had been removed (or resigned) from the Cabinet, typical patterns of social policy formation included spending departments aiming to lower the size of cuts demanded by the Treasury. Occasionally these conflicts affected not only the scale but also the profile of policy change.

The ideological framework of breaking the influence of vested interests (trade unions in particular), restoring the power of the central state, and creating a 'free economy' (Gamble 1988) became manifest in many policy areas, such as privatization of nationalized industries or changes in taxation which favoured the better off (decreases in marginal income tax rates, increases in indirect taxation, and more extensive tax breaks for homeowners and employees in receipt of company-based benefits). The 'informal welfare state' (Rhodes 2001), that is, employment relations, trade union legislation, and labour market regulation, were subjected to significant forms of restrictions, manifested in a deregulated labour market and a significant decline of employment protection by the mid-1990s (Graham 1997). By comparison, apart from selling off council housing and the introduction of 'quasi markets' in health and social care (Le Grand and Bartlett 1993), the structure and scale of the 'formal welfare state' was less affected by policy change than government rhetoric might have suggested (e.g. Taylor-Gooby 1996, 1989). For example, social spending levels in 1995 were substantially higher than in 1980, even if adjusted by demographic change and variations in unemployment (Siegel 2002). However, over time some apparently incremental reforms brought about significant alterations in the British social policy landscape (see Chapters 4–6). In short, driven by the centre (Prime Minister, Treasury) the preference for social policy retrenchment was dominant within British Conservative governments of the 1980s and 1990s. The influence of other actors, such as critical Cabinet members or trade unions, or lobby groups, was marginal and diminished further. Moreover, during the 1980s there was little need to adjust policy priorities because of solid majorities in the House of Commons (see below) and opposition parties weakened by internal conflicts (Deakin 1994). Some of the reasons why actual change trailed policy priorities will be discussed shortly.

The situation for the CDU/CSU in the early 1980s was similar in some respects, but different in many others. As in the UK, cost-containment was high on the agenda. The fact that the growth of social spending had overtaken economic growth was regarded as potentially undermining both economic and social stability (Schmidt 1998*a*: 102). Unlike the Thatcher government, the CDU/CSU was primarily interested in financial consolidation rather than restructuring traditional welfare state arrangements, the reason being differences in patterns of party support and ideological backgrounds (Schmid 1990). A more heterogeneous social base, including a strong working class representation, has contributed to a perennially ambiguous position on social policy, with the party torn between Catholic social theory and conservative trade unionism on the one hand, and market liberalism on the other (Michalsky 1985). Concerned about social insurance contributions and the extent of employment protection, during fiscal crises the party's 'economic wing' would join employer organizations and the junior government partner, the Free Democratic Party (FDP), eager to advocate cutting back public spending in order to lower the cost of labour. However, a major architect of the post-war West German social policy structure, during the 'golden age' between the 1950s and early 1970s, the CDU/CSU outbid the Social Democratic Party (SPD) in the scale of proposed welfare expansion. In the 1980s and early 1990s the party's 'social policy wing' remained the agenda setter in social legislation (Zohlnhöfer 2001). Informally, and at times formally, its policy preferences were supported by the SPD which also favoured incremental adjustments and overall preservation of traditional structures and social insurance in particular.

Compared with its British conservative counterpart, the stronger 'workerist' tradition within the CDU/CSU can be exemplified with reference to Norbert Blüm (CDU) who remained both the Minister of Labour and Social Affairs and a trade union member during all four Kohl governments. An example of the informal consensus on matters of social policy across the major parties is the fact that a member of the SPD was promoted to Permanent Secretary within Blüm's ministry in 1988, and remained in this position (as the only social-democratic Permanent Secretary) during the remaining period of conservative–liberal governments (Schmidt 1998: 78). Hence, instead of the CDU/CSU, ideologically the market–liberal FDP was closer to British Conservative governments of the 1980s and 1990s. Holding between 5 per cent and 10 per cent of the popular vote the FDP traditionally played the role of 'kingmaker' until the late 1990s, exerting considerable influence on policy formation. However, the FDP's preference for more targeted public and greater scope for private provision in social policy was relatively easily sidelined, at least until the mid-1990s, by the government's 'social policy' wing.

As for corporatist actors, institutional arrangements (see below) and tightly earnings-related and thus 'wage replacement' benefits provide a strong incentive for German trade unions to be involved in social insurance and to defend traditional features (Clasen 2001). In the 1980s and most of the 1990s, even employer organizations, particularly those representing large business, supported the basic framework of German social insurance over cheaper, more market-based, but potentially more conflict provoking alternatives of social protection (Nissen 1988; Mares 2003). In short, despite a more adversarial socio-economic context since the mid-1970s, a fairly solid broad preference in favour of incremental adjustment or 'smooth consolidation' (Offe 1991) prevailed over occasional suggestions for far-reaching reform.

Precipitated by economic and other reasons, by the mid-1990s this broad consensus eroded and was succeeded by disagreement both across and within the two major parties over the direction of social policy reform (e.g. Leisering 2000). Within a much more conflict-ridden atmosphere, a common diagnosis of problems prevailed regarding the arguably detrimental effects of social insurance contribution rates (payroll taxes), increasing the cost of labour, and thus perceived to be threatening the economic competitiveness of German companies. Beyond this, however, very little cross-party agreement remained. In the mid-1990s the 'social policy' wing within the CDU/CSU began to lose its position as agenda setter. By contrast, the business wing within the CDU/CSU, strongly supported by employer organizations and the FDP (Jochem 2001), gained political clout. Advocating deeper cuts and structural reform in social provision, more severe retrenchment was duly implemented, and more planned, during the second half of the 1990s. Partly out of electoral expediency, the SPD objected to and repealed some of the cuts after the general election in 1998. However, initially pursuing classic redistributive social policy reforms, the red–green coalition subsequently engineered a policy U-turn and introduced cuts and also some structural changes (Gohr and Seeleib-Kaiser 2003; Egle et al. 2003). This path is evidence of both electoral politics and internal conflicts within the SPD (and within the Green Party, its junior partner in government) over the direction of social policy. Basically, a shrinking trade union oriented faction in favour of preserving traditional social policy structures was faced by a 'modernizing' faction which was more open to breaking new ground, including the partial transfer of social risk management to non-statutory sources. There is ample evidence that the 'modernizers', led by Chancellor Schröder and the party leadership, have gained ground in recent years. However, internal party controversies have characterized both legislative periods (Gohr 2003; Egle and Ostheim 2003).

That no particular policy preference can be identified as dominant within the government's social policy agenda can partly be attributed to the SPD's failure to engage in a process of systematic programmatic renewal during its time in opposition (Busch and Manow 2001; Gohr 2001). In fact, conflicts between 'modernizers' and 'traditionalists' flared up in earnest only after the general election in 1998. By contrast, debates over new social policy priorities within the Labour Party had begun after its unexpected defeat in the general election in 1992, so that policy reorientation had been completed before, or in some areas fairly shortly after, gaining political power in 1997. Following a Cabinet reshuffle in July 1998, New Labour's broad social policy orientations were uncontested, as was the Treasury as the main driver of the reform agenda. There is ample literature on the causes of Labour's policy reorientation, its adoption of some of the Conservative Party's policy menu, and its pursuit of what has been called 'third way' policies, especially in the area of social policy (see Hay 1999; Powell 1999; Rhodes 2000; White 2001; Lewis and Surender 2004). Subsequent chapters will discuss some of these aspects in specific policy sectors. For the moment, suffice to say that Labour's adoption of a more market-based, cost-containment oriented, employment centred, and means-tested (targeted) social protection regime marks a significant break of policy priorities compared with party positions prior to the 1992 election. As a consequence, British social policy reform since the late 1990s has been guided by a set of motives and preferences considerably more coherent and consistent than in Germany. This does not imply that legislation has always created sustainable structures (see Chapter 5 on pensions, for example). However, with a Labour Party broadly endorsing the political economy structures created by its predecessor, and having adopted many previous Conservative Party positions on social policy, a new 'liberal consensus' (Taylor-Gooby 2001) has emerged in the UK supporting a fairly stable policy course. The opposite trend can be observed in Germany, where the programmatic distance between the two major German parties was fairly narrow until the early 1990s but has widened since, making the formation of policy preferences more dynamic and the direction of social policy formation more volatile and less predictable.

3.2. EMBEDDING WELFARE STATE REFORM: THREE SETS OF INSTITUTIONAL INFLUENCES

Institutions provide collective actors with capacities to formulate and implement policy. At the same time institutions influence policymaking both directly in terms of presenting formal 'rules of the game' for policymaking processes (Immergut 1992), and indirectly and less tangibly by affecting the formation of normative orientations (Thelen and Steinmo 1992). Analytically, three sets of institutional settings can be assumed to have impinged on welfare state reforms: formal policymaking structures, programme-specific institutional settings, and linkages between social policy programmes and national political economies.

3.2.1 Formal policymaking structures

Party competition and governing parties are faced with very different frameworks for policymaking in the two countries. Put simply, the Westminster system bestows strong central control and provides very little formal obstacles for ruling parties. The first-past-the-post electoral system produces single-party governments which, depending on the majority in the House of Commons, enjoy a strong policymaking position due to the principle of parliamentary sovereignty. The influence of local authorities has traditionally been weak and was further curtailed under four consecutive Conservative governments. The creation of an independent monetary policy committee within the Bank of England in charge of setting interest rates, as well as devolution of some political power to Scotland and Wales, has decentralized policymaking in some fields. However, crucial policy domains such as economic policy, taxation, and social security have remained firmly in the hands of central government. In short, political power in the UK is firmly located at the centre, providing ruling parties with considerable scope for introducing more than incremental change, with the proviso that, by implication, options for deflecting blame are more limited than elsewhere, with the government being held accountable for the success or failure of policy outcomes.

In contrast, the influence of political institutions is such that the German state has been characterized as 'semi-sovereign' (Katzenstein 1987). Indeed, a multitude of 'co-governing forces and veto players' (Schmidt 2003: 41) can potentially steer the process of government policy to a considerable extent. Proportional representation has tended to produce two-party government coalitions, with the Chancellor and federal ministries at the core of executive authority. However, other collective actors play important policy roles, such as the independent central bank (formerly the *Bundesbank*, now the European Central Bank) which has been in charge of interest rate setting without political interference. As the guardian of Basic Law, the Constitutional Court has frequently set limits for government policy, at times influencing both the direction and the scale of policy, as Chapters 5 and 6 demonstrate. Moreover, German federalism implies tax revenue sharing and locates the responsibility for certain policy areas (such as education or child care) not at federal level but within the sixteen regional states (*Länder*). It also gives the *Länder* a strong political representation via the second chamber (*Bundesrat*) which co-legislates over matters which are deemed to require uniform standards across the country, including most areas of social policy provision, albeit not all. Many labour market policies can be implemented without *Bundesrat* consent, for example. However, often possessing a veto position of strategic importance, the *Bundesrat* can make policymaking extremely cumbersome, particularly at times of rival majorities in the two houses of parliament. This was the case in the late 1970s and early 1980s, and between 1996 and 1998, allowing the opposition parties to exploit their majorities in the *Bundesrat* in order to block or shape policy via negotiations in committees mediating between the two loci of policymaking (Silvia 1999). Similarly, the current red–green government has been confronted with a strong conservative *Bundesrat* majority since April 2002, once again making policy reform at times very difficult (Schmidt 2001).

The above does not imply that policy reform or policy change can simply be attributed to the constellations of 'veto players'. For example, examining the ideological distances between veto players and their internal cohesiveness (Tsebelis 2002) would, in itself, not explain why the German government in the 1980s failed to exploit its *Bundesrat* majorities for more structural reform in social policy. Equally, the introduction of deeper cuts and more far-reaching change in social policy in the second half of the 1990s, that is, at a time when the *Bundesrat* represented a much more effective veto player, is difficult to fathom. Policy reform does not depend on the mere presence or absence of veto players per se, but on preference formation and political strategies adopted by collective actors, in the context of contingent conditions. In short, the considerable differences in formal institutional policymaking structures in the two countries allow, in principle, British government parties much more scope for more far-reaching and speedier change. However, differences in formal institutional capacities do not in themselves explain differences in the scale of change along similar directions or variations in policy profiles.

3.2.2 *The welfare state as independent variable: programme-specific features*

This book investigates reforms within three areas of the welfare state which are assumed to be functionally equivalent: supporting unemployed people, providing income maintenance during retirement, and assisting families. And yet, institutional structures of public intervention in these domains differ considerably across countries. This is important for two reasons. As discussed in Chapter 2, changes in institutional settings are at the centre of the analysis. In which ways and to which extent have social policy structures been transformed over time, and how can transitions (or continuity) be explained? In other words, programme-specific features are part of what might be called the 'dependent variable' for the investigations to follow. At the same time, existing institutional settings are also 'independent variables'. Political choices in the past produced certain institutional structures and characteristics which include some but exclude other actors, provide contexts for collective action and negotiations, bestow incentives, and influence actors' perceptions of challenges and opportunities. In other words, policy processes can be expected to differ because of differences both across countries and across institutional characteristics of particular policy domains.

Two of the policy fields investigated in this book have a long history within their respective welfare states. Governed by principles of compulsory social insurance, pension provision and unemployment support originated between the 1880s and 1927 when unemployment insurance was finally introduced in Germany. Today, social policy in the UK is generally regarded as dominated by tax-based programmes and the contributory principle as weak. Indeed, social insurance contributions are less important than in Germany and direct and indirect taxes a more relevant source of funding (Kautto 2001). However, just over half of all spending on cash benefits in the UK continues to be contributory-based (DWP 2004), with the largest part being devoted to the basic state pension. The share was larger in the 1960s (at about 70 per cent) but it would be misleading to argue that contributory funding has become marginal within the British welfare state.

There are other characteristics which make British social insurance distinctive. As is well documented (e.g. Fraser 2002; Harris 2003), historically National Insurance (as it became after the Second World War) is rooted more in poverty alleviation than in maintaining living standards for industrial workers. In its post-war reconstruction, erstwhile separate social insurance schemes were amalgamated into the single comprehensive National Insurance. Contributions, as well as benefits, were flat-rate in order to enable also lower paid employees to contribute to the system and to leave room for additional non-statutory forms of social protection over and above subsistence level. Fiscal problems in the 1950s and 1960s led to the introduction of changes in funding arrangements, with contributions becoming fully proportional to earnings in the 1970s. Benefits too became (partially) proportional to wages with the introduction of earnings-related supplements to unemployment and sickness benefits in the 1960s and a supplementary pension system in the 1970s (Chapter 5). However, British steps towards embracing the concept of wage replacement remained half-hearted, with modest earnings-related supplements based on fairly restrictive eligibility conditions. In the 1980s, the experiment with the principle of wage-replacement was terminated (Chapter 4).

The National Insurance Fund (NIF) is fully under the control of central government and does not involve contributors (employees and employers) in its management. In turn, because of modest and flat-rate (rather than earnings-related) benefits, there is not much of an incentive structure for contributors to be involved in matters of social insurance. This structure favours a prevailing public belief that there is no real distinction between taxes and contributions (Stafford 1998) and ambiguities as to whether contributions paid to the NIF confer any firm entitlement to cash support. The notion of reciprocity is certainly much less dominant in British National Insurance than in German wage-replacement oriented social insurance (Mau 2003). Briefly, after the Second World War social insurance became the dominant type of social policy provision in West Germany. Today, the bulk of cash benefits remains funded by contributions which are paid by employers and their employees, each paying half of a fixed proportion of employees' earnings into separate funds, covering health and long-term care, pensions, unemployment, and work related accident insurance (the latter is fully funded by employers). Crucially, cash benefits including pensions and unemployment transfers are earnings-related and oriented at the principle of status or income maintenance (*Lebensstandardsicherung*), that is, income replacement for lost earnings which preserve, at least to some extent, the standard of living that individuals enjoyed before receiving benefit. Furthermore, social insurance funds are self-administered in the sense that contributors (employees and employers) cooperate in the management of agencies (and funds) which are separate from state revenue, albeit joined by state representatives within unemployment insurance. However, the government rather than self-management remains responsible for legislation affecting critical aspects, such as contribution or benefit rates or eligibility and entitlement criteria.

Public and policy debates about solidarity and distributive justice reflect these cross-national differences in benefit orientation and administrative structures. For example, in the UK the image of taxpayers versus (fraudulent) benefit claimants is routinely evoked. By contrast, social policy debates in Germany conventionally refer to a 'community of contributors' whose interests are not identical with those of general taxpayers. What is more, the 'community of contributors' might refer to a specific sub-community because of the existence of separate funds according to different types of risk, employment status, or occupational affiliation (Clasen 1997). The fact that eligibility to transfers is confined to those who have contributed to the system has been regarded as one of the features instilling trust and hence as a source of support for the institutional resilience of German social insurance, at least until the 1990s (Offe 1991).

Both the administrative involvement of social partners and, more importantly, the wage-replacement character of benefits, implies that public pensions and unemployment support have a much higher profile and figure more strongly on the agenda of social partners in Germany than in the UK. The fairly strict earnings-related notion of support turns transfers into deferred or 'social' wages in Germany, acquired via earmarked contributions. Accordingly, the role of pensions and unemployment benefits within the respective industrial relations systems and national political economies of the two countries has differed considerably (see later).

In sum, compared with the UK, the strong wage-replacement character of entitlements fosters strong vested interests in maintaining existing structures and can thus be expected to have influenced the direction and shape of retrenchment policies in the 1980s and 1990s. Within unemployment insurance, curtailments can be assumed to be comparatively more discriminating in Germany, where core contributors are both in a strategically better position for, and more strongly interested in, resisting cutbacks. Within pension insurance, despite similar pay-as-you-go structures, the involvement of contributors, the level of contributions, and the generosity of benefits which are more tightly determined by lifetime earnings (see Chapter 4) can be assumed to provide more barriers to reform due to 'lock in effects' and a stronger 'path dependence' of German policy reform compared with the UK.

Finally, funding structures are yet further institutional features which can be assumed to have influenced reform processes and outcomes. In the UK the single NIF is effectively a component of general state revenue. Consequently, fiscal concerns and conflicts on how to restrict spending tend to focus on overall expenditure or broad policy sectors, for example, social security, but not on the NIF in particular.

By contrast, debates on public finances in Germany are often programme-specific due to actual or prospective annual deficits in particular funds (e.g. pensions) which have to be balanced by government tax revenue or require specific cost-containment efforts. Indeed, until well into the 1990s, much social policy reform in Germany was triggered by problems of revenue in particular social insurance sectors. Typically, governments resorted to at times complex manipulations of separate social insurance funds and general tax revenue for political purposes. For example, intent on avoiding an increase in the total level of social insurance contributions, raising taxation, or cutting spending, governments might balance a deficit in pension insurance by lowering unemployment insurance contributions and simultaneously raising pension contributions. More complex instances of this so-called 'shifting-yard' policy have shaped reforms in unemployment insurance (Chapter 4). Basically, the more intertwined and compartmentalized funding structure of social insurance in Germany provides a complex set of incentives and opportunities for cost-containment policies, potentially involving insurance funds as well as tax revenue at federal, *Land*, or local level, and giving rise to political negotiations and interest coalitions which can cut across party political lines.

The impact of these programme-specific features (or policy legacies) influencing policy processes has been emphasized particularly within the 'historical institutionalist' school of new institutionalism (Steinmo et al. 1992; Hall and Taylor 1996). Cross-national comparisons have linked policy outcomes not only to the relative organizational position and institutional responsibilities of collective actors, but also to the ways in which institutions influence actors' preference formation and strategies. Pierson (2000) points to reasons why policy feedback can have a strong influence on the dynamics and sequencing of reform. Once institutional structures have been established, the repertoire of feasible reform options becomes more limited and policy reforms tend to become 'path dependent'. Existing features make a particular path more conducive and provide resistance to pressures that might make alternative outcomes otherwise more attractive. Processes of 'self-reinforcement' and a 'status quo bias' (Pierson 2000) can be explained with reference to institutional incentives and constraints, such as high initial set-up costs, learning effects, coordination effects, and adaptive expectations.

This approach has provoked accusations of 'institutional determinism' (Wood 2001a; Crouch and Farrell 2002). However, path dependence does not imply that there is only one feasible policy outcome, but that past events make certain outcomes more likely than others. Explaining continuity and change, Myles and Pierson (2001) have convincingly demonstrated the usefulness of the concept for the understanding of comparative pension policy reform. Chapter 5 will illustrate that respective pension 'policy legacies' were indeed crucial factors which influenced differences in direction and patterns of policy reforms in Germany and the UK. However, in other policy domains path dependence seems to have less explanatory power. For example, in Chapter 4, institutional features are important factors also in unemployment support, but conceptualizing what exactly constitutes a 'path' in the first place seems more difficult than in pension policy (also Seeleib-Kaiser 2003). Within family policy, path dependence in particular and institutionalist approaches more generally seem less useful analytical tools than interest based explanations, combined with dynamic contextual influences (see Section 3.3).

3.2.3 Institutional complementarities and functional equivalents—linking social protection and political economies

A third institutional aspect is the interface between social policy programmes and other aspects of national political economies. Social policy programmes are dependent on the economic and political context within which they operate. For a start, their fiscal viability rests on state revenue, the volume of which is influenced by the performance of the economy and the level of employment. In turn, welfare state regulations influence employment rates, gender differences in paid work, or transitions in and out of work. More specifically, certain sectors of national political economies or 'production regimes' (Huber and Stephens 2001), including industrial relations, labour market regulation, or financial governance structures, can be regarded as interlinked with sub-systems of social protection. Drawing on Soskice (1991; also Hall and Soskice 2001), Huber and Stephens (2001: 23) distinguish between 'coordinated' and 'liberal' production regimes, reflecting different patterns of relations between enterprises, financial institutions, labour, and governments. 'Coordinated' production regimes are characterized by a higher degree of cooperation across and between economic actors and governments, a denser degree of institutionalization, and processes of coordinated wage setting. By comparison, in 'liberal' production regimes 'arms-length, market-determined transactions' prevail, as well as short-term equity capital markets, maximization of shareholder values, and decentralized wage bargaining. Hall and Soskice (2001) make Germany a prototypical example of a coordinated market economy (CME), characterized by long-term financial investments in companies, close relationships between businesses and their major suppliers and clients, strong employee representation at company level and extensive coordination among firms based on encompassing business associations, and a publicly subsidized training system. Industry-wide collective bargaining between social partners without state interference (*Tarifautonomie*) bring about binding wage settlements and equalizing wages at equivalent skill levels across particular industries.

By contrast, keeping 'banks, firms and the government in different spheres' (Rhodes 2000*a*: 24), the British political economy is characterized by a dominance of short-term stock market finance capital, weak levels of business coordination and state interventionism, as well as decentralized, craft-based unions' representation, favouring voluntaristic plant-based rather than sector-wide wage bargaining. Deregulated markets function as the principal mechanism for economic activity, discouraging employers from long-term investment in the skills of their employees. Repressive trade union legislation in the 1980s and 1990s and the absence of national

apprenticeship and training systems contributed to an even more deregulated liberal market economy (LME). Because of a financial system that
promotes rapid turnover, short-term profit orientation is dominant, as well
as an emphasis on flexibility, cost reduction, and relatively low levels of
skills and a sizeable low wage sector contributing to relatively large wage
dispersion. Its 'comparative advantage' lies in price rather than quality
competition (Wood 2001: 250).

Linking the study of models or 'varieties' of capitalism (Hall and Soskice
2001) with the debate on the origins and trajectories of distinct welfare state
regimes (Esping-Andersen 1990), recent analyses have aimed to identify
'institutional complementarities' (Ebbinghaus and Manow 2001: 2) between particular components of social protection and aspects of national
political economies. This is perhaps most obvious in the area of industrial
relations and social insurance. For example, analysing the historical co-
evolution of the two spheres in Germany, Manow (1997) has shown that
certain institutional features of social insurance (its self-administration in
particular) provided the labour movement of the early twentieth century
with specific opportunities (jobs and resources) which, in turn, made trade
union membership more attractive. Moreover, the specific design of social
insurance, that is, a parity-based collaboration between employee and
employer organizations, favoured the development of strong centralized
trade unions and provided a forum for conflict resolution reaching beyond
matters of social insurance. During the 1970s and 1980s the bipartite
structure of pension insurance, for example, facilitated a broad consensus
between social partners (and the government) for employment restructuring with the help of early retirement options (Ebbinghaus 2001).
At the expense of the long-term sustainability of unemployment and
pension insurance, relatively generous social insurance benefits served
two important economic functions: allowing companies to shed less productive labour and helping trade unions to protect those still in work from
wage competition from those made redundant (Manow 1997; see also
Ganßmann 1991).

It might well be that what was once a socially effective system producing
positive economic externalities (productivity increases), has since become
counterproductive for the economy and the sustainability of the welfare
state (Manow and Seils 2001; Kitschelt and Streek 2003). More relevant
here is to note the 'tightly coupled' domains of German social insurance on
the one hand and industrial relations on the other (Hemerijck et al. 2000).
This link might be expressed as the notion of a 'social wage', that is, the
entitlement to a wage replacement benefit rendered by employment-based
contributions to social insurance, complemented by a high level of employment protection. No equivalent connection between industrial relations

and social insurance exists in the UK. Unable to cope with mass unemployment in the 1920s, early trade union run schemes collapsed and the British labour movement began to lobby for improved benefits. However, by the time of the major restructuring of the British welfare state in the 1940s, trade unions had decided against any involvement in the administration of social insurance in favour of a state-run system (Crouch 1999). Instead of an occupational-based and tightly contribution-based scheme as in Germany, British social insurance became a 'weak' citizenship model (Crouch 1999: 448) with low contributions and low levels of benefit. This absence of a notion of a 'social wage', that is, the divorce between the labour movement and social insurance, is distinctively characteristic of the British political economy and has arguably contributed to the difficulties of economic management for much of the post-war period (Rhodes 2000*a*). Exacerbated by a fractured and decentralized trade union and wage bargaining structure, the absence of a 'social wage' at the centre of a social consensus made it impossible to 'link advances in welfare provision with a medium- to long-term commitment to wages and price stability' (Rhodes 2000*a*: 36). In short, for German workers', wages, social insurance-based 'deferred wages' and employment protection are interlinked domains. In the UK industrial relations have focused exclusively on wages, complemented by weak and increasingly diminishing levels of employment protection,'while social protection has traditionally been disconnected from workers, 'economic security' (Bonoli 2003).

A related example of particular linkages between political economies and social policy, and the implicit assumption that the connection influences social policy reform outcomes, has been put forward by Estevez-Abe et al. (2001). The authors provide cross-national evidence of systematic connections between employment protection, unemployment protection, and prevalent skill profiles. In Germany the level of employment protection is high and unemployment protection relatively generous, compared with weak levels of both in the UK. At the same time, firm- and industry-specific skills are characteristic within the German labour force, acquired through on-the-job training and apprenticeships and vocational training schools respectively, compared with a prevalence of general and more portable skills independent of particular industries in the UK. These constellations provide employees and employers with different incentive structures. In the more fluid and less socially supported British labour market, workers can protect themselves against labour market insecurities by investing in general and highly portable rather than specific skills, making general (rather than vocational specific) education more attractive. In turn, firms tend to make use of technologies which do not require specific skills but employ the more abundant and flexible general skills

(Estevez-Abe et al. 2001: 162). By contrast, relying on combinations of firm-specific and industry-specific skills, particularly large German employers have a strong interest in public provision of vocational training (Wood 2001: 251) and other policies which reduce the costs of providing and maintaining adequate rewards for workers willing to acquire skills required for specific industries. Relatively inflexible labour markets, with a 'high-skill, high-wage equilibrium', represent incentives for employers to invest in their employees' skill acquisition (Fioretos 2001: 221). In turn, workers would support policies which ensure an adequate return for their investment in specific skills, such as good job security (employment protection) and adequate income maintenance for periods between jobs (unemployment benefits). As a consequence, just as in matters of early retirement, 'colluding interests' between social partners (Ebbinghaus 2001; Mares 2003) might be expected to have created a barrier towards strong retrenchment of unemployment protection. By comparison, there is little reason why British employers should have objected to a curtailment of unemployment support. On the contrary, lower levels of out-of-work benefits might have been welcomed as putting pressure on reservation wages and contributing to the creation of a flexible and deregulated market economy as the basis for the particular competitive advantage in the UK (see Section 3.4). Given a 'tighter coupling' between social protection and the German political economy, and a congruence of interests between large German employers and trade unions on skill preservation, reform initiatives might have involved less retrenchment in Germany than in the UK. Moreover, reform profiles can be assumed to be different. Retrenchment in Germany might have been more discriminatory, targeted at peripheral groups rather than core workers, whereas there is little reason to expect differentiated retrenchment efforts in the UK.

Finally a caveat: as Crouch (2003) points out, institutionalist approaches, such as the 'varieties of capitalism' or 'production regimes', invite deterministic notions of path dependence and suggest functionalist accounts of policy development. Indeed, national production systems are more heterogeneous than implied, and subject to shifts over time. In Germany, for example, traditional industrial relations structures have become much more volatile recently due to new divisions within, and shifting power resources between, employer organizations and trade unions (Streek and Hassel 2003), as well as controversies between trade unions and German governments (Streek 2003). In short, the erstwhile consensual German political economy model seems to be under considerable strain, reflected also in more dynamic and less predictable outcomes of social policy formation since the mid-1990s, as subsequent chapters will show.

The opposite is true for the UK. As discussed, traditionally social protection and industrial relations have been largely disconnected domains. However, years of retrenchment of the 'informal welfare state', combined with sustained economic and non-inflationary employment growth since 1993, have bequeathed the Labour government an economic, political, and institutional landscape considerably different from previous decades. As a result, there is now a greater 'functional compatibility' (King and Wood 1999) between the more deregulated and liberalized British market economy and a stronger employment-oriented and targeted social security system. Having subscribed to the 'competitive advantages' brought about by a flexible, low-cost-oriented economy, the current Labour government has reinforced policies which would produce a closer fit between, or 'dovetailing', of social security programmes and demands of the 'large low-wage, low-skill sector of the economy' (Rhodes 2000*a*: 57). Indeed, Rhodes (ibid.) argues that policies such as the promotion of in-work benefits, modest levels of means-tested support, and new 'activating' benefit criteria have locked Britain's formal and informal welfare systems 'into an institutional ensemble sustaining a particular form of competitiveness and economic growth that is highly resistant to change'. As subsequent chapters show, the linkage between political economies and structures of social protection does indeed go some way to explaining the particular profile of policy reforms. This applies to unemployment support in particular, and to a lesser extent to pensions, where other institutional aspects (policy legacies; see Section 3.2) were more important. Institutional elements (e.g. the Constitutional Court in Germany) also proved relevant in family support. However, policy dynamics in this domain owe much to the dynamics of political preferences in the context of secular changes in economic and social conditions.

3.3 CONTEXTS AND CONTINGENCIES

As Scharpf (2000: 767) pointed out, in recent years the 'multi-veto characteristics of German political institutions' have been made responsible for constraining much required structural change. However, in earlier decades the same institutional framework was portrayed as a contributory factor to the successful macro-economic management, and the lack of similar institutional embeddedness made responsible for British ineffective macro-economic 'stop-and-go policy' (Rhodes 2000*a*). In other words, the impact of institutions is not static but depends on dynamic socio-economic contexts. Moreover, changes in social, political, economic, and cultural contexts can influence power positions, as well as policymakers' strategies and their preferences. For example, as Chapter 6 will show, sustained rising female employment exerted pressure, and facilitated gradual party policy reorientation in favour of more public provision addressing the reconciliation of family life and paid work. More sudden changes, such as public scandals or landslide electoral majorities, might increase the legitimacy for certain action and thus open up windows for policy change.

At times, electoral fortunes are influenced by contingent events. For example, presiding over mass unemployment and unimpressive economic performances, the popularity of the Thatcher government in the early 1980s was boosted by the war over the Falkland Islands. In addition, internal divisions within the Labour Party, resulting in anything but a coherent position on social policy, presented the government with a tactical advantage. Thus, rather than battling for political survival as had initially been feared, the government was re-elected with a massive majority in the general election of 1983, potentially providing a favourable position for more far-reaching reform initiatives (Table 3.1). In Germany, the fall of the Berlin Wall and Helmut Kohl's insistence on speedy unification irrespective of medium-term economic or social consequences helped secure a strong majority in favour of the incumbent government. Labour governments of the late 1990s relied on extremely comfortable majorities in parliament and far-reaching reform initiatives seemed much less risky for the first red–green government in Germany than for the second, having secured re-election by an extremely narrow margin in 2002.

However, secure majorities combined with an ideological disposition towards curbing welfare programmes are not necessarily sufficient conditions for actual retrenchment. In the early 1980s, popular opinion in Germany was relatively amenable to cost-containment policies, with a majority of the population accepting cuts in pension entitlements as a means to safeguard the pension system (Alber 1989: 307). However, during the 1990s, public opinion decidedly rejected cuts in core welfare state programmes (Roller 1996). Besides, politically the two major German

Table 3.1. Parliamentary majorities after general elections, 1979–2002

	1979	1983	1987	1992	1997	2001
UK	Conservative	Conservative	Conservative	Conservative	Labour	Labour
	43	144	102	21	177	165
	1983	1987	1990	1994	1998	2002
Germany	CDU/CSU-FDP	CDU/CSU-FDP	CDU/CSU-FDP	CDU/CSU-FDP	SPD-Green	SPD-Green
	58	41	134	10	93	9

parties have traditionally declared themselves as defenders of key social policy structures, leaving little room for open retrenchment without the respective ruling party having to pay a heavy electoral price (Kitschelt 2001). For example, the explicit curbing of social entitlements (sickness pay, pensions) arguably contributed to the 1998 election defeat of the incumbent Kohl government. In the UK, despite an ideologically more determined government commited to diminish the role of public provision, Thatcher administrations in the 1980s hesitated to advocate openly radical reforms because of assumptions about the welfare state's popularity (Deakin 1994). Public attitude surveys indicate that such reservations were well founded (Taylor-Gooby 1988; Hills 2004). Particularly the NHS but also other services, such as education, were strongly and consistently supported by the electorate throughout the 1980s and 1990s. Even radical curbing of unemployment protection was not without the risk of inciting popular backlash. As Hills (2004: 151) shows, suspicions of benefit fraud and abuse have been widespread within the British population. At the same time, however, there has been broad support for unemployed people. Ever since 1983 when annual surveys began, the statement that benefits for the unemployed are 'too low and cause hardship' has attracted considerably and consistently stronger agreement than the notion that benefits are 'too high and discourage work'. Opinions became less sympathetic towards the unemployed and much more volatile only after the 1997 election, potentially reflecting (or facilitating; see Hills 2002) the Labour government's stricter work-focused unemployment support programme (see Chapter 4). Other contextual conditions either exert pressure or facilitate options for social policy reform. Most important are perhaps changes in economic and labour market performance.

Economically, German and British governments followed broadly parallel paths in the 1970s and 1980s, but trajectories diverged dramatically in the 1990s. The second oil price crisis in the early 1980s induced deep economic recessions and unprecedented levels of mass unemployment in both countries (Fig. 3. 1). Economic performance improved in the second half of the 1980s, with stronger growth rates in the UK, albeit accompanied by steep levels of inflation. The liberalization of credit controls and politically motivated fiscal policy (a further round of personal income tax reductions) added to an overheating of the British economy, leading up to a dramatic economic decline towards the end of the decade. In general, the economy followed a 'boom-and-bust' pattern with rapid and strong oscillations typical of the development of the British economy, particularly since the 1970s. By comparison, a tight monetary policy pursued by the *Bundesbank* contributed to lower fluctuations and steadier levels of inflation and interest rates in Germany.

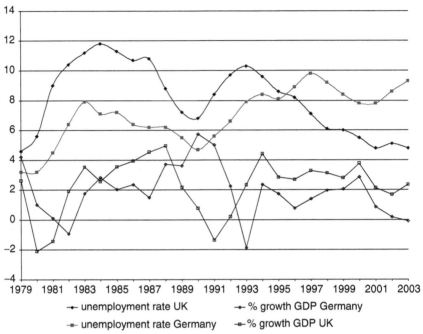

Fig. 3.1. Annual unemployment rates and real GDP growth, UK and Germany, 1979–2003

(*Source*: OECD 2004*a*; Euromonitor 2004; International Monetary Fund 2004).

In the early 1990s, trajectories diverged. The UK had entered yet another dramatic phase of economic decline, with negative growth, steeply rising unemployment, annual inflation of almost 10 per cent, and exorbitantly high interest rates in order to counter speculative runs on the British currency before leaving the European Exchange Rate Mechanism (ERM) in 1992. By contrast, the fall of the Berlin Wall triggered a very different trend in Germany. Initially German unification fuelled a short but strong economic boom in West Germany, fed by unmet demand in the territory of the former German Democratic Republic (GDR). In the long run, however, the adverse economic impact of unification was immense for both parts of the new country—and a significant contextual change with far-reaching consequences for social policy reform.

This was not immediately evident, though. On the contrary, the extension of traditional West German institutions to the territory of unified Germany suggested structural stability rather than change. Economically, however, the political management of unification created massive long-term problems, with severe implications for Germany's political economy.

Introduced speedily with the hope of preventing an even more rapid migration from East to West, monetary union implied a steep rise in labour costs for East German companies, with an 'overnight appreciation of the local currency by about 400 per cent' (Wiesenthal 2003: 40). In addition, with wages in the new *Länder* gradually climbing to up to 90 per cent of West German levels, East German companies were confronted with sudden increases in production costs while running at a productivity level of about 30 per cent of the West. As a result, about 80 per cent of firms in the East went out of business (Alber 2003: 20). The former East German labour force of close to 10 million people shrank to about 6 million within two years, implying demands for huge levels of public transfers from the West. Accordingly, expenditure on income transfer programmes, labour market schemes, retirement and early retirement pay, as well as unemployment, support rose sharply.

The economic problems in the eastern part of the country proved long-lived, with adverse consequences for the German economy as a whole (Ganßmann 2004). Thus, Germany today may have become institutionally integrated but continues to consist of two separate economic spheres, with different structures and problems (Czada 1998). After early improvements and increases in labour productivity reaching almost 80 per cent of the West German level, annual economic growth in the East has trailed below already modest West German rates. Average unemployment rates in the East are currently above 20 per cent, more than twice the West German average. Employment in the West has remained roughly stable since 1992, but declined in the East, with a particularly steep decrease since 1999 (Koller 2003). Transfers and new debts of up to €100 billion per year finance the east of the country. As a proportion of GDP, Germany's state debt rose from 41.5 per cent in 1991 to 61.5 per cent in 1997, with corresponding interest payments increasing from 11.4 per cent of the budget in 1991 to 18.9 per cent in 1999 (Wiesenthal 2003: 43). Equivalent to about 4 per cent of West German GDP (*Der Spiegel*, 15 April, 2004), the scale of annual West–East transfers have been identified as having contributed two-thirds of the current economic recession in Germany.

In short, economic and political conditions since the mid-1990s have become increasingly adverse and provide a sharp contrast with the 1980s. During the second half of the 1980s, West German unemployment had largely been curbed and economic growth was well above the European Union (EU) average. A broad party consensus in social policy prevailed and the industrial relations system facilitated compromises which produced increases in productivity of up to 4 per cent per annum (Statistisches Bundesamt 2004*a*), at the expense of growing labour market exit for older workers (Bäcker et al. 2003). Since 1992, Germany has been faced with mass unemployment and low GDP growth, making the country the weakest economic performer in the EU. Moreover, the erstwhile cross-party consensus over social policy turned into conflict, the social partnership system has become seriously threatened (Streek 2003; Streek and Hassel 2003), and large German corporations have increasingly switched to short-term profit maximization and transferring investments outside of Germany (Ganßmann 2003a).

In sharp contrast, socio-economic conditions during the 1990s became more favourable in the UK (see Fig. 3.1). As discussed earlier (Section 3.2.3), the political economy of the UK does not rely on corporatist governance structures, the degree of employment protection is low, and labour markets have become increasingly flexible and deregulated since the 1980s. Since 1993, unemployment has steadily declined without adding inflationary pressure. Unlike traditional 'stop-and-go' macro-economic policy, characterized by strongly fluctuating parameters of economic activity, the path has been one of steady growth within a context of low inflation and generally low interest rates. Despite somewhat lower growth rates after 1999, compared with the deterioration in Germany the British economy performed well with unemployment remaining relatively low (see Fig. 3.1). Today, a growing low-wage sector is supported by a minimum wage and the extensive use of wage subsidies. While labour productivity remains below Germany and other major economies, annual increases between 1993 and 2003 were consistently higher in the UK (2 per cent on average; ONS 2004) than in Germany with (1.1 per cent; Statistisches Bundesamt 2004a).

Also employment rates in the two countries increasingly diverged. Figure 3.2 shows that the overall employment/population ratio in Germany deteriorated markedly after 1990, to a level even lower than in the late 1970s. The sustained improvement in the British labour market since 1993 has been achieved by both increases in female employment and the reversal of the decline of male employment (however, labour market inactivity for prime-aged and particularly low-skilled British men continued to increase; see Clasen et al. 2004). By contrast, male employment in Germany continued to decline to an extent which has not been compensated by rising female employment.

High employment facilitates the economic 'feasibility of large welfare states' (Ganßmann 2003), generating household income, adding tax revenue, and lowering transfer expenditure. However, higher levels of employment might involve high rates of part-time working or short working weeks. A 'labour mobilization index' (Nickell 1997; Ganßmann 2003) is thus a more instructive indicator of the relative pressure resulting from labour market developments. Such an index can be calculated as the

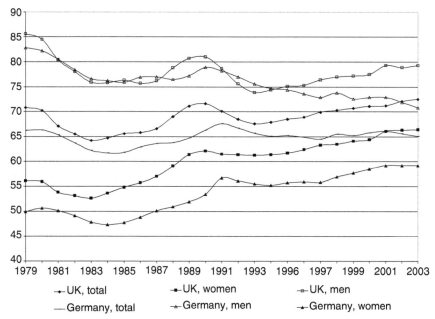

Fig. 3.2. Employment/population ratios, Germany and the UK, 1979–2003
(*Source*: OECD 2004*a*)

product of average annual working hours and employment/population ratios, divided by the maximum full-time working hours (for convenience assumed to be 40 hours per week and 52 weeks per year). Derived from OECD data, Table 3.2 indicates a sustained decline of annual working hours in Germany (previously West Germany) in contrast to a more stable development in the UK, followed by a more recent decline.

Table 3.2. Average annual working hours, Germany and the UK

	Germany	UK
1980	1739	1769
1985	1659	1762
1990	1566	1767
1995	1520	1739
2000	1463	1708
2003	1446	1673

Source: OECD 2004*a*.

The labour market mobilization indices for the two countries suggest a strong degree of divergence since the mid-1980s. Although remaining below the levels of the late 1980s, and despite a prevalence of women working part-time (see Chapter 6), the development in the British labour market has been very favourable or, to put it differently, created little economic pressure for welfare state retrenchment. By contrast, Fig. 3.3 suggests that the West German economic improvement in the late 1980s was achieved without much impact on the labour market (with increasing employment rates cancelled out by shorter working hours). During the 1990s, further decline of annual working hours, in addition to declining male employment, has not been compensated by increases in female employment, most of which was part-time (see Chapter 6). In short, the labour mobilization index is yet another illustration of the growing problem pressure for German governments, potentially putting more emphasis on policies of cost-containment.

Putting the two countries in a wider cross-national perspective, Ganßmann (2003) underlines the contrasting contextual conditions, with the UK characterized by the highest level of labour mobilization out of thirteen European countries in 2002, compared with the lowest level in Germany except for Belgium and Italy. Of course, it can be argued that, in principle, low levels of labour mobilization can be compensated by increases in productivity, which has indeed risen in Germany during the

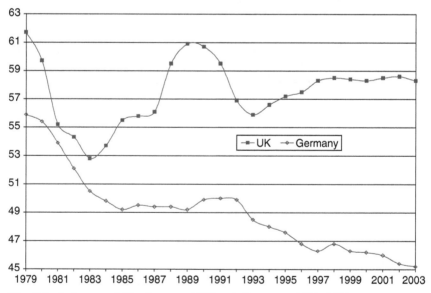

Fig. 3.3. Labour mobilization rate, UK and Germany, 1979–2003.

Source: Own calculation based on data from OECD 2004*a* (see text).

1990s (Ganßmann 2003), but at a much slower pace than in the UK (see earlier).

At a macro-level, the increasingly contrasting economic and labour market trends in the two countries contributed to divergent trajectories of social spending in the 1990s. However measured (Alber 2003: 19), as a result of the deep economic recession, social expenditure as a proportion of GDP increased in the early 1980s in both countries (Fig. 3.4). However, by the end of the decade German spending had been brought down to a level below 1982 when the conservative–liberal coalition first took office, indicating successful financial consolidation. The economic recession and rising unemployment towards the end of the decade caused social spending to rise in the UK, and subsequently to decline when the economy picked up. By contrast, the consequence of German unification, followed by a deep economic recession in the old *Länder*, implied a more sustained rise in social spending.

In the new *Länder*, the social expenditure ratio reached 65 per cent in 1992 and has since remained well above 50 per cent, 'topping Sweden by far' (Leibfried and Obinger 2003: 205). With the exception of a small 'solidarity' surtax (7.5 per cent on income tax), the German government refrained from funding this increase via taxation. Instead pension insurance

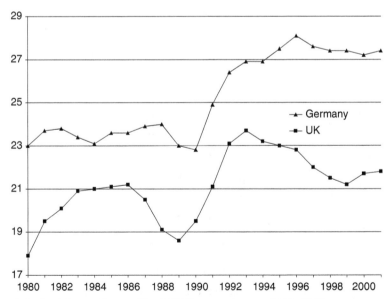

Fig. 3.4. Social spending as % of GDP, annual rates, 1980–2001

(*Source*: OECD Social Expenditure database, 2004; West Germany until 1990).

and unemployment insurance rates were raised, adding to non-wage labour costs which had already edged upwards during the 1980s, thereby contravening the government's explicit aim of containing social insurance contributions (Schmidt 1998: 65). In the mid-1970s, the aggregate social insurance rate (payroll tax) stood at about 30 per cent of gross wages (up to certain contribution ceilings), rising to about 32 per cent by 1978, and to 34 per cent by the time the first conservative government took office in 1982 (Fig. 3.5). Despite having reduced unemployment, by the end of the decade the rate had reached 36 per cent. In other words, the cost of labour had increased before the onset of German unification. However, during the 1990s social insurance contributions rose even more steeply, eventually reaching a record level of 42.1 per cent by 1998, and have only marginally declined since (Fig. 3.5).

The principal reason for this steep increase is not simply German unification, but the government's underestimation of the sustained cost of the latter combined with the decision to shoulder the financial burden of the collapse of the economy in the East via the social insurance system rather than general taxation. As discussed, redundancies on a massive scale in the former GDR, persistent mass unemployment, and an

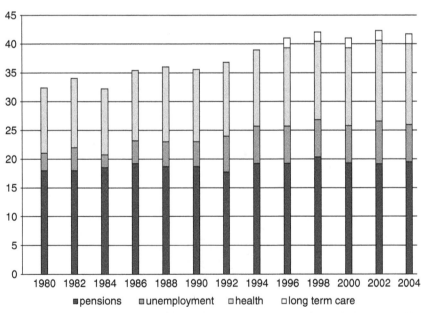

Fig. 3.5. Aggregate social insurance rates, in % of gross wage, Germany, 1980–2004.

(*Source*: BMGS 2004).

under-performing economy produced extreme pressure on public finances. In addition, the economic recession beginning in late 1992 and the Maastricht Treaty imposing strict qualifying criteria for European Monetary Union (EMU), including a limit of 3 per cent annual public deficit as qualifying condition, created fiscal problems of an unprecedented scale. As a result, having initially brought the government, employers, and unions closer together, the short phase of a reluctant unification-induced expansion of social and labour market provision, not least aimed at stemming East–West migration, came to an end and the government resumed policies of cost-containment. However, unlike the 1980s, the new and much harsher economic climate was matched by new conflict lines between social partners and the two major political parties. With the post-unification boom over, rising social insurance costs were perceived by employer organizations as seriously undermining the competitiveness of German business at a time of increasing economic internationalization and European integration. Their demands for more radical retrenchment and cutting non-wage labour costs were supported by the FDP and by the business wing within the CDU/CSU. Their growing influence became manifest when the government initiated cutbacks in core social policy programmes (e.g. sick pay), thereby triggering a breakdown of hitherto relatively amicable relationships with trade unions and massive public demonstrations against welfare state retrenchment in 1996. Further government proposals, including a planned cut in pension entitlements, contributed to the defeat of the Kohl government in the 1998 election (see Chapter 5).

In short, the economic consequences of German unification had a huge impact not only on the German economy but also on power relations within parties, party competition, and industrial relations. Paradoxically, initially unification delayed rather than enforced social policy reform. As discussed in Chapters 4 and 5, despite increasing fiscal problems, a broad perception prevailed that the West German institutional framework had enabled successful incremental adaptation to economic pressure in the 1980s. Thus, since the economic and labour market disruptions were not expected to last, there was little immediate advocacy for structural change. This notion evaporated however after the mid-1990s, and ever since social policy formation has become much more volatile.

Finally, it should be pointed out that increased social insurance contributions, as the new cross-party problem diagnosis from the mid-1990s, was not the only result of the political management and lasting economic impact of unification. For example, in 1995 the government introduced a contributory funded 'fifth pillar' of social insurance, the long-term care insurance, adding another 1.7 per cent to total labour costs (see Fig. 3.5). In addition, efforts to stem the exit into different forms of early retirement have been largely ineffective. For example, in recent years there have still been fewer men entering regular retirement than (early) retirement after unemployment (VdR 2003).

3.4 CONCLUSION

Looking back over twenty-five years one could justifiably argue that, in many respects, the UK and Germany have changed positions. Back in the 1980s, German economic and labour market performance was generally more favourable than in the UK, and overall trends less dramatic and volatile. The economic recession in the early 1980s seemed to have been successfully overcome by the end of the decade. Much social policy reform was based on a broad cross-party consensus of adapting but maintaining existing structures, often via seemingly technical and incremental adjustments. Broad agreements between the two major parties, supported by a functioning industrial relations system, facilitated a relatively stable course of retrenchment without endangering basic institutional frameworks of social policy provision.

By contrast, British government policy during 1980s and early 1990s was ideologically driven, unilateral, and intent on achieving substantial retrenchment and structural change. Located within a context of neo-liberal policies and 'boom-and-bust' periods of economic development, government measures were often deliberately confrontational, aimed at curbing the influence of vested interests generally and the role of trade unions in particular. Traditional welfare state programmes were regarded with suspicion, and subjected to substantial retrenchment in the long run. However, overall social expenditure was less successfully curtailed than in Germany, not least due to less favourable economic and labour market trends.

During the 1990s economic and political contexts changed dramatically. In addition to two major economic recessions, German unification proved to have a lasting and destabilizing effect on economic outcomes, party competition, and industrial relations. An erstwhile broadly stable path gave way to stop-and-go policy in social policy, U-turns, and a pattern which has been described as 'stumbling towards reform' (Bönker and Wollmann 2001). Today consensus has been limited to a cross-party problem diagnosis (high non-wage labour costs) and a broad agreement that incremental policy change has become ineffective and structural change required. The readiness to engage in far-reaching institutional welfare state change is stronger than it has been since the 1950s. However, few common policy priorities can be identified across parties, or indeed within them.

A reverse trend can be identified in the UK. Much more favourable economic and labour market conditions, and some institutional change (e.g. the independence of the Bank of England), have led to a more consistent path of policymaking. Having accepted the more deregulated, liberal, and flexible political economy created by its predecessor, the Labour government has developed policies broadly along the same direction and linked policy domains, such as unemployment support and labour market programmes (see Chapter 4), more effectively than in the past. Public policy programmes may not have become more sustainable (such as pensions; see Chapter 5) but an increasingly coherent policy course has been pursued.

Given these changing socio-economic contexts, more pressure might be expected to have led to structural reform in the UK during the 1980s than in the 1990s. The reverse might be assumed for Germany. However, other potential influences discussed earlier, such as electoral politics or public attitudes, are likely to have impinged on policy formation. Other contextual factors could be added as well. For example, sharp increases in poverty and income inequality might have played a role in the UK but less so in Germany where income distribution, wage dispersion, and poverty rates have traditionally been lower. Chapters 4–6 will investigate in which policy domain such contextual conditions and dynamic policy priorities have influenced reform paths, in conjunction with the three sets of institutional parameters discussed: formal policymaking structures, programme-specific settings, and linkages between social protection programmes and other aspects of national political economies.

4

Supporting unemployed people: income protection and activation

In modern welfare states unemployed people receive two types of public support. Income transfers replace lost earnings and labour market programmes help with the return to paid work. These measures are not independent of each other. Benefit receipt is generally conditional not only on eligibility requirements, such as having paid sufficient social insurance contributions or need, but also requires the willingness and capacity to enter paid employment and the availability for work. The latter indicates that labour market integration is the ultimate aim of unemployment support. However, work requirements can be defined, and 'tested', in various ways, including participation in job-search programmes, training, or other schemes which are deemed to foster transitions from benefit into paid employment, recently referred to as 'welfare-to-work' or activation policies. The focus in this chapter is on major changes in the regulations which affect rights and responsibilities of unemployed benefit claimants and thus on both benefits and activation policies.

This chapter shows that the direction of policy change over the entire period has been fairly similar, consisting of both benefit retrenchment and a more prescriptive and work focused social support system as a result of 'benefit activation'. However, the pattern of retrenchment in the UK was global and led to a homogenization of unemployment support. The German pattern was more differentiating and also included selective improvements. As a result, unemployment protection in Germany continues to distinguish between a better-off, but shrinking, core clientele for whom there has been relatively modest retrenchment and a growing periphery which has been affected much more, with the gap between the two groups widening. Moreover, in the UK there has been more restructuring and a steady and substantial shift towards means-testing, whereas institutional reorganization has occurred only recently in Germany. In addition, activation policies started much later and in a less forceful fashion than in the UK. Section 4.1 provides a fuller picture of these trends and variations in policy direction and policy patterns. Sections 4.2 and 4.3 discuss the policymaking processes which brought about these outcomes in Germany and the UK, respectively. Section 4.4 summarizes major causes for cross-national similarities and differences.

4.1 PROGRAMME STRUCTURES, DIRECTIONS, AND POLICY PROFILES

In the light of assessing major patterns of reform and structural change, this section briefly sketches out some general characteristics of the German and British systems of unemployment protection, indicating change in a dia-chronic comparison of characteristics in the 1980s and 2004 (for more details, see Clasen 1994, 2002; Reissert 2005; see also Appendix A and B).

4.1.1 Germany

Until very recently the German system of unemployment protection con-sisted of a two-tier structure on unemployment benefits, with a third tier (general social assistance) available for those without, or insufficient, sup-port of either form of unemployment transfer. The first layer (*Arbeitslosen-geld*, ALG) is closely guided by insurance principles. It is payable to persons who become unemployed and have worked in insured employment for at least twelve months. It is financed from compulsory contributions which, subject to a ceiling, are proportional to gross earnings (3 per cent in 1980; 6.5 per cent in 2004) and equally split between employers and employees. In 1980, the benefit rate was equal to 68 per cent of previous earnings, payable for a standard maximum duration of twelve months (Table 4.1).

For those with exhausted ALG entitlement, or who did not qualify for ALG but had been in insured employment for a minimum of seventy days (in 1980), the secondary system of unemployment benefit (*Arbeitslosenhilfe*, ALH) applied. As with ALG, the level of this benefit was earnings-related, but at a lower rate of 58 per cent of gross earnings. In this sense ALH had a wage replacement character. However, ALH was financed by general taxation rather than contributions. What is more, eligibility was dependent on a means-test (taking the income of spouses into account), and the benefit was payable indefinitely, provided unemployment and lack of resources persisted. In short, ALH combined insurance principles (link to previous earnings) with needs-based characteristics (means-test).

Both ALG and ALH (the latter on behalf of the federal government) were administered by the Federal Labour Institute (*Bundesanstalt für Arbeit*, BA; renamed *Bundesagentur für Arbeit* in 2004), which is an inde-

Table 4.1. Major programme characteristics of unemployment support, 1980 and 2004, Germany

	1980	2004
Benefit level	ALG: 68% of previous earnings ALH: 58%	ALG: 67% (60% if no children) ALH: 57% (53% if no children)
Entitlement ALG	Maximum 12 months	12–32 (depending on age and contribution record); (from 2005: 12; maximum 18 for over 55 year olds)
Eligibility ALH	Also for those with shorter contribution record	Abolished
Structure	Three-tier (ALG, ALH, and SA)	Two-tier (2005) ALG I and ALG II
Activation	Weak	Strong (1996; 2003) (but no mandatory participation for ALG claimants)
Overall aim and character	Status-oriented reintegration; relatively favourable suitability criteria	Labour-market integration; stricter activation criteria

pendent public authority subject to federal legislation. A tripartite organization comprising of representatives from employers, trade unions, and the state, the BA and its regional and local labour offices are responsible for transfer payments, comprising of unemployment compensation and also other benefits such as short-term working allowance, which is a temporary compensation for workers with reduced working hours due to economic difficulties. The BA is also in charge of the bulk of active labour-market programmes in Germany, which are financed out of the same source as ALG (and other transfers), with the federal government having to balance the annual BA budget if deficits occur. The latter was the case when unemployment rose in the early 1980s, and for each year in the 1990s (with annual subsidies from general taxation ranging between 2 and 22 per cent of the BA budget). This particular funding structure has several implications. First, for individual unemployed persons, access to labour-market programmes was (until recently) largely determined by benefit receipt, with ALG (and ALH) claimants in a privileged position as prime clientele of the BA. Second, the joint funding structure tended to create expenditure patterns which squeezed funds for active labour-market programmes at times of high unemployment and thus increased demand-led benefit spending (Schmid et al. 1987). In periods when unemployment fell, more room for expansion for active programmes was created because of reduced pressure on the BA budget. Third, the requirement to balance annual deficits in the BA budget provided strong cost-saving incentives for the federal government. Indeed, as is shown later, the state of the annual BA budget was a major determinant in labour-market policymaking.

Finally, until recently social assistance (SA or *Sozialhilfe*) was a third form of potential support for unemployed people. As with Income Support in the UK, *Sozialhilfe* in Germany provides a guaranteed minimum income to all persons in need (not only unemployed) subject to a means-test. However, the German system is regulated at federal level, but funded and administered by local authorities and municipalities. Thus, in regions with high levels of long-term unemployment, and for many unemployed people without or with only insufficient support from ALG or ALH, significant pressure is exerted on local authorities' budgets. Reissert (1998) refers to a 'vicious circle' arising from this compartmentalized treatment of unemployed clientele. High regional unemployment tends to push up local social assistance spending, which tends to deplete resources for regional public investment which, in turn, fosters further employment losses and unemployment. The persistence of high levels of unemployment in the 1980s thus prompted many local social assistance offices to transfer employable social assistance claimants to programmes which would provide earnings, at least for some time, and re-establish entitlement to ALG (Clasen et al. 1998). The number of social assistance claimants participating in different types of local employment programmes climbed from below 120,000 in 1993 to about 200,000 in 1996 (Heinelt and Weck 1998: 52). Buhr (2003:158) refers to official surveys which indicate that the number subsequently rose to 400,000—which was about 10 per cent of total unemployment and close to half of all SA claimants considered to be available for employment.

Contrasting major programme characteristics in 1980 with those in 2004 (Table 4.1), a process of selective cutbacks is suggested in Germany, as well as improvements for older contributors with longer contribution records. The level of income protection for claimants of ALG, the primary form of support, has only changed slightly, and hardly at all for claimants with children. Until recently, institutional parameters also remained rather stable. As will be discussed, the merging of ALH with SA (which came into force in 2005) does however represent a radical change. Suitability criteria, defining jobs deemed acceptable for unemployed people, had already become tighter in the 1970s and 1980s (Clasen 1994) and some local offices would require recipients of SA deemed able to work to engage in employment-related schemes. However, general and encompassing

activation policies (affecting job-search conditions and work-related obligations) started later than in the UK and remained less prescriptive in comparison.

4.1.2 The United Kingdom

Compared with Germany, three features distinguished British unemployment protection in 1980. First, the delivery of both contributory and
means-tested benefits was centralized, top-down, and integrated. Although
insurance based benefits were funded differently and were technically
separate from non-contributory transfers, the government determined the
terms and conditions of both.

Second, there was no separate funding arrangement for unemployment
support. Instead, unemployment benefits were paid out of the NIF, which
was also the source for other contributory benefits, particularly the basic
state pension.

The third characteristic was a weak contributory basis and (after 1981)
the absence of earnings-related unemployment compensation. Unlike in
Germany and other European countries in which insurance benefits
adopted a more explicit wage replacement character in the 1950s and
1960s, British steps in this direction remained half-hearted with the introduction of a so called earnings-related supplement on top of flat-rate benefit
in 1966 (Clasen 1994). Due to the modest generosity and small margin
between the standard unemployment benefit and means-tested support (in
fact, both rates have been identical for years), it has always been fairly
common for recipients of insurance benefits, particularly those with a
non-working partner or dependants, also to be claiming means-tested benefits, such as housing benefits. Moreover, the share of unemployed who did
not meet the contribution conditions, or who had exhausted their entitlement, and were thus reliant on means-tested benefits, has traditionally been
higher than in Germany. The scheme thus functioned much less as a form of
wage-replacement than in Germany, and most other European countries. As
discussed in Chapter 3, British trade unions were thus less involved in
debates surrounding unemployment compensation compared with their
French or German counterparts, for example, who regard contributory
benefits as a component of the wage package.

The three central characteristics outlined above apply also to the current
scheme. However, there has been a considerable decline in benefit generosity in relation to average full-time adult earnings (DWP 2004*b*), the
earnings-related supplement has disappeared, and the maximum entitlement to contributory support was halved in 1996. In the same year, previously separate insurance and means-tested support became incorporated
into a single system, Jobseekers Allowance (JSA), which grants contributory

Table 4.2. Major programme characteristics of unemployment benefit (1980) and Jobseekers Allowance (2004), UK

	1980	2004
Benefit level	21% of average male earnings	12%
Benefit structure	Flat-rate plus earnings-related supplement	Flat-rate (lower rate for under 25-year-olds)
Additions	For dependants	Abolished
Entitlement	12 months	6 months (contributory JSA)
Qualifying conditions	Fairly lenient contributory criteria	Tighter
Activation approach	Weak	Strong and encompassing (partly mandatory) (1989; 1996; 1998)

support for a maximum of six months followed by means-tested support. Table 4.2 compares some other programmatic features of insurance-based unemployment protection in 1980 with the current scheme.

4.2 SCALE AND PROFILE OF CHANGE IN COMPARATIVE PERSPECTIVE

Additional comparative information on the generosity and coverage of benefit support, as well as benefit activation, can shed further light on the direction, scale, and pattern of reform (Clasen et al. 2001). Comparisons of the 'replacement rate' (degree by which benefit compensates for lost earnings) are often used, but are not straightforward (Kvist 1998). Apart from the definition of earnings, calculations depend heavily on assumed socio-economic characteristics of benefit claimants and decisions about the inclusion or exclusion of potential benefits in addition to the primary form of unemployment protection (Gallie and Paugam 2000: 381–5). For example, the standard level of JSA is very low in the UK compared with other European countries. However, unemployed people often apply to additional means-tested support such as Council Tax benefit and housing benefits, which can be as high as unemployment benefit. Indeed, once help with housing costs is included, replacement rates in the UK improve considerably in international comparisons (OECD 1999*a*).

The OECD has developed a summary indicator of unemployment benefit entitlement which combines a range of (gross) unemployment replacement rates for workers with full employment records at two earnings levels, three family situations, and of unemployment spells (OECD 2002*a*). It indicates a modest and progressively declining generosity of unemployment protection in the UK (see Table 4.3). The index for Germany is not generous either within a European context, but above the British level and remaining fairly stable over time. In a broader comparison of twenty OECD countries, the British and German systems represented middle positions in the mid-1970s. By 1999 the rankings of both had dropped to fifteenth for Germany, while the UK had become the least generous country (Nickell 2003; see also Korpi and Palme 2003).

As for coverage, Table 4.4 shows that the role of insurance-based support was much more important in the early 1980s than twenty years later in both countries. Dwindling during the 1980s, the share of

Table 4.3. Replacement rates of unemployment protection (OECD summary index)

	1979	1985	1989	1993	1997	2001
UK	24	21	18	19	18	17
Germany	29	28	28	28	26	28

Source: Based on OECD summary measure (gross rate based on three family types, two earnings levels, and three durations of unemployment) (OECD 2002*a*: figure 3.4, OECD 2004*c*; see also text).

Table 4.4. Beneficiary rates (benefit recipients as share of registered unemployed)

	1980	1981–4	1985–9	1991–3	1994–6	1997–2000	2001
UB or JSA (contributory)	48	31	28	30	24	14	16
IS or JSA (means-tested)	40	53	60	60	69	73	70
ALG	53	48	39	49	48	43	40
ALH	14	20	25	23	26	32	34
Unemployment SA	9	9	17	17	13	17	17

Source: For UK: based on Clasen (1994: 41); DSS Social Security Statistics (various years); and DWP (2004*a*: Table C1 for 1993 onwards)—claimants divided by annual claimant unemployment
For Germany: share of recipients amongst average annual stock of unemployed; calculations based on Reissert 2005 and Bundesanstalt für Arbeit, ANBA, various years (estimates data for 1980 and 1981)
For West Germany until 1993: social assistance figures not fully comparable due to different survey methods (recipients stating 'loss of employment', 'unemployment' as the main stated reason for claiming; from 1994: registered as unemployed; also introduction of special assistance scheme for asylum seekers in 1993 (Statistisches Bundesamt, Fachserie 13, Reihe 2)—note that a significant share of social assistance claimants are also in receipt of ALG or ALH (see text).

unemployed in receipt of (first-tier) insurance-based support (UB/JSA and ALG respectively) improved a little in the recession of the early 1990s, but has dropped considerably since the mid-1990s. At the same time, the scope of means-tested support grew progressively in the UK, representing the predominant form of unemployment support today. This trend can also be illustrated with reference to funding sources. As a percentage of total transfers to unemployed people, the share of contributory-based funding declined from 45 per cent in 1979 to 25 per cent in the mid-1980s, and from 16 per cent in the late 1980s to 9 per cent in 2000 (DSS 1999). In short, the character of social protection for unemployed people in the UK has significantly shifted from a mixed social insurance and needs-based support, towards one which is predominately based on needs principles (see also Clegg and Clasen 2003).

In Germany, the coverage of the first tier of insurance based unemployment compensation (ALG) amongst the stock of unemployed also diminished and the second-tier ALH has become much more important, as well as general social assistance. It can thus be argued that unemployment support has also become more needs based in Germany. However, ALG remains important for a considerable share of the unemployed (and the vast majority of those entering unemployment; Reissert 2005). Moreover, as discussed, ALH is not entirely governed by needs principles. While eligibility is subject to a means-test, its rate is proportional to previous earnings. Taken ALG and ALH together, the wage replacement character (and insurance principle) is still relevant for well over two-thirds of all unemployed. Moreover, about a third of all unemployed social assistance claimants also received either ALG or ALH in the 1990s (Statistisches Bundesamt, various years). In short, the scale of declining contributory support in Germany is much less pronounced than the UK. This changed, however, in 2005 when ALH was replaced by the means-tested ALG II, implying a dramatic restructuring within unemployment support with a majority of claimants becoming dependent on benefits which no longer reflect former earnings but current needs and means.

Quantitative indicators in the field of activation policy are harder to come by than those for cash transfers. Shifts between rights and obligations are difficult to express in expenditure or case load figures. However, changes in expenditure on active labour market programmes as a whole might at least provide an idea as to the potential effort of employment integration schemes in each country. These were rather similar in the 1980s; however, adjusted for unemployment, West Germany had spent considerably more than the UK by the end of that decade (Table 4.5). In the aftermath of unification, German spending increased steeply, while British efforts declined considerably below the EU average. Latest available

Table 4.5. Spending on active labour market policy (% of GDP)

	1980	1985	1986–90	1991–4	1995–7	1998–2001	2002
UK	0.6	0.7	0.8	0.6	0.4	0.4	0.4
Germany	0.7*	0.7	0.9	1.5	1.3	1.3	1.2
EU average	—	0.9	0.9	1.1	1.1	1.1	1.0†
UK: divided by u**	0.10	0.06	0.09	0.06	0.05	0.07	0.08
Germany: divided by u**	0.13	0.10	0.15	0.23	0.15	0.16	0.15

Source: OECD 2001*b*, 2002*b*, 2004*b*; from 1991 for the whole of Germany.
*figure for 1982: G. Schmid 1998: 159; **divided by annual ILO unemployment rate;
†without Luxembourg; data for 2001 for most countries (Greece for 1998).

figures (OECD 2004*b*) indicate that the UK remains rooted at the bottom among EU countries. After the mid-1990s, the difference between the two countries remained significant but diminished somewhat due a decrease in German expenditure and a slight increase in adjusted British figures.

However, active labour market includes a range of different pro-grammes, such as training, job creation, work experience, job matching, and counselling and job search schemes. Concentrating only on major items, Tables 4.6 and 4.7 provide an indication of the changing profile of spending in both countries over time. Unfortunately, international data do not separate spending on job search schemes from administrative costs. The OECD simply lists public employment services (PES) and adminis-tration costs as a single item. Nevertheless, remarkable for the UK is the decline of job creation since the mid-1980s and the diminishing scope of

Table 4.6. Profile of labour market policy expenditure—major measures (% of GDP)

		1985	1986–90	1991–4	1995–7	1998–2001	2002
PES and	UK	0.14	0.15	0.20	0.19	0.13	0.17
administration	Germany	0.21	0.22	0.24	0.23	0.23	0.23
Labour market	UK	0.09	0.17	0.15	0.14	0.05	0.02
training	Germany	0.20	0.31	0.52	0.38	0.34	0.32
Subsidized	UK	0.22	0.17	0.03	0.03	0.01	0.03
employment	Germany	0.17	0.17	0.42	0.39	0.32	0.22

Source: Own calculations based on data from OECD Employment Outlook (1992, 1996, 2000, 2004); until 1991 Great Britain and West Germany; UK figures: 1985 is 1985–6, etc. (for definitions, see OECD 2001*a*). PES and administration includes placement, counselling and vocational guidance, job-search courses, job mobility measures, etc., as well as administrative costs. Measures disregarded in the table are youth measures (targeted at transition from school to work) and special schemes for disabled job seekers.

Table 4.7. Profile of labour market policy expenditure (% of total active spending)

		1985	1986–90	1991–4	1995–7	1998–01	2002
PES and	UK	20	19	33	47	33	42
administration	Germany	30	24	16	18	18	19
Labour market	UK	13	21	25	35	13	8
training	Germany	28	34	35	29	26	27
Subsidized	UK	31	21	5	8	3	8
employment	Germany	24	19	28	30	25	18

Source: Data from Table 4.7 divided by rows 1 and 2 respectively of Table 4.5 (see also *Source* of Table 4.6).

training. Devoting considerably more resources to both programmes, the steep increase after unification is significant in Germany, but also the decline since the mid-1990s.

Table 4.7 considers the relative scale of different spheres of spending. It confirms the dramatically diminishing scope of both job creation and training programmes in the UK, matched by a considerable shift towards job-search related programmes since the 1980s (assuming that administration costs have remained fairly stable). Thus, expenditure data suggest that the growing emphasis on activation policies in the UK after 1997 has been on intensified job-search efforts rather than training, the relative role of which has even diminished further.

In sum, common trends of welfare state reform in unemployment support but also distinctive national profiles can be discerned. Both countries have dropped significantly in international rankings of benefit generosity, and replacement rates indicate continually declining generosity in the UK when compared with average earnings. The growing share of unemployed people dependent on means-tested support implies a structural shift in the relative scope of distributive principles upon which monetary support rests. This is most obvious in the UK where the notion of contributory support has all but disappeared and means-testing has become the ubiquitous form of cash benefit for the unemployed. By contrast, a division between a core and a periphery in the 'divided' German welfare state (Leibfried and Tennstedt 1985; Offe 1991) remains a feature in unemployment support. However, as will be discussed later, reforms have shifted the boundary between the two. Although the level of support declined by only a small margin, and hardly at all for parents, the core (ALG recipients) has shrunk somewhat while the periphery has widened. The ALH system has been successively pushed towards a more marginal position, culminating in the merging with SA and the creation of ALG II in 2005. The latter has transformed 'a central element of the country's prized social security system. From 2005, the group of the unemployed that will receive benefits that are linked to previous earnings will become a minority' (Hassel and Williamson 2004: 13).

Nevertheless, although the protection is less extensive than it was especially for older workers, claimants of unemployment insurance benefits in Germany continue to receive relatively generous payments and for them previous earnings remain a criterion for job suitability criteria (for six months). By comparison, any division within unemployment support in the UK has all but disappeared. As will be shown later, these different patterns of retrenchment, that is, global retrenchment and structural shift towards a needs-based support in the UK versus selective retrenchment (and selective expansion during the 1980s) in Germany, came about as a result of different reform trajectories.

As for activation policy, the option of applying work tests and transferring unemployed people from benefit receipt into labour market and work experience programmes have existed in Germany for a long time and have increasingly been made use of by local authorities responsible for SA claimants (Buhr 2003). In the 1990s, new work test options were introduced for other unemployed groups, prompting some commentators to emphasize similarities between British and German activation efforts (Leisering and Hilkert 2000; Mohr 2004). However, while administrative practices might have become more similar and the overall policy direction might be the same, remaining cross-national differences should not be ignored. First, redefining job suitability criteria and putting more onus on unemployed claimants were already evident in the 1970s and 1980s (Clasen 1994), but major steps in this direction were only made in the second half of the 1990s (see later). Second, whereas the UK does not differentiate between benefit claimants, different suitability criteria, work test options, and possibilities for transfer from benefit to labour market programmes apply to different groups of unemployed in Germany, traditionally dependent on the type of benefit received. Third, unlike the New Deal programmes for young people and long-term unemployed in the UK (see Section 4.3), there is still no routine mandatory transfer from benefit receipt to a labour market scheme in Germany. Once again, this might be changed for future ALG II recipients under the age of twenty-five, but currently such action is merely optional. Finally, as subsequent sections will show, the remit of the British activation agenda is much more encompassing than that of Germany.

As a next step, the identified directions, scale, and pattern of change will be related to reform processes in the two countries from the early 1980s.

Only major legislative changes will be discussed here, which are listed in Appendices A and B. Since different phases and directions of change can be identified, the discussion for each country is divided into three time periods, capturing reforms implemented during the 1980s, between 1990 and the end of conservative rules in the UK (1997) and Germany (1998), and finally changes introduced by the German red–green government and New Labour since then.

4.3 REFORMING UNEMPLOYMENT SUPPORT IN GERMANY

4.3.1 Selective cuts and targeted improvements (1982–9)

In the early 1980s, the second major post-war recession triggered West German unemployment levels to rise to unprecedented levels (see Fig. 3.1). Because of diminishing revenue and rising benefit expenditure, the budget deficit of the BA rose steeply in 1981, triggering cuts in both unemployment protection and active programmes. Such a response by the then social-democratic led coalition under Helmut Schmidt was in accordance with policies which had been introduced in the mid-1970s and which followed a maxim that savings should be made where deficits occur (Webber 1984). Of course, there were alternative ways of balancing the BA budget. Apart from raising contribution rates (more firmly), the BA's revenue basis could have been changed by also making the self-employed and tenured public sector employees pay into the system. A long-standing demand voiced within the SPD and trade unions in particular, the latter would have required an institutional reform which, however, was not seriously considered. Instead, the actual pattern of reform remained within the context of routine answers to fiscal deficits in the BA and avoided conflict with the unions at the same time (Clasen 1992: 290). The pattern of retrenchment left the position of core workers largely untouched but curtailed benefit rights for groups more peripheral to the labour market (job starters, casual workers, and others with less stable contribution records; see Appendix A). This pattern became a trademark for reform initiatives in the 1980s and also the 1990s under both centre–left and centre–right governments.

However, as a result of high unemployment the BA deficit grew during 1982, inducing the FDP—the junior and more market liberal party in government—to demand more substantial cuts, including a blanket reduction of unemployment rates (to 50 per cent of previous earnings during the first three months of unemployment). These suggestions contributed to the eventual breakdown of the centre–left government, with the FDP leaving the coalition and aligning with the CDU/CSU in a new interim government in the autumn of 1982, which later went on to win the general election in early 1983. Despite the demands made by the FDP and calls by the previous conservative opposition for more substantial cost-saving, the new government simply introduced measures which had already been planned by the previous government (Clasen 1994). In 1983 and 1984 it maintained thus not simply a course of retrenchment, but adopted the previous pattern of small and dispersed cuts which mainly disadvantaged peripheral workers (see Appendix A), while refraining from benefit retrenchment which might affect core workers. The only exception was a relatively small cut in benefit rates restricted to claimants without children (Appendix A). This decision can be attributed to the growing family orientation of the conservative social policy agenda since the late 1970s (see Chapter 6).

Between 1984 and 1987 the conservative–liberal government appeared to switch policy direction from selective retrenchment to selective expansion, easing access to ALG and progressively extending entitlement from twelve to, eventually, thirty-two months for some groups among the unemployed (Appendix A). However, in a second change direction, the pattern of selective cost-saving measures was resumed after 1987, cutting expenditure on training and job creation programmes (G. Schmid 1998) and introducing benefit restrictions for groups with less continuous contribution records (see Appendix A). These changes in policy direction, and the continuation of the particular pattern of policy, privileging core workers (with families) and concentrating retrenchment efforts on the margin of the labour market, can partly be explained with reference to the constellation of preferences within the government coalition. But the specific institutional setting for unemployment policy is a contributory factor. As for the policy direction, the motivation within the government coalition in favour of a more severe and global form of benefit retrenchment was only weak. Unlike the Conservative Party under Thatcher at the time, the CDU/CSU was much less cohesive regarding its social policy orientation, with different factions pulling in opposite directions. As discussed in Chapter 3, during the 1980s, the 'social policy' wing within the CDU/CSU was intent on preserving traditional welfare state structures (Schmid 1990; Winter 1990). This 'employee' orientation was most prominently represented by Norbert Blüm, a trade union member and Minister of Social Affairs in all four Kohl governments until 1998. The more business-oriented and market-liberal wing of the conservative party was able to push for some deregulatory employment policies, but the social policy faction remained the prime agenda setter in the domain of social policy within relevant party and parliamentary committees (Zohlnhöfer 2001: 661).

The dominance of this wing in the field of unemployment support became manifest on three occasions. After the general election in 1983, it successfully resisted the FDP's demand for a global benefit cut (see earlier). Amidst the second round of cutbacks towards the end of the 1980s, the FDP called for a reduction of ALG entitlement for unemployed claimants below the age of twenty-five (to nine months). Again, the proposal remained unsuccessful against a broad informal coalition (including the social policy wing of the CDU/CSU, the oppositional SPD, and trade unions) set on defending the insurance and wage replacement principle within the ALG scheme.

However, a third defeat by the FDP in the mid-1980s, at that time arguing for a reduction in BA contribution rates, indicates that the policy pattern has also to be understood with reference to the specific institutional setting and the administrative separation and intertwined fiscal interdependencies between the three types of benefit provisions for unemployed persons in particular. According to official German data, unemployment reached an unprecedented level with more than two million people out of work in the early 1980s. By then the impact on the material situation of core workers and their families had become a focus of protests by trade unions and other groups, such as church organizations. In addition, the combination of the growth of long-term unemployment and tighter eligibility criteria reduced the share of ALG claimants by the mid-1980s (see Table 4.4). While this eased fiscal pressure on the BA, pressure on tax-funded ALH expenditure and local social assistance budgets grew. This situation led to mounting criticism against federal policy not only from the opposition but also from individual conservative municipalities and *Länder*. This protest was strengthened when, as a consequence of the combined effect of the factors mentioned earlier and the growth of employment after 1982 (adding revenue), BA deficits of over DM8 billion in 1981 declined and had turned into a surplus of more than DM3 billion by 1984 (Clasen 1994: 208).

The paradoxical situation of BA reserves at a time when unemployment remained well above the two million mark posed serious problems of legitimacy. However, rather than requiring strategies of 'blame avoidance', this situation provided several opportunities for political 'credit-claiming' (Weaver 1986). First, BA reserves enabled the government to expand labour market programmes (G. Schmid 1998) and at the same time to cut non-wage labour costs by lowering the contribution rate to the BA. Second, the government engaged in a form of welfare expansion by selectively extending ALG entitlement. By restricting this option to older workers with long contribution records, the government explicitly appealed to traditional criteria of deservingness (better rewards for better contributors) as well as to notions of social fairness (older workers deserve better support because of a lower chance of re-employment). Third, the policy eased labour market pressure since the extended ALG entitlements became a major route out of employment into a quasi-form of early retirement (see Chapter 5). Reissert (2005) refers to studies which show that one-third of total expenditure on unemployment protection payments was paid to people who left the labour market at the end of their unemployment spell. In other words, the government, in agreement with social partners, 'instrumentalized' (Reissert 2005) the ALG system for purposes of early labour market exit (see also Oppen 1997).

Finally, extended ALG entitlement resulted in a cost transfer from tax funded ALH to contribution-based ALG (Clasen 1992: 294). In other words, largely as a result of the particular institutional structures of unemployment protection in Germany, the government was able to perform an apparent conjurers trick of welfare expansion while at the same time saving (tax) spending on social security. In short, the impact of changes in employment and unemployment on the BA budget, in combination with the specific institutional setting of unemployment support in Germany, facilitated policies of retrenchment and expansion (Jochem 2001). More particularly, it enabled the social policy wing of the CDU/CSU (Zohlnhöfer 2001: 669) to determine policy patterns in line with their interests which, in the 1980s, corresponded closely with the traditional German focus on wage labour centred social policy (Vobruba 1990).

This illustrates the importance of the institutional setting which connects different domains of German social insurance with each other via federal tax subsidies, giving rise to the so-called 'shifting-yard' (*Verschiebebahnhof*) policy. For example, the decision to reduce pension insurance payments by the BA on behalf of unemployed claimants (1983) saved expenditure on the part of the BA but decreased revenue for pension insurance. Equally, the expansion of ALG entitlements a few years later allowed the government to entitle all mothers to child rearing pension credits (see Chapter 6) because the former reduced tax-funded federal ALH expenditure, making funds disposable for the latter. In short, an assessment of German unemployment support policy has to take account of institutional horizontal interlocking across social insurance branches via federal subsidies, as well as vertical interdependencies between federal, regional, and social insurance funding for different types of benefits. No equivalent institutional setting exists in the UK.

4.3.2 German unification, acceleration of retrenchment, and late activation (1990–8)

Rather than prompting structural reform, German unification led to the transfer of traditional West German welfare state programmes to unified

Germany. In response to the massive collapse of employment in the territory of the former GDR, the scale of labour market policy rose significantly (see Table 4.5). The increase in expenditure was partly covered by steeply increasing contribution rates to the BA (see Fig. 3.5) and partly by accumulating unprecedented deficits in the BA budget. Despite this considerable fiscal pressure, unification merely suspended the continuation of the policy pattern and direction of the 1980s. A turn was made towards what might be called activation policies which were developing elsewhere in Europe at the time, including the UK but also Denmark and the Netherlands (Cox 1998; Clasen 2000), only entered the German agenda towards the end of the 1990s, and structural change in benefit programmes even later.

Why did unification foster structural stability? Supported by the growth of demand in the eastern part of the country, the West German economy experienced an economic boom in the early 1990s, followed by a recession in 1993, that is, at a time when fiscal pressure was easing in most other parts of Europe. This delayed business cycle caused the debate on unemployment to be dominated by cyclical economic aspects rather than questions of employability or work disincentives (Zohlnhöfer 2001: 662). Rather than benefit schemes, public attention was drawn to the massive expansion of job creation, training, and short-term work measures during the early 1990s. The ratio by which labour-market programmes reduced open unemployment rose from 16 per cent in 1998 to 49 per cent in 1991 (G. Schmid 1998: 168). Reissert (2005) estimates that of the four million people who had lost their jobs in the former GDR between unification and 1992, 'almost 3 million had not affected the unemployment register' as a consequence of a range of labour-market measures, early retirement, and migration to the western part of the country (1.2 million). In short, while a welfare-to-work approach was slowly emerging elsewhere in Europe, a reverse work-to-welfare policy was pursued specifically in the eastern part of Germany.

However, German unification initially also altered traditional interest coalitions and policy orientations. Heinelt and Weck (1998) argue that sentiments of responsibility towards contributing to a successful unification process, fears of social unrest and the expectation of even stronger migration into the old *Länder* favoured support for institutional stability and an expansive labour-market policy across all political parties and both sides of industry. There was a prevailing conviction that the West German labour-market policies had proved successful in the 1980s, and that mass unemployment in the 1990s would be a temporary problem. Moreover, employer representatives and market-oriented policymakers feared that the exceptional situation of German unification would potentially strengthen traditional trade union demands for programmatic change (e.g. widening the revenue base of the BA). As a consequence, increases in contribution rates were conceded as the option which would retain existing structures.

The economic boom in western Germany began to subside in late 1992 while the east German economy did not pick up as expected. Public deficits grew further and the *Bundesbank* raised interest rates, providing impetus for a switch from expansion to cost-saving measures. In the following year policy debates were influenced by the Maastricht convergence criteria for Economic and Monetary Union (EMU). In addition, the government and employer organizations triggered a debate about Germany as a location of investment (*Standort Deutschland*) which was arguably becoming less attractive because of high wages and rising social insurance contributions. Indeed, the contributory funding of the welfare state became increasingly perceived as a structural impediment to economic recovery. In the wake of this debate the consensus sustaining expenditure for large scale labour-market policy in the territory of the former GDR began to crumble and cost-saving efforts re-emerged. In line with the policy pattern of the 1980s, the government proposed cuts in spending on labour-market programmes and also selective reductions in ALG and ALH levels to take effect in 1994, once again hitting those without children more than parents. In addition it was proposed to limit entitlement to ALH for two years, and to abolish the scheme for those without prior receipt of ALG altogether. These plans were successfully challenged by the *Bundesrat* as unduly transferring costs from the federal government to the *Länder* and municipality level. No longer dominated by a CDU/CSU majority, it should be noted also that some conservative-led *Länder* in the *Bundesrat* were highly critical of the proposed changes. As a compromise, ALH entitlement remained unaltered for the majority of claimants, but was scaled back for those without prior receipt of ALG (see Appendix A).

In the mid-1990s, the speed of retrenchment picked up and activation policies became more prominent. For ALH claimants, a gradual decrease in benefit rates for long-term receipt was introduced in 1996, as well as stricter rules regarding active job search and work requirements. For some commentators these policies indicated a 'fundamental change of perspective' (Heinelt and Weck 1998: 56). Previously the normative orientation had been to aim for job offers which corresponded with individual skills and acquired status. By contrast, the new legislation indicated a shift towards a system of income protection, but no longer wage replacement or status-adequate employment integration. Perhaps even more indicative of this trend were regulations which came into force in 1998 under the new Social Policy Act III (*Sozialgesetzbuch III*, SGB III) which replaced the former Labour Promotion Law. Previously claimants had been able to refuse job offers below their former level of earnings or qualification if the new job was deemed to jeopardize a return into more adequate employment. Expecting individuals to adapt to changing demands on the labour market, the new legislation defined suitability criteria more narrowly merely in monetary terms (see Appendix A).

It should be noted that new regulations were not entirely restrictive but included selective improvements. However, unlike in the 1980s, this time the latter focused on those in non-standard forms of employment. For example, a partial unemployment benefit, replacing earnings from one of possibly several part-time jobs, was introduced, the coverage of seasonal workers was widened, options for transferring from unemployment into self-employment were made more generous, and the acceptance of low-paid employment were made more conducive (for details, see Reissert 2005). These changes can be seen as in accordance with the redefinition of the above suitability criteria, that is, aiming at labour-market reintegration regardless of previously held employment. As such, they might be interpreted as changes in unemployment support mechanisms aimed in accordance with, and supporting, changing employment structures, such as a growth of flexible and more atypical forms of work.

Otherwise, however, the previous policy direction and pattern of selective retrenchment was resumed in the mid-1990s, with policies beginning to focus on questions of employability and work requirement. SA and ALH claimants were most affected by this turn towards activation and work testing, but new suitability criteria affected also long-term ALG claimants (see above). As far as unemployment compensation was concerned, there were no more new improvements for core workers. Instead, for the first time the rate of ALG for those with children was reduced, even though the reduction was marginal (1 per cent) and ALG claimants continued to be spared major losses compared with ALH recipients. How can these patterns be explained?

One major factor was certainly the impact of unification and the sustained need for large-scale transfers to the former territory of the GDR in order to cushion the collapse of the labour market. The economic recession after 1993 and the failure of the east German labour market to pick up exacerbated fiscal pressure, while the self-imposed European convergence criteria limited the scope of action further. All these factors provided a very different economic and political context compared with the 1980s. More specifically, the BA budget had no reserves to spend at any time but reported record annual deficits. Contribution rates had been increased steeply in 1991 and further increases were ruled out when the conservative–liberal government began to perceive non-wage labour costs as a major problem hampering economic competitiveness.

This altered context influenced the constellation of interest representation within the government. Zohlnhöfer (2001) refers to three reasons why the social policy wing lost its previous dominance in questions of labour-market policy, and why it conceded cuts in unemployment protection more specifically. First, a majority of the faction perceived some deregulatory polices implemented in the 1980s (e.g. in the field of temporary work) as having had a positive impact on job growth and had thus become more amenable to measures which would enhance labour-market flexibility. Second, the negotiations over the introduction of the long-term care insurance scheme at the time (see Götting et al. 1994) deflected attention away from debates about unemployment protection. In order to make some gains in the former, concessions were made in the reform of the latter. Finally, the power of the social policy wing had waned due to changes of personnel in relevant committees after the early 1990s. Finally, while the *Bundesrat* proved to be an important ally for the conservative social policy faction in 1993 (watering down ALH plans), hardly any legislative changes introduced since then required its consent.

Such reasons help to explain why the conservative–liberal government returned to retrenchment policies and inflicted deeper cutbacks than in the 1980s. But they do not explain why ALG rates were not scaled back more decisively, as had been advocated by the FDP in the 1980s. Both fiscal pressure was greater and opportunities for more radical retrenchment seemed better, due to the loss of influence of the social policy faction and the growing strength of the pro-market faction within the conservative government. However, structural factors such as interdependencies between Germany's political economy and its core social security systems (Ebbinghaus and Manow 2001) continued to make global retrenchment an inappropriate policy. Represented by trade unions and by sizeable factions within both major political parties, it is suggested here that traditional norms of social justice and types of redistribution prohibited more severe cuts in ALG payments. As discussed in Chapter 3, benefit entitlement for core workers are regarded as part of the 'social wage' and thus a constitutive element within the German 'coordinated market economy' (Hall and Soskice 2001*b*: 21). Competing internationally in high quality product markets, and thus relying on a high skill/high wage constellation, makes export industries subscribe to relatively high levels of wage replacement benefits, at least for the short-term unemployed. With the German industrial relations system, ALG payments function as a form of 'side-contract' (Ganßmann 1991), lowering the risk of undermining collectively regulated wage rates. Better benefits for core workers safeguard investments in the formation of industry-specific skills (Estevez-Abe et al. 2001), ease labour-market transitions (including options for labour-market exit for older workers), facilitate employment restructuring, and thus the reconciliation of conflicts between both sides of industry. In short, the nexus between the core of unemployment support with employment and industrial relations in Germany helps to explain the particular profile of retrenchment, within which ALG recipients continued to fare relatively well during the 1990s.

4.3.3 Shifting grounds within the red–green coalition and late structural reform (1998–2003)

Having increased to 4.2 million people out of work, unemployment was a central theme in the run-up to the general election in 1998. In addition to other pledges, cashcard sized plastic cards were distributed during the election campaign, a publicity device which had also been used by the Labour Party in 1997; the SPD vowed to reduce unemployment to 3.5 million within four years. However, unlike its counterpart in the UK, there had not been any programmatic reorientation of social policy aims within the SPD during its time in opposition (Gohr 2001). In labour-market policy a 'status adequate' employment reintegration (Heinelt and Weck 1998) remained the guiding principle, as well as the need to maintain a sizeable 'second' labour market, that is, publicly subsidized employment, as long as unemployment levels remained high. Accordingly, the new red–green government expanded job creation schemes, especially in eastern germany, and heeded election promises by revoking some of the cutbacks which had been implemented by the previous conservative–liberal government (e.g. affecting sick pay and employment protection). Other measures widened the scope of jobs covered by social insurance. Within labour market policy, the new government eased access for older unemployed to training and job creation schemes and lowered the degree by which redundancy money from employers reduced unemployment benefit. As a response to a ruling by the Constitutional Court in May 2000, and reinstating a regulation which had applied before 1982, the government treated one-off payments (Christmas bonus, holiday pay, etc.) as regular earnings which raised the real level of unemployment benefits. However, the ruling did not apply to ALH claimants, many of whom were also hit by the decision to abolish the benefit for those without prior receipt of ALG. In short, the differential treatment of unemployed people by benefit type initially continued under the red–green government.

In parallel to the waning power of the social policy wing within the CDU/CSU, groups in favour of defending traditional social policy structures also gradually lost influence within the SPD. Oskar Lafontaine, as the dominant champion of a demand-oriented Keynesian economic policy, resigned as Finance Minister in 1999. After his departure, internal debates within the SPD gained prominence between the so-called 'modernizers', advocating a more supply-side 'third-way' oriented public policy, and 'traditionalists', favouring traditional social policy structures. The latter were supported by vociferous trade unions which remained highly suspicious of any signs of a deregulatory policy and moves which would introduce stronger wage dispersion. But calls for a policy shift were fuelled by the agenda-setting Schröder–Blair paper in 1999 (Jeffery and Handl 1999) and controversies and recommendations made by other policy circles kept labour-market policy in the public eye. For example, the notion of the need to shift from an 'active' to an 'activating' labour market policy emanated from the 'benchmarking' group attached to the corporatist 'Alliance for Jobs' (*Bündnis für Arbeit*). This group was also responsible for coining the idea that labour-market policy should 'promote and oblige' *(fördern und fordern)*, which can be seen as an equivalent of the 'rights and responsibilities' concept of the third way in Britain (Clasen and Clegg 2004).

The fact that these debates were not accompanied by legislative action can partly be attributed to weak problem pressure at the time (Blancke and Schmid 2003). The economy grew reasonably well and unemployment was declining, making the political target level of 3.5 million by 2002 seem feasible. However, in 2001 unemployment began to rise sharply again and the general election in 2002 was looming. In the autumn of 2001 the government introduced the so-called *Job-Aqtiv* act (Appendix A). The new legislation introduced stricter job-search activities, job profiling, and made reintegration contracts for unemployed benefit claimants obligatory. It also eased access to wage subsidies, training programmes, and business start-up options. Ostheim and Zohlnhöfer (2004) point out that the latter aspects were examples of the EU's European Employment Strategy (EES) directly impacting on the formulation of German labour-market policy. Previously, no EU influence on German policymaking in this field can be observed. However, the fact that EES guidelines figured prominently in the *Job-Aqtiv* legislation does not imply a shift of political power from the national government to the EU. Instead, given that policymaking in other fields, for example regarding part-time employment or disability policy, were devoid of EU references, the German government can be argued to have selectively instrumentalized EU guidelines (Ostheim and Zohlnhöfer 2004). This does not deny that EU policy has shaped German labour-market policy discourse in recent years. On the other hand the government might have expected EU guidelines to raise legitimacy for policy aims which had already been decided upon (Büchs and Friedrichs 2005). In fact, more than a direct EU influence, the *Job-Aqtiv* legislation underlined the SPD's gradual departure from a traditional demand-oriented labour-market policy towards adopting a supply-side orientation, illustrated by the falling number of participants in active programmes (BMGS 2004: table 8.14).

In this context, the detection of manipulated job-placement records produced by the BA in early 2002 opened a 'window of opportunity' for more structural reform. The so-called Hartz commission (named after its chairman Peter Hartz, a personnel manger at VW) was set up to make policy recommendations by the summer of 2002, that is, a few months before the general election. The timing proved crucial. As part of its election campaign the government vowed fully to implement the commission's recommendations immediately after a potential election victory. This put the social policy wing within the SPD and trade unions in a difficult position since attacking the proposals, announced in the summer of 2002, was considered as potentially limiting the government's re-election chances. As a consequence, once they were published there was little open disagreement with the Hartz recommendations and, after its extremely narrow electoral victory in the autumn, the returning red–green coalition introduced the first largely uncontroversial chunk of the proposals. These aimed mainly at organizational changes intended to make placement and labour-market services, more effective, to promote private job services, and to facilitate small-business start-ups. Geographical and other work-related aspects of job-search rules became more strictly defined, and the level of disregarded capital lowered for the means-test which applies to ALH claimants (Schmid 2003).

During the course of 2002 and 2003 the socio-economic context worsened dramatically (see Fig. 3.1). Economic growth rates had declined to 0.8 per cent in 2001 and to 0.2 per cent in 2002. For 2003 a slow recovery was widely expected. Instead, the German economy contracted by -0.1 per cent, the worst performance since 1993. Unemployment rose from below 4 million in early 2002 to close to 4.5 million a year later. The volume of employment declined to the lowest level in ten years, and the public deficit for 2003 (-4 per cent) turned out to be even higher than in 2002 (-3.5 per cent). All this provided strong political support for those within the coalition who had become increasingly persuaded by the cause for more structural reform, including the Chancellor. In this context, Schröder announced the so-called 'Agenda 2010' in March 2003, which included a wide range of cost-saving measures within several welfare state areas and a weakening of employment protection legislation. Within unemployment protection significant retrenchment and structural changes were planned for 2004 and 2005 (see Appendix A).

In his speech to the parliament, Schröder claimed that these policies represented the 'only way to both improve the incentive to take up employment and also be able to reduce non-wage labour costs'. Heated discussions within both government parties ensued, special party congresses were set up, and trade unions reacted strongly against the plans. However, portrayed as hindering much needed reforms, defenders of existing welfare state structures were put under extreme pressure when Schröder raised the stakes by attaching his political future to a successful passing of the reform plans. In order to secure a government majority in the *Bundestag*, some concessions were made to critics who objected to long-term unemployed people having to accept any type of legal job, irrespective of pay or other suitability criteria. However, those concessions were later revoked so that the proposals would be acceptable to the CDU-led majority within the *Bundesrat*. Eventually agreed upon in December 2003, the new regulations began to be implemented from 2005 onwards (see Appendix A). They bring about significant reductions of ALG entitlement (but not rates) and the merging of ALH with SA into ALG II, a single new means-tested benefit. Despite some transitory arrangements (e.g. supplements payable for up to two years after exhaustion of ALG), the latter implies lower benefit rates for most previous ALH claimants, and the loss of eligibility particularly for claimants with partners in work because of the introduction of stricter means-testing compared with the current ALH. The change also implies a strong shift towards activation principles, a new emphasis on case management, and active participation of job seekers, and new suitability criteria which require ALG II claimants, in principle, to accept any legal job offered. For unemployed under the age of twenty-five, much tougher benefit sanctions for those refusing a job or training offer will be implemented, with eligibility to ALG II likely to be made conditional on accepting suitable work, training, or an integration programme offered.

The acceleration of the speed of reform, and the breaking of new ground by introducing new benefit structures, requires explanation. The extremely weak economic context since 2002 can be regarded as a catalyst. Only days after the general election in September 2002 the government had to concede that public deficits were significantly larger than had been assumed and that the self-imposed EU limit of 3 per cent of GDP would not be met in the forthcoming year. The popularity of the coalition government plummeted, followed by humiliating defeats in *Länder* elections in early 2003. During the course of the year it was becoming obvious that the government would fail to meet the EU criteria for the second time. In short, the fiscal pressure and thus threat of political survival was stronger than it had ever been since the start of the red–green government in 1998.

This situation played into the hands of those within SPD (and Green Party) who had already adopted new 'interpretative patterns' (Bleses and Seeleib-Kaiser 2004) of how to respond to pressures such as economic internationalization, Maastricht convergence criteria, and the underperforming German economy. Increases in social insurance rates had been ruled out as economically counterproductive and leading actors within both parties had already been persuaded by the cause for structural reform. The Chancellor and his allies were able to use fiscal pressure as leverage to weaken internal (and trade union) opposition. The BA scandal at the beginning of the election year of 2002 had opened a window of opportunity. The use of 'commission' policy, manifested in the selection of the Hartz commission members, its allocated time frame, and the deliberate use of leaks to the media improved conditions for far-reaching reform. In addition, opponents were either weak at the time (such as the trade unions suffering from an ill-fated strike action by IG-Metall in eastern Germany in June 2003) or had disappeared. For example, after the 2002 election, the Ministry of Labour and Social Affairs, a stronghold of traditional social policy orientation, was dissolved and large parts integrated in the new Ministry of Economics and Labour, headed by Wolfgang Clement, a more business-oriented social-democrat. Nevertheless, the introduction of the Hartz recommendations, and especially of the new ALG II in 2005, was faced not only with trade union opposition but also with increasingly public hostility (especially in the new *Länder*) during 2004. The fact that the red–green government did not back off from its plans though might be regarded as a sign that 'a political crisis has finally arrived that is as deep as the economic crisis—and deep enough to persuade the SPD to adopt a policy of liberal reform, against its own traditionalist constituencies, so as to reach out to centrist voters afraid that otherwise decline will continue indefinitely' (Kitschelt and Streek 2003: 29).

4.4 THE UNITED KINGDOM

4.4.1 Benefit retrenchment, the erosion of unemployment insurance, and early activation (1979–90)

Consolidating public expenditure was an even more overriding policy aim for the British government in the 1980s. In addition, especially after the removal of some more moderate Cabinet members in 1981, the Thatcher administration was considerably more committed to and driven by a neo-liberal public policy agenda than the Kohl government. Promoting self-reliance, privatization, and 'rolling back the boundaries of the public sector', as it was announced in the first budget speech in 1979, were explicit policy aims. And yet, other than council house sales, no specific plans for welfare state reform had been made before the election in 1979 (Timmins 2001: 362). Once unemployment started to rise in 1980, improving work incentives by widening the gap between benefit income and earnings became a major reference point for subsequent social security policy. Demand-led unemployment benefit expenditure rose significantly, and would have done so even more had it not been for some significant benefit alterations. For example, in 1980 insurance benefits for the unemployed (and other claimants) were cut by 5 per cent in lieu of making transfers taxable two years later. Since the previous Labour government had toyed with a similar plan in the 1970s, and influential advisory bodies were in principle in favour of taxing short-term insurance benefits (i.e. excluding pensions), it was not difficult to legitimize this decision.

Also the second major legislation affecting the unemployed, the abolition of the earnings-related supplement (ERS), met with surprisingly few protests. The implications of the move, contributing to a significant shift from contributory to means-tested support for the unemployed in the 1980s (see Table 4.4), might not have been fully appreciated at the time. In addition, the real value of the supplement had been allowed to decline under Labour and Conservative governments in the 1970s and, by the early 1980s, the system was 'in a mess' (Micklewright 1989: 540). Concentrating on other cuts affecting strikers and occupational pensioners, the TUC gave the ERS abolition scant attention. Other potential critics, such as the Child Poverty Action Group (CPAG), were slow to react and seemed ambivalent about the defence of a principle which reproduced market income differentials in the welfare sector. Debates in parliament on whether the abolition of ERS constituted a breach with the insurance principle (Clasen 1992: 286) indicated an 'ambiguity inherent in social insurance' in the UK (Bolderson 1982: 292). All this illustrates the weakly embedded notion of earnings-related contributory support within the British social policy architecture, which is also reflected in public attitudes that indicate more support for basic universal unemployment protection in the UK than in Germany (Cebulla et al. 2000; Mau 2003). According to Timmins (2001: 374), Chancellor Geoffrey Howe defended the abolition as a return to Beveridge's flat-rate principles. However, the main driver of the reform was not restoring a particular notion of distributive justice but to save money and to address the 'why work' problem, that is, to widen the gap between benefits and income form work, with which 'ministers remained obsessed' (Timmins 2001: 375).

These cuts were not necessarily unpopular at a time of rising unemployment in the early 1980s (Donnison 1982: 208). Real wages, particularly at the lower end of the scale, were falling due to increases in indirect taxation. As a consequence, adjusting benefit levels in order to maintain work incentives, the government fuelled a debate on benefit fraud and work-shyness (Golding and Middleton 1982) and portrayed antisocial behaviour on the part of welfare state claimants as part of the unemployment problem.

On the other hand, benefit eligibility and entitlement rights for older unemployed claimants of means-tested benefits actually improved (see Appendix B), albeit only moderately and aimed at reducing the unemployment count and facilitating labour-market exit.

By the end of the conservative government's first term in office in 1983, the number of unemployed people in receipt of means-tested support had more than trebled (to 1.7 million; McGregor 1985: 235) and the relevance of contributory support declined (Table 4.4) as a consequence of several further cuts between 1984 and 1998 (Appendix B). And yet, in recognition of a public popularity of the insurance principle, the government continued to claim that there was 'a clear role for unemployment benefit as a contributory, national benefit' (DSS 1985: Cmnd 9517: 37). Besides, simply abolishing contributory unemployment benefits would have put into question a tax policy which increased National Insurance contributions (and indirect taxation) in order to compensate for the loss of revenue from income tax as a result of having substantially reduced tax rates for higher income earners (Wilkinson 1993).

In addition to consolidating social security funding, concentrating resources to those in greatest need had become another strong policy objective by the mid-1980s. The introduction of Income Support as the major form of means-tested support (Berthoud 1987) brought about further retrenchment for unemployed people, and replaced benefit rights for (almost) all under eighteen years of age with a guaranteed place on a youth training scheme (Roll 1988). However, the level of training was often patchy, generally viewed as of little value by participants and open to abuse by employers (Trickey and Walker 2001: 187). Relying on a traditionally voluntarist approach to training (Whiteside 1995), a range of new labour-market programmes were introduced or extended in response to high unemployment in the early 1980s (Meager 1997: 72). However, after Thatcher's third general election victory in 1987, programmes were scaled down (King 1993, 1995). More importantly in the context of this chapter, the emphasis within labour-market policy switched from training to job-search activities, enhancing work incentives and subsidizing work placements for the long-term unemployed.

The origin of what later became so-called activation policies at EU level can thus be traced to the late 1980s in the UK, with job-search assistance as the preferred alternative to training. Already in 1986 a compulsory 'Restart' interview for the unemployed after six months out of work was introduced. In 1990 such interviews became more frequent and a Restart course was made obligatory for the long-term unemployed and those who rejected offers. More generally, new rules were introduced in 1989 which stipulated that all benefit claimants had to provide evidence that they were 'actively seeking employment'. After a maximum period of thirteen weeks, the wage for a job ceased to be a criterion on which a job offer could be turned down. Previously claimants were not expected to accept jobs which paid less or were on less favourable conditions than those generally observed by agreement between associations of employers and employees (Ogus and Wikeley 1995: 127).

In sum, the aims of deregulating labour markets, creating wider wage dispersion, enhancing work incentives, and cutting social security spending were strong motives affecting unemployment support policy during Thatcher's second and third terms in office. All objectives pushed for benefit retrenchment and a labour-market policy which eschews publicly provided employment in favour of enhanced job-search efforts, emphasizing individual responsibility on the part of the unemployed. Any differentiation between job seekers by type of benefit receipt, as in Germany, would have seemed inappropriate. As a consequence, the first contributory pillar of unemployment support was significantly scaled down in terms of both generosity and coverage (see Table 4.4). This trend was partly facilitated by the absence of formal constraints in British policymaking, and by programme-specific structures, such as the centralized benefit system and the traditionally close proximity between contributory and means-tested support. There is only a weak incorporation of the wage-replacement principle within British social security, and no earmarked social insurance contributions are made to separate funds. In comparison with their German counterparts, British unemployed people appear to perceive the receipt of assistance-based benefits as less stigmatizing (Clasen et al. 1998). In other words, a social insurance system less closely coupled with labour-market policy can be regarded as having contributed to a compliance with a growing emphasis on traditional poverty orientation within unemployment support and a creeping erosion of contributory-based support (Clasen 2001).

4.4.2 *Continuity and a move towards compulsory activation (1990–7)*

During the 1990s the focus of reform switched almost entirely from aspects such as benefit eligibility and entitlement towards work-based requirements and obligations (see Appendix B). In fact, the introduction of the Jobseekers' Allowance (JSA) in 1996 was the only significant change in unemployment protection, albeit in a structurally significant way since it laid the foundation for a radical reconnection between cash benefits and labour market programmes which gained speed and scope under the Labour government in the second half of the 1990s.

In the absence of significant policy changes until 1996, rhetorically and administratively the policy direction remained the same as in the 1980s. In general, unemployed benefit claimants were asked to be more active in their job search and to adapt expectations to 'more realistic' wages. The relative value of unemployment benefit (as a share of average full-time adult earnings) had declined from 21 per cent in 1979 to below 15 per cent in the late 1980s (DWP 2004*b*). For the government this decline was not seen as a cause for concern since the relevant comparison was 'between the rates of benefit and the level of wages paid in the kinds of jobs which claimants are likely to obtain' (Deacon 1997: 38). Wage and income inequality had significantly widened since the early 1980s (Joseph Rowntree Foundation 1995), regulatory mechanisms such as Wages Councils been abolished, and the role of trade unions considerably weakened. In short, actively supported by employer organizations interested in improving competitiveness by lowering labour costs, and not impeded by institutional impediments, the deregulation of the British labour market included declining levels of unemployment benefits, thereby maintaining the distance to equally declining wage levels.

The economic recession in the early 1990s led to a rapid increase in social security spending generally and unemployment support in particular (Brewer et al. 2002: twenty-five). However, curbing benefit levels further seemed politically difficult after the series of cuts which had been imposed in the 1980s. The Treasury repeatedly suggested indexing benefit rates below the level of inflation in the early 1990s. However, such proposals were dismissed by the then Secretary of State, Peter Lilley, as inflicting hardship and throwing claimants into poverty. Savings would thus have to be found elsewhere, for example by further targeting benefits at those deemed in need and by enhancing incentives to move off benefit and into employment (Timmins 2001: 524–5). Measures such as imposing stricter work tests, which potentially reduce the inflow to benefits and foster the outflow into jobs, might thus be seen as an alternative to benefit restrictions during the 1980s.

Another concern remained on the agenda. Having risen steadily during the 1980s, the dependency on means-tested transfers amongst the unemployed almost doubled between 1990 and 1993 (Evans 1998: 288). While principally in line with the notion of targeted benefits, this trend was regarded as potentially undermining work incentives due to the interaction between benefits and wages at the lower end of the labour market. As a response, the government widened the gap between social security support and earnings by making in-work benefits for parents more generous (see Chapter 6) and by introducing small-scale job subsidies such as 'back-to-work' bonuses (Meager 1997). This strategy began to connect unemployment benefit claimants more closely with labour-market policy, a trend which became ever more pronounced during the 1990s.

The endpoint of Conservative policies seeking to tighten benefit conditionality and enhancing job-search behaviour was the introduction of the JSA in 1996. The reform implied both retrenchment and structural change in the wake of merging two previously separate schemes into one (see Appendix B). The reform was expected to save expenditure, with about a quarter of a million people becoming worse off due to benefit exclusion or reduction (Unemployment Unit 1995). More generally, the creation of the common JSA framework represented a further demotion of insurance-based support and a form of homogenization in the sense that the type of benefit receipt had become all but irrelevant within British unemployment support policy. Irrespective of the reasons for unemployment, needs-based income protection had become the norm and new mechanisms deemed to facilitate labour-market integration were introduced for all benefit claimants, such instruments as 'Jobseekers Agreement', 'Jobseekers Direction', and the more prescriptive definition of 'actively seeking work' (Appendix B).

The JSA met with opposition both inside and outside the House of Commons. However, the Labour Party did not commit itself to repealing the scheme after a possible election victory. With hindsight, this is not surprising given that in the mid-1990s a cross-party consensus had emerged around the problem of 'welfare dependency', the emphasis on a 'stricter benefit regime', and supply-side labour market policies. This is also evident in the light of the structural similarity between the New Deal and *Project Work*, which the Major government introduced on a trial basis in two localities in 1996. This was a compulsory (thirteen weeks) work experience scheme aimed at people under the age of fifty who had been out of work for at least two years. Hailed as a great success in the 1996 Conservative Party Annual Conference, it was to be expanded to another twenty-eight areas, and its nationwide introduction was announced as an answer to Labour's New Deal programme in the run-up to the 1997 general election.

4.4.3 New Deals and the turn from unemployment towards worklessness (1997–2003)

After Labour's victory in the 1997 general election, the new government maintained its predecessor's policy course and accelerated it, augmented by improvements for low paid workers and by more comprehensive and coherent labour-market programmes. The move towards a more prescriptive, work-oriented social security policy represented a clear break with Labour Party aspirations and policy proposals of the 1970s and 1980s. Under Tony Blair as party leader and then Prime Minister, the government proclaimed the need for a 'new contract' between citizens and the state. While it was the government's obligation to provide opportunities for entering paid employment, benefit claimants had to become more 'proactive', and were obliged to accept training, work, or education offers (DSS 1998b: Cm 3805). Aimed at enhancing employability and with the moral underpinning of participation in paid employment as the norm for all in an 'active society' (Walters 1997), the Blair government explicitly aimed to create a new balance between 'rights and responsibilities' by strengthening the latter, coupled with better quality training and improved take home pay, via wage subsidies, for those accepting low-paid employment.

Beginning in 1998 the Labour government introduced and subsequently modified elements of the New Deal programmes which became the central component of the above strategy (see Appendix B). The programmes did not alter benefit rates, but considerably increased the conditionality attached to benefit receipt. Several schemes for different groups of working-age benefit claimants were devised, with different eligibility rules and degrees of obligations attached (see Trickey and Walker 2001; Walker and Wiseman 2003). Briefly, the most explicit degree of mandatory transition from benefit into labour-market programmes can be found in the New Deal for young people (NDYP—for all people between eighteen and twenty-four), and the programme for long-term unemployed people. This latter was remodelled in 2001 and, as the ND twenty-five+, now applies to claimants out of work for eighteen (within the past twenty-one) months. Both schemes involve the assignment of personal advisers and the drawing up of individual 'action plans'. Individual counselling is designed to improve motivation, build self-esteem, and ensure that placements and training are appropriate to individual needs. Programmes consist of three stages. The 'gateway period' of four months provides individual intensive job-search assistance. Those who do not find work are transferred to one of four 'options' which last six months or more (second phase). These are subsidized employment, full-time education, or (for young people only) voluntary or environmental work. Unlike any previous programmes, the take-up of one of these four options is mandatory, and non-compliance sanctioned by benefit reduction or withdrawal. All options involve at least some degree of training. Employers receive a weekly subsidy per participant and a flat-rate contribution towards training costs. Failing to enter unsubsidized work after completing one of the options, further guidance and, if required, training follows (the 'follow through' stage).

Crucially, the New Deal programmes extended their remit beyond unemployment (Clasen 2002). In fact, the aim is principally to integrate all working-age recipients of cash transfers into employment, unless prevented by reasons such as ill-health. This has to be seen against the background of a steep rise since the 1980s in the number of working-age people in receipt of benefits and not classified as unemployed, such as lone parents (Millar 2003*a*: 116) and men claiming sickness or disability benefits (Alcock et al. 2003). The latter includes prime age working men, and particularly those with no or low qualifications (Nickel and Quitini 2002). The steady increase in the number of these economically inactive, but not unemployed, groups became a growing cause of policy concern during the second half of the 1990s (HM Treasury and DWP 2001). This then is the background for the extension of the New Deal programmes to groups who previously were not included in labour-market integration schemes (see Appendix B). Compared with particularly young and long-term unemployed benefit recipients, the degree of obligation for these groups is generally lower. Nevertheless, recent policy changes have introduced an increasingly work-focused benefit regime for all working-age benefit claimants (see Appendix B).

But the New Deal programmes are but one aspect within Labour's welfare-to-work strategy. Incomes of those in work were raised by the introduction of a minimum wage and several types of tax credits (wage subsidies) targeted at different groups, such as lone parents, disabled people, families, and recently also single people (Walker and Wiseman 2003). In fact, the scope of the minimum wage and tax credits, as measures which aim to 'make work pay', are of a much larger magnitude than the New Deal programmes. The British government's forecast for 2001–2, for example, was to spend £900 million on the latter but more than £5 billion on tax credits for low earners, and the number of low-wage families in receipt of tax credits doubled between 1997 and 2003 (see Chapter 6).

As supply-side instruments, the New Deal programmes focus on problems of employability. Rather than stimulating labour demand, attitudes to work and expectations regarding employment and wages are portrayed as determining employment chances (Peck and Theodore 2000: 731). In this respect, it is not surprising that under the Labour government the level of expenditure on active labour-market policy has not increased, nor altered its emphasis, but continued to focus on elements such as job placement and job search at the expense of employment creation or training (Table 4.5 – 4.7). To what extent policies have succeeded in raising employment levels or improving the job chances of benefit claimants is beyond the focus of this chapter (see Card et al. 2004; Walker and Wiseman 2003). In the context of this study the scope of policy reorientation on the part of the Labour Party policy is of more importance. As a whole, the New Deal and other policies highlight Labour's acceptance of the need for a flexible and deregulated labour market, and its strategy aimed at integration into employment which might be low paid and thus requires public subsidy. During the 1980s and early 1990s one of the Party's objectives had been to improve the material situation of benefit claimants and to turn back the creeping growth of means-testing, which was regarded as sapping self-esteem and diminishing work incentives. Even in-work benefits or wage subsidies were condemned as sustaining 'the evil of low wages' (Field 2002: 98). In other words, the party has undergone a U-turn from 'defenders of collectivism to proponents of neoliberal economic policies' (Wood 2001a: 398).

Putting unemployment policy within a wider context, it might be argued that the Labour Party of the 1990s might simply have come to terms with the British liberal market economy, that is, the fact that collectivized industrial relations have never taken root in the UK, that companies depend upon short-term finance from equity markets, and that a switch towards a more high skill–high wage economy might not only be faced with structural problems but regarded as inferior in a new context of a more globalized economy (Rhodes 2000a; Wood 2001b). Any previous aspirations of a more Keynesian demand-oriented public policy paradigm were thus abandoned in favour of a supply-side agenda as part of a learning process which started in the early 1990s and accelerated after the fourth successive electoral defeat in 1992 (Roder 2003). Indeed, New Labour's perception of a flexible British labour market and political economy as conferring certain 'comparative advantages' (Hall and Soskice 2001b) has made supply-side options more amenable than in other countries governed by modern social democratic parties (Hall 2002; Clasen and Clegg 2004). This does not rule out changes in policy direction or paths (Shaw 2003), or determine specific policy choices or patterns within broad policy directions (Crouch and Farrell 2002). However, Labour's broad policy reorientation, combined with the absence of significant policy veto points, makes policy outcomes such as maintaining moderate benefit levels, needs-based support, and activation policies focused on job-search efforts much more likely than alternative approaches.

Several factors can be identified which contributed to Labour's adoption of a more prescriptive activation approach and the acceptance of means-tested benefits. One of the influences was economic research and theory which implied that the introduction of stricter work tests, more restricted benefit entitlement, mandatory training, or other appropriate measures would improve the employability of particularly long-term job seekers and increase the actual supply of labour (Layard 2000). Any deadweight associated with these measures was likely to be compensated by employment generating wage moderation effects. The assumption that more 'employable' benefit claimants would increase the effective competition for jobs and contribute to non-inflationary employment growth gained prominence within the Labour Party by the mid-1990s and seems to have influenced government policy after 1997 (Finn 2000). Indeed, increasing employability became something of a buzzword in Labour's rationale for the New Deal programmes (Philpott 1999) as a way of not only improving employment chances but combating systematic disadvantage among specific groups, and young people in particular. While the stock of youth unemployment declined after 1993, the risk of unemployment before the age of twenty-five actually increased, as well as the average duration of unemployment spells for young men. This and the perceived adverse consequences of long-term benefit dependency and social exclusion can be regarded as major reasons for the particular policy focus on youth unemployment (Stafford 2003).

Besides, a move towards a new unemployment policy regime, which included a higher degree of compulsion, became a chance of political credit claiming. Previous conservative governments had been reluctant to embark on anything which could have been construed by critics as a move towards a US-imported 'workfare' strategy. This caution seemed justified given that since the early 1980s more than half of the British population had consistently regarded unemployed people as victims of external circumstances. However, this perception changed dramatically after 1997 with a sharp rise in the proportion of those who perceived benefits as too generous and as discouraging active job search (Hills 2001, 2004). In short, imposing more obligations on unemployed people seemed much less of a political gamble than in the first half of the 1990s. In addition, concentrating on the young unemployed and explicitly keeping public expenditure low were political tactics which helped prevent accusations of fiscal imprudence or lack of targeting. Last but not least, the continuously improving labour market facilitated a portrayal of the New Deal as successful. In short, the second half of the 1990s provided several opportunities which aligned favourably with Labour's motives in the pursuit of a more work-oriented unemployment support system (Clasen 2000).

As to possible external influences, Labour's welfare-to-work strategy corresponds with the European discourse on making social protection systems more 'employment friendly' (European Commission 1998) and some of its features resemble closely recommendations which were formulated as part of the EES. However, the shift in Labour's perception was likely to be more influenced by US than European debates—both in terms of conceptual discourses on welfare rights and obligations, as well as regarding political strategies adopted by the Clinton administration (King and Wickham-Jones 1999; Deacon 2002). Also the previous conservative governments were influenced by US debates on 'welfare dependency' and there is a long history of social policy contact, influence, and transfer between the two countries (Holmwood 2000). The US debate with its emphasis on private responsibility and the notion of benefits potentially exerting a corruptive influence resonated in speeches made by ministers in the UK since the late 1980s (Timmins 2001: 446). On a policy level, US programmes directly influenced the design of several British labour-market programmes introduced in the 1980s (King 1995) and the perceived contribution of Clinton's welfare reforms to the electoral success of the US Democratic Party played a relevant role in the development of Labour's welfare-to-work agenda in the 1990s (Walker 1999; Deacon 2000).

4.5 COMPARATIVE CONCLUSIONS

As discussed in Chapter 2, theoretical accounts of policy reform often talk past each other not only because they operate at different levels of abstraction, but also because of the use of different indicators of change. For example, Heinelt and Weck (1998) identify a departure from the traditional notion of 'status adequate' labour-market reintegration in Germany, which is explained with reference to changing 'core beliefs' (Sabatier 1993) within different advocacy coalitions in the mid-1990s. Using different indicators for change, Bleses and Seeleib-Kaiser (2004) point to processes of economic internationalization inducing political parties already to adopt a 'new interpretative pattern' for policy formulation in the 1970s. Such analyses are primarily interested in identifying and investigating the causes for particular turning points in policy direction, say from labour-demand to labour-supply or from de-commodification to re-commodification. For the purpose and interest of this book, these types of analyses are only partially instructive for two reasons. First, within the general direction of retrenchment there have been instances of expansion (e.g. for older unemployed persons in Germany during the 1980s) which tend to be ignored or downplayed in analyses bent on illustrating broad tendencies such as welfare state curtailment. Second, within a common shift towards retrenchment in both countries (e.g. Mohr 2004), policy restructuring and different policy profiles have emerged which, for cross-national research on welfare state reform, seem at least as interesting as policy directions. Why, for example, were benefit rates scaled down more in the UK than in Germany? Why has the insurance character steadily eroded in the UK and to a lesser extent in Germany? Why has the division between core unemployment benefit clientele and periphery almost disappeared in the UK but not in Germany? Why did the UK embark sooner and with more force on activation policies? As outlined in Chapter 2, and illustrated in Sections 4.3 and 4.4, addressing such questions requires consideration of the dynamics of party preferences and shifts in power relations on the part of policymakers on the one hand, but also of options and constraints offered by institutional means, as well as contingent and situational factors which offer opportunities for reform, on the other. Once again, for analytical purposes, it seems useful to assess them separately.

4.5.1 Motives

Comparing the early 1980s with current configurations of unemployment support, a clear trend of benefit retrenchment can be observed in both countries, combined with a more obligation focused eligibility orientation. This trend in policy direction can certainly be linked to party positions, particularly in the UK where a neo-liberal emphasis on curbing expenditure, concerns over work disincentives, and labour market deregulation under successive Thatcher governments contrasted sharply with the ideological preferences of the previous Labour government. In Germany, the dividing line between advocates of neo-liberalism and those in favour of selective cutbacks and expansion in order to uphold traditional structures, cut across party positions. Until the early 1990s, the latter included the 'social policy' faction within the CDU as the dominant agenda setter, but also the SPD and trade unions keen on safeguarding institutional stability and avoiding more drastic retrenchment. German unification disrupted this setting and sapped the strength of the 'welfare state oriented' advocacy coalition (Heinelt 2003: 139), but not immediately. At first, unification gave rise to a form of reluctant but consensual deficit spending and subdued conventional conflicts of interest. Once the magnitude of the collapse of the east German labour market and its long-lasting effect became apparent, however, reinforced by the economic recession in 1993 the impact of globalization discourses and the Maastricht criteria, internal divisions weakened the social policy wing within the CDU/CSU. This context also eroded the traditional cross-party alliance on social policy, thus facilitating the switch from a labour-demand to labour-supply orientation, more severe benefit retrenchment, and steps towards activation.

Policies introduced since 1997 and 1998 respectively suggest that centre–left parties in both countries had undergone a change of perspective in labour market policy, illustrated by the position towards wage subsidies in the UK, or towards job creation programmes and a publicly subsidized 'second labour market' in Germany. With references to the content of party manifestos and programmes, Roder (2003) draws attention to parallel processes of programmatic reorientation within labour-market policy at the time of opposition and early processes of adaptation of conservative positions towards the welfare state can be identified (Gohr 2003). For example, from the mid-1990s onwards the SPD began to be critical towards the scale of welfare state expenditure, to emphasize the role of flexible markets and individual efforts, and to accept the government's position that social insurance contributions were jeopardizing German economic competitiveness. However, cross-national differences were discernible. Compared with the Labour Party, policy reorientation had only started within the SPD and not been completed by the time of gaining political power. SPD participation in government at *Land* level fostered heterogeneous interests within the party (Bush and Manow 2001; Gohr 2001), and made successive electoral failure at federal level less painful and programmatic reorientation thus less pressing than in the UK. Labour's 'welfare-to-work' approach had become a consensual and major reference point by the run-up to the election in 1997, and continued to inform legislation from then onwards. By contrast, the SPD initially revoked deregulatory policies and benefit restrictions introduced by the Kohl government before embarking on retrenchment and activation-oriented legislation in its second term. There are other reasons for differences in the dynamics of preference formation, such as the dominance of party competition along economic arguments in the UK and the apparently irreversible loss of credibility of the Labour Party during the 1980s, followed by the unexpected defeat in the general election of 1992 which triggered a process of introspection and facilitated a new policy course. By comparison, both major centrist parties in Germany competed as credible welfare state protectors (Kitschelt 2001) and defenders of key social policy areas such as social insurance programmes. This left little political room for open retrenchment. Indeed, the demonstrations against the Hartz IV legislation in the summer of 2004 illustrate the prevailing electoral risks for any party intent on structural reform in core social policy areas. However, having finally gained power in 1998, and faced by an adverse and further deteriorating social–economic context after 2000, programmatic modernizers also gained strength in the SPD, while defenders of traditional welfare state structures became increasingly sidelined.

4.5.2 *Contexts and opportunities*

Electoral aspects and internal shifts of power balances within parties impacting on changes in policy orientation are helpful for an understanding of changes in overall policy direction. However, they do not in themselves explain national policy patterns or differences in the scale of change. For this, institutional and mediating factors play an important role. As to the latter, Blancke and Schmid (2003) refer to the dynamics of political and fiscal pressure, for example, as well as opportunities opening up for decisive policy moves. Indeed, situational or contextual factors, such as declining unemployment, electoral cycles, and shifting public attitudes towards benefit claimants, were shown to be relevant factors which help to explain why New Labour was able to reinforce and extend activation policies more than the SPD in Germany (see also Clasen 2000, 2002). The placement scandal of the *Bundesanstalt für Arbeit* in 2002 opened a window of opportunity for social policy modernizers. There are two caveats though. First, contingent factors are both dynamic in nature and neither constraining nor facilitating per se. For example, annual deficits in the BA budget triggered responses which, in principle, could have led to programmatic reform of its revenue structure or increasing contributions rates. However, preferences in the 1980s and 1990s made these options politically undesirable. Second, contingent factors and the formation of policy priorities are not independent from each other. For example, following the short-lived boom in the early 1990s, the subsequent economic recession in conjunction with the Maastricht criteria put a constraint on deficit spending. Combined with the fiscal consequences of unification, this affected the distribution of political power within and across both major parties in Germany and influenced learning and repositioning processes of individual party members. In short, external influences introduced a new dynamic which impinged on social policy formation.

4.5.3 Institutional means

Policy preferences and dynamic contextual factors together go some way to explaining broad policy directions, as well as the timing and scale of reforms introduced. But national policy patterns are also determined by institutional means which policymakers have at their disposal. In the field of unemployment support, all three institutional elements discussed in Chapter 3 come into play. First, a comparatively stronger neo-liberal policy agenda in the UK was supported by institutional capacities, such as a first-past-the-post electoral system, single-party governments, and strong central control in the House of Commons especially after the elections of 1983 and 1997 (see Table 3.1). By contrast, as discussed in Chapter 3, formal policymaking structures in Germany provide many more stumbling blocks, even if a similarly determined ideological preference as in the UK had prevailed at the time.

However, once again, institutional structures do not function as political veto points per se but have to be linked to the formation of political preferences and interests (Jochem 2003). For example, shifting majorities in the German *Bundesrat* would have predicted more structural change in the 1980s rather than in the 1990s when retrenchment was more substantial. As Zohlnhöfer (2001) demonstrates, the switch of policy direction in the 1990s is attributable to the waning influence of positions represented by the social policy wing of the CDU/CSU. As shown, internal party dynamics within the SPD contributed significantly to shifts in the direction of unemployment policy after 1998. Similar shifts in policy direction cannot be identified in the UK either before or after the 1997 election. Once 'wet' Cabinet members had been removed during Thatcher's first term, almost all policy changes affecting unemployment benefit claimants brought about retrenchment. Of course, even the ideologically fairly cohesive Conservative government in the UK cannot be regarded as a monolithic party or 'individual' veto player (Tsebelis 2002). At times social security policy was subject to differing interests on the part of the Treasury and the DHSS (later, DSS) (Deakin and Parry 1993). This affected, for example, decisions on benefit indexation in the early 1990s. Under New Labour, such an internal veto has been weakened because the position of the Treasury strengthened for three reasons: an overriding concern with controlling public spending and avoiding tax increases during Labour's first term in office; the transfer of certain responsibilities from spending departments to the Exchequer (see also Chapter 6); and New Labour's adoption of a philosophy of social inclusion through paid employment, which is very much in accordance with the Treasury's traditional line on social policy (Parry 2000).

Second, as demonstrated, programme-specific funding structures provide an important supportive institutional influence on cross-national policy variation. Unlike in Germany, social insurance in the UK is firmly linked to the rest of public social expenditure and the government has central control of both insurance and assistance benefits, thus avoiding policy fragmentation and major conflicts of interests within the public sector. By contrast, in the German multilevel governance structure there tends to be an incongruity between savings and costs. Within unemployment support, active and passive labour market programmes tend to crowd each other out and cuts in one type of benefit generally have knock-on fiscal effects on other types of cash support for the unemployed (Schmid et al. 1987). Intertwined funding structures also offer options of cost transfer ('shifting yard' policy) between different social insurance branches. The creation of ALG II in 2005 will significantly lower but not eliminate incentives for the options for such strategies within unemployment support.

Finally, earnings-related benefits which function as 'deferred wages' in Germany have no equivalent in the UK. This creates few incentives for British trade unions to be actively involved, or even particularly interested, in matters of unemployment insurance (Clasen 2001), while popular perceptions do not relate strongly to a notion of contributory benefits as representing 'earned' social rights and thus as significantly different from benefits based on the principle of 'need' (Mau 2003). There is no doubt that the changes implemented in 2005 represent a paradigmatic shift for unemployment support policy in Germany, including a weakening of the wage replacement notion of unemployment support (see Appendix A). On the other hand, the function (and level) of ALG remains unaltered for the core of (short-term) unemployed people. Despite the radical restructuring of unemployment support decided upon in late 2003, the German government regarded the suggestion of cuts in ALG rates as economically and socially unjustified, unlikely to improve work incentives, and potentially undermining a 'clearly discernible' distance between contributory-based benefits and means-tested support in order to legitimate mandatory membership in social insurance (Bundesregierung 2004: 38). This contrasts strongly with the British homogenization of benefit support where differentiation based on previous employment histories has all but disappeared.

In other words, an explanation for persistent cross-national differences impacting on national patterns of policy change in unemployment support (e.g. selective or global retrenchment) would be incomplete without taking account of 'institutional complementarities' (Hall and Soskice 2001*b*: 17), in this case between transfer benefits and forms of labour-market regulation and industrial relations. As discussed in Chapter 2, the historical development of Germany's social insurance system cannot be isolated from evolving structures of collective bargaining and industrial relations (Manow 1997) and existing interdependencies between these spheres continued to underlie reform outcomes during the 1980s and 1990s. In the case of German unemployment insurance, such linkages have guided retrenchment efforts away from core workers and towards more peripheral groups in the labour market. By contrast, in the UK, there is no 'tight coupling' (Hemerijck et al. 2000) between social insurance and industrial relations (Crouch 1999). Historically, the British labour movement has been far more detached from unemployment insurance than their German and continental counterparts (Rhodes 2000*b*). This then also provides different contexts for the political reorientation for German and British centre–left parties in the 1990s (Hall 2002). A pattern of global benefit retrenchment, as well as the levelling down of unemployment support to poverty level, the squeezing out of contributory support, and the switch from benefit towards activation policies was much more feasible in the UK because it brought about a stronger alignment between the structure of unemployment support and the increasingly deregulated and flexible labour market.

It is thus different types of social insurance themselves which, in combination and interdependency with the political economies in which they are embedded (Korpi and Palme 2003: 431), help to understand patterns of retrenchment and restructuring. Finally, as the chapter has demonstrated, cross-national differences are dynamic in nature. In the early 1980s, the scale of insurance-based support in the UK was larger and means-tested support less common than it is today. Thus, even though British social security has traditionally been more concerned with questions of poverty relief and less oriented to wage labour than in Germany (Kaufmann 2003), this should not be regarded as a static influence on policymaking but as a feature which in itself should be subjected to empirical analysis.

5

Retirement pensions

Old-age pension programmes and policies differ from unemployment protection in several ways. For one, policy changes are often designed in such a way that future rather than current pensioners are affected. Changes in retirement ages or new pension formulae are often phased in or come into effect in the medium term. Second, the policy domain is potentially more sensitive due to a larger constituency. Public opinion polls in both Germany and the UK show that pensioners are regularly perceived as more deserving of state support than unemployed benefit claimants. Third, pension entitlement rests on long contribution records and on built-up commitments which are expected to be honoured. In many countries pension rights enjoy a high degree of legal protection, which render cutbacks not impossible but politically sensitive and suggest periods of phasing in, transitional regulations, and strong political justifications for change (Rüb and Nullmeier 1991: 460). As a consequence, under conditions of fiscal austerity and adverse demographic developments, apportioning losses between current retirees, future pensioners, and current contributors requires skilfully managed reform processes (Bonoli 2000; Hinrichs 2002), spreading losses, and providing partial compensations in order to 'avoid blame' (Weaver 1986) for unpopular decisions. In sum, because of a higher profile and political sensitivity, as well as programme-specific features, notions of 'path dependence' (see Chapter 3) and the 'new politics of the welfare state' (Pierson 2001a), that is, the political management of welfare state retrenchment, might be more useful concepts for the understanding of contemporary pension reform than unemployment support policies.

However, as in unemployment protection, many pension reforms have not merely been about retrenchment but also about restructuring. Examples of retrenchment are changes in pension indexation or a straightforward cut in the replacement rate. Equally, raising the age of retirement can be considered as retrenchment. But other reforms might change the 'character' of a benefit system (Clegg and Clasen 2003) without bringing about retrenchment or expansion at the aggregate level, at least not in the short term. Examples are the introduction of politically regulated and subsidized private pensions, supplementing a scaled down public provision. While this is certainly a form of restructuring of a country's pension landscape, to which extent, and for which groups, it also represents retrenchment often requires empirical investigation. A small change in the pension formula can have significant distributive effects which, compared with the previous situation, implies lower pension entitlements for some but improvements for others. Equally, introducing a minimum pension level or a stronger (or lesser) degree of pension crediting for certain periods or activities (e.g. for child rearing, caring, time spent in education) makes a pension system less (or more) 'wage labour centred' (Vobruba 1990), shifting the balance between distributive principles of 'individual equity' (monetary contributions determining entitlement) and principles of 'solidarity', that is, interpersonal ex-ante redistribution (Hinrichs 2000). Such policies might make arrangements more favourable for some groups (parents, low earners) but bring about retrenchment for others (monetary contributors). However, the latter might be compensated by raising the level of tax subsidies. In short, retrenchment is an important concept but, on its own, a rather narrow and restrictive indicator of welfare reform. Clearly, simply focusing on either changes in pension spending or on replacement rates tells us little about the ways in which pensions are being restructured (Hinrichs and Kangas 2003).

Which types of retrenchment and which options for restructuring are more feasible than others depend on existing national pension systems, which differ considerably in the UK and Germany in respect of both institutional settings and policy objectives. Germany belongs to a group of countries which rely on 'social insurance' pensions, providing earnings-related benefits as the predominant form of income in retirement. By contrast, the UK is a classic representative of a 'multipillar' pension country, where public pensions are, by and large, of a flat-rate character and cover basic needs only, with non-statutory types of retirement income topping up public pensions to a considerable degree for large sections of society. These structural differences have contributed to different policy responses in the face of common problems, such as demographic ageing, new employment patterns, or increasing capital mobility (see also Bonoli 2003*a*).

Ever since the late 1950s, the German social insurance pension system has aimed to provide income security in accordance with the level of achieved individual living standards during employment. Other sources of retirement income have been regarded as supplementary to the main pillar of a mandatory public pension. In contrast, British public pension policy has predominantly been aimed at providing a basic level of support which, ideally, should supplement other sources of income in retirement such as occupational or private pensions. Indeed, the idea of a wage-related public pension materialized only in the late 1970s and has since been discarded. Since these and other factors are important for an understanding of pension policymaking, Sections 5.1 and 5.2 discuss the basic features of pension systems in both countries, the wider context in which they are embedded, and provide a stylized diachronic comparison of the scale of change between 1980 and recent years. This is followed by a discussion of major policy changes in the two countries (Sections 5.3 and 5.4), split, as in Chapter 4, into three periods which provided different socio-economic and political contexts for reform.

5.1 PROGRAMME STRUCTURES AND THE PUBLIC/PRIVATE MIX

5.1.1 Germany

Typical for a 'corporatist welfare state' (Korpi and Palme 2003) several first-tier mandatory pension schemes exist in Germany for different occupational groups. For example, there is a contributory scheme for miners and other programmes covering professionals, craftsmen, and farmers, as well as a tax funded scheme for tenured public sector workers (*Beamte*). However, often overlooked in international comparisons, these schemes are relatively small while the two largest schemes have become rather comprehensive and encompassing over time. In fact, by the late 1990s the two major mandatory public social insurance pension funds (for blue- and white-collar workers) covered more than 90 per cent of all gainfully employed persons (Schmähl 2003*a*). Moreover, since the 1960s there has been cross-subsidization between these two schemes and any remaining regulatory differences in regard to contributions and benefits have disappeared (Rüb and Nullmeier 1991: 442). Self-employed workers can opt into the statutory scheme.

Those in insured employment make earnings-related contributions to social insurance pension funds up to a ceiling (see Table 5.1), with employers and employees sharing the burden equally. Eligibility to social insurance pensions in Germany presupposes a minimum of five years of contributions and reaching retirement age of, normally, sixty-five years of age. However, there are several pathways into early retirement at age sixty (women, disabled, unemployed) or sixty-three for workers with a contribution record of thirty-five years (Börsch-Supan et al. 2002: 166). In 1980, all of these options implied the receipt of a full pension. In subsequent

Table 5.1. Major features of and changes within German public pension insurance, 1980 and 2003

	1980	2003
Joint contribution rate	18	19.5
Contribution ceiling*	140%	170%
Coverage (of all gainfully employed)	Above 90%	Above 90%
Tax subsidies[†]	15.6	27.8 (2002)
Expenditure as % of GDP	11.9	12.1 (2001)
Level of 'standard' pension[‡]	70.3	68.6
Role of means-tested benefits[§]	2.6 (16.3)	2.3 (7.3) (2000)
Crediting for:		
education	13 years	Abolished (2005)
child rearing	—	3 years per child
Early retirement (after unemployment and other conditions)	No deductions from full pension	Deductions apply and age of earliest exit raised (by 2008)
Indexation based on	(Nominally) gross average wages	Net average wages plus 'sustainability factor' (2006)
General minimum pension	No	Yes (means-tested)
Public subsidies for private pension	—	Yes

Notes: *percentage of average monthly full-time earnings, own calculation based on BMGS 2004: tables 7.8 and 1.12; for 2003 based on average earnings in October; [†] % of expenditure, includes all tax subsidies (including child rearing credits, etc.); own calculation based on VdR 2004; expenditure (BMGS 2004: table 7.2); [‡] see text; [§] share of social assistance claimants over 60 (HzL) divided by persons over 65 (in brackets: claimants over 65 as share of all social assistance claimants); Statistisches Bundesamt. Fachserie 13 (various years and VdR).

years, changes made (or will make) early retirement financially less attractive and raised the age of early entry (see Appendix C).

    Ever since a major pension reform in 1957, the statutory pension system has been guided by the notion that individual payments should reflect relative living standards achieved in working life, and thus be determined by individual lifetime earnings in relation to average earnings of all insured persons. This 'productivist design' (Hinrichs 1998: 4), that is, a tight linkage between entitlement and contributions based on employment, has nurtured a perception of pensions as a form of 'deferred wage' and 'acquired right' by contributors. This also explains why pension policy is high on the agenda of trade unions who are strong defenders of traditional structures. More generally, all major political parties and also employers have, until the mid-1990s, supported existing arrangements and opted for incremental adjustment rather than structural change.

But German pension insurance is not exclusively guided by principles of individual and intergenerational equity (Hinrichs 1997). Solidaristic elements are present in the form of tax subsidies which cover non-contributory periods or provide pension credits in return for certain recognized activities or periods of economic inactivity (such as unemployment, sickness, military service, or time spent in education). Since the mid-1980s, time spent caring for children or frail family members also has been awarded pension credits. Table 5.1 indicates that the crediting for some groups (parents) have become more generous over time, while others (those with university degrees) have lost out.

Pension levels were generally indexed in line with changes in average gross earnings, but by the late 1970s this practice had already been abandoned de facto and in 1992 indexation became formally based on changes in net, rather than gross, average earnings. In the 1980s, an assumed contribution record of forty-five years and average lifetime earnings resulted in a (standard) pension level of 70 per cent of average net earnings (or about 65 per cent for average earners with forty years contribution). However, due to increases in non-standard forms of employment, different patterns of labour market participation between men and women, and thus differences in lifetime earnings, there is a wide dispersion of actual pension payments, with significantly higher average amounts paid out for men than women and salaried workers compared with those in waged employment. In fact, about half of all male and about 90 per cent of all female retirees receive a pension which is below the standard pension (Schmähl 2003a: 177). Equally, until recently there has been no general minimum pension. Nevertheless, the recourse of pensioners to social assistance is relatively low, and has declined since the early 1980s (Table 5.1). For single female pensioners, this is partly due to derived pension rights (such as survivors' pensions). Equally, publicly subsidized private pensions were only introduced fairly recently (see Appendix C).

In the late 1990s public pensions (mainly from social insurance funds) provided between 75 per cent and 83 per cent of pensioner household income in west Germany and about 95 per cent in the east. While occupational and private pensions are fairly widespread, particularly in the western part of the country (covering almost half of the workforce), in 1999 they provided less than 10 per cent of current pensioners' income in the west, and less than 2 per cent in the east, with income from assets covering only about 5 per cent (less than 2 per cent in the east; Schmähl 2003a: 160–1). This puts Germany in sharp contrast with the UK.

5.1.2 The United Kingdom

The British public pension system differs from the German scheme with respect to its architecture, its overall aim, and factors driving reform since the 1970s. Unlike in Germany, there are no separate pension contributions and no separate pension funds. Instead, employees make contributions (of 11 per cent of earnings between a lower and an upper level; 1 per cent above) to the National Insurance Fund (NIF). Employers contribute another 12.8 per cent (with no upper earnings level). Representing about 80 per cent of spending, pension payments are by far the largest single component of the NIF budget (Glennerster 2003: 134). First introduced in 1908 as a means-tested programme, public pensions became a contributory benefit available for men at the age of sixty-five (women at sixty) in 1946. The current basic state pension (BSP) requires a long contribution record for a full payment, but extensive crediting (for periods of full-time education, unemployment, sickness, or looking after children) generates comprehensive coverage (see Table 5.2). However, while over 90 per cent of male pensioners currently receive a full BSP, only 51 per cent of women do so, and most of them based on their late husband's contribution compared to merely 12 per cent of women with a full BSP based on their own contribution record (National Pensioners Convention 2004). In short, just as in Germany, the receipt of pension income is unevenly distributed. Apart from the skewed receipt of BSP, women are also less likely to be members of occupational pension plans (see later). At the same time, women represent three-quarters of single pensioners, but over four-fifths of single persons claiming a means-tested pension (O'Connell 2003).

Maintaining its traditional character as a modest subsistence flat-rate pension, the value of the BSP increased to about 20 per cent of average male gross earnings in the late 1970s. At that time, pension payments were indexed in line with prices or average earnings, whichever rose faster. However, since 1981 the state pension has subsequently been indexed to prices only. As a consequence, the level of the state pension relative to earnings has declined considerably (Table 5.2), and (for a single pensioner) is forecast to represent only 7 per cent of gross average male earnings by 2050 (Emmerson and Johnson 2002: 301). However, once means-tested benefit income is taken into account it can be argued that the actual minimum income provided by the state is closer to 40 per cent for a single pensioner and 56 per cent for a couple (Emmerson and Johnson 2002: 309). The most important of these means-tested benefits is the Pension Credit (PC) which in early 2004 guaranteed an income of £102 per week for a single person (£121 for a couple), equivalent to a supplement to the BSP of between 30 per cent and 40 per cent. In late 2003, almost 4.9 million individuals

Table 5.2. Major features of and changes within public British pensions, 1980 and 2003

	1980	2003
Coverage of BSP[*]	97%	98%
Replacement rate of basic state pension (BSP)[†]	30%	20%
Indexation of BSP based on:	Earnings or prices (whichever higher)	Prices
Second-tier public pension	SERPS; earnings-related	State Second Pension (S2P); new formula; flat-rate (from 2007)
Value of SERPS	25% of best 20 years	20% of lifetime earnings
'Inherited' SERPS by surviving spouse	100%	50%
Contracting out of SERPS possible for:	Approved defined benefit occupational pensions	Also funded schemes and personal pensions
Public pension expenditure as a share of GDP[‡]	5.1%	5.4%
Pensioners in receipt of means-tested benefits[§]	57% (1979)	32%

Notes: Information where not stated is from DWP (2003, 2004*c*);
[*]pensioner units (single or couples) in receipt of BSP;
[†]value of basic state pension for a single person divided by average full-time male net earnings (for couples the value was 31 per cent in 2003), New Earnings Survey;
[‡]OECD (2001*a*) and Emmerson and Johnson (2002: 316) figure refers to 2000 and includes means-tested benefits for pensioners;
[§]pensioners in receipt of at least one form of means-tested benefit (DWP 2004*c*).

were eligible to receive a PC, which was close to 45 per cent of all pensioners in the UK. However, between a quarter and a third of eligible pensioners fail to claim the benefit, so that their income is below the official minimum (O'Connell 2003). Other means-tested benefits include housing benefit (received by about 20 per cent of pensioners) and Council Tax benefit (supporting 30 per cent of those over retirement age with the cost of local tax). In total, about a third of all British pensioners are currently dependent on some form of means-tested support, which is well below the rate in the late 1970s (Table 5.2), but expected to rise substantially in the future.

The complexity of the system is compounded by the state earnings-related pension scheme (SERPS) which the Labour government introduced in 1975 in response to a growing divergence between those with and those without occupational pension coverage. About half of all current pensioners receive some form of SERPS income, albeit generally at low rates (on average about 20 per cent of the BSP) because the scheme was only enacted in 1978. By the late 1990s, the total cost of SERPS expenditure was equivalent to 15 per cent of BSP expenditure (Emmerson and Johnson 2002). Ever since its inception, it has been possible to 'contract out' of SERPS, encouraged by a reduced rate of National Insurance contributions and favourable tax treatment of contributions made into an occupational or personal pension plan. Improved tax incentives for private provision and a less favourable benefit formula introduced in 1988 resulted in about three-quarters of those eligible having contracted out of SERPS by the early 1990s. Since 2002 no further pension rights have been accrued in SERPS which was replaced by the State Second Pension (S2P). According to a new formula, this scheme is targeted at low earners (up to half average earnings), and intended to become a second flat-rate top-up payment to the BSP in 2007. The effects of all these changes is a considerable flattening out of public pension provision for all those who earn below three-quarters of average earnings, with the combined public pension entitlements providing an income equivalent of about 25 per cent of average adult earnings for those retiring in 2018 (Hills 2003: 19).

The total level of public pension expenditure, that is, BSP, SERPS, and means-tested benefits, amounted to little over 5 per cent of GDP in 1980 and has increased only moderately since then. This represents less than half of public pension spending in Germany (Table 5.1). It also suggests differences as to the prospective future cost of public pensions in the two countries—the forecast is a sharp rise in Germany due to the combination of demographic ageing and the design of the public pension scheme. Also the UK is affected by low fertility (see Chapter 6) and demographic ageing though, to a some-what lesser extent than Germany. In addition, the modest scale of the public pension system combined with reforms introduced since the 1980s, imply a decline of British public pension expenditure over the next forty years and thus a very different scenario from Germany (Table 5.3).

However, this medium-term sustainability of British public pensions has to a large extent been secured by a considerable cost of foregone public revenue (Hills 2003: 24). If rebates for contracting out of SERPS as well as tax incentives for personal and occupational pensions were included, total public expenditure on retirement pensions in the UK would be consider-ably higher. For example, in the mid-1990s total spending for these purposes, which did not count as public expenditure, amounted to about £20 billion (Evans 1998: 285) compared to direct pension expenditure of £30.2 billion (DWP 2004a). In 2001, total public direct and indirect (tax) pension related expenditure has been calculated to be equal to 8 per cent of GDP (Wikeley et al. 2002: 587).

Table 5.3. Projected demographic pressure on public pensions

		2000	2010	2020	2030	2040
1. Old age dependency ratio	Germany	24.1	30.2	34.4	46.3	54.3
	UK	24.1	25.3	31.1	40.4	47.2
2. Spending as % of GDP	Germany	11.5	11.8	12.3	16.5	18.4
	UK	4.2	5.2	5.1	5.5	4.0

Source: 1. OECD (2002*b*; population over 65 years divided by population between 15–64 years);
2. Disney et al. (2004); assuming GDP growth of 2 per cent per annum (not including means-tested benefits to pensioners in UK of about 1 per cent).

Nevertheless, differences in public pension structures have influenced reforms in different ways. Demographic factors and rising social insurance contributions have fuelled concerns about the fiscal and economic sustainability of public pensions in Germany, particularly since the 1990s. In the UK, debates about public pensions have long been influenced by the scale of private pension provision which was already considerable in 1979 but has grown since (see Table 5.4) Noticeable is that almost a tenth of all retirement income stems from earnings, and 24 per cent for recently retired persons in 2002 (DWP 2004*c*). Table 5.4 also illustrates the growing scale of disability benefits which acts as one pathway out of employment, particularly for older men (Alcock et al. 2003; Clasen et al. 2004).

Finally, it should be noted that different patterns of housing tenure need to be taken into account for cross-national comparisons of income sources

Table 5.4. Public and private income for average pension unit (singles and couples), UK

	Proportion of pensioners with income from:		Share of average pensioners' income coming from:	
	1979	2001	1979	2001
Public pensions and benefits	97	98	61	51
Occupational pensions	40	60	16	26
Personal pensions	—	8	—	3
Investments	62	69	11	10
Earnings	n/a	8	16	9
Disability benefits	4	21	*	*

Source: DWP (2003) and my own calculations based on DWP (2003)
* no separate data, disability benefits included in 'public pensions and benefits'.

amongst pensioners (Frick and Grabka 2003). The UK has one of the highest rates of home ownership in Europe, whereas Germany has one of the lowest. More than 60 per cent of pensioners in the UK are owner occupiers, and the vast majority of them have paid off their mortgages (Emmerson and Johnson 2002: 320). The growth of home ownership is one reason why poverty amongst British pensions 'after housing costs' has declined since the mid-1990s, whereas poverty 'before housing costs' has remained largely unchanged (Brewer et al. 2004).

5.2 PROFILES AND DIRECTION OF CHANGE COMPARED

A comparative assessment of public pension policy has to take account of the relative scope of public and private pension provision in the two countries as it existed at the start of the period under investigation. Pedersen (2003) showed that out of seven West European countries, the reliance on public transfers was highest in Germany in 1980 compared with only a small role played by occupational and private pension income. By contrast, as shown earlier, the role of occupational pensions in the UK was already considerable in 1980, and the scale of private pensions about three times as large as in Germany. Since then, the gap has widened further based on a steep rise in the prevalence of both private and occupational pensions, between them covering almost half of all British retirement income in the mid-1990s, compared with a little over a fifth in Germany (Pedersen 2003). As a corollary, the average generosity of public pensions is comparatively high in Germany and low in the UK. In the mid-1990s public transfers in retirement represented about 70 per cent of average net equivalent income of German employees (a rise from 60 per cent in 1980), compared with a stagnating level of just below 40 per cent in the UK. These differences in scale and significance of public pensions might be expected to impact on the degree of change and profile of reforms introduced since the late 1970s. In principle, a large and growing private pension sector might facilitate cuts in public spending. In contrast, even small-scale cutbacks might be difficult to implement in a country with a predominance of public pension for retirement income.

And yet, German governments have been able to curb pension expenditure considerably. As a share of GDP, total pension expenditure rose only marginally (0.1 per cent) between 1980 and 1995, and much less than in any other European OECD country, except for Ireland, the Netherlands, and Luxembourg where spending declined. Adjusted by changes in demographic patterns German pension expenditure even decreased, whereas

British spending increased (Siegel 2002: 207). However, had it not been for cuts in the basic state pension and SERPS, expenditure would have risen much more. Indeed, under original legislation from the late 1970s, spending on SERPS has been estimated to have reached £41 billion by 2030. Legislative changes in the 1980s and 1990s reduced this to about £12 billion (Banks and Emmerson 2000). Similarly, applying legal parameters as they existed in the late 1970s, pension transfers in Germany would have been up to 20 per cent higher in the 1990s (Alber 1989: 300; Schmid 1997: 77). Taking account of further cuts since then, studies (cited in Hinrichs and Kangas 2003: 579) show that pension benefits of cohorts retiring after 2020 are forecast to be about 20 per cent lower than pensions of those who retired in 1996. In short, using the counterfactual, the cumulative long-term cost-containment effect of retrenchment policies has been considerable in both countries.

Sections 5.3 and 5.4 will show that institutional characteristics of public pensions (policy legacies) have influenced distinctive national reform profiles. For example, separate pension contributions earmarked for a fund which involves social partners in its administration, as well as the strongly earnings-related character of public pensions, fostered a cautious pattern of incremental change in Germany, with governments inclined to search for consensus and negotiated compromises and carefully balancing the interests of current contributors and pensioners. In the UK, retrenchment of public pensions was politically less risky due to a different programme structure, with a single NIF, effectively integrated in overall public sector spending and closely controlled by the government, a weak earnings-related public pension, and the significant presence of private arrangements.

Indeed, a first glance of changes in programme structures (Tables 5.1 and 5.2) suggests that in Germany generally small cost-containment policies prevailed with little effect on formal pension replacement rates. However, as discussed, current and future pension payments would have been considerably higher without legislative change. In addition, retrenchment has affected some groups in particular (job starters, employees with university degrees, and early retirees), and will lower the standard pension level in the long run. As in unemployment support, structural change was introduced only recently, but will bring about a new balance between public and private provision as the result of the process (Hinrichs 2003).

In the UK the scale of retrenchment within public pensions has been larger. The replacement rate of BSP has declined substantially and will fall further. The generosity of SERPS was significantly cut back in the 1980s and 1990s. More recently the scheme was abolished and replaced by a new programme which will become a flat-rate system. As discussed, the short-lived foray into earnings-related public pensions in the UK has to be put into context. Even by the 1970s private pensions in the UK represented a significant proportion of retirement income for average earners. Conservative governments since then have been able to shift the balance further in favour of non-statutory provision, scaling down public pensions in return for financially attractive exit options into private alternatives. As will be demonstrated, the resulting change in the British pension landscape contributed to a major reorientation of Labour's pension policy.

5.3 REFORMING PUBLIC PENSIONS IN GERMANY

5.3.1 Consensual adaptation and adjustment (1982–9)

Pension policymaking during the 1980s was situated within a very different context than in earlier decades. After the paradigmatic reform of 1957 which afforded public pensions a wage-replacement character, the positive economic context and a considerable budget surplus within public pension funds induced political parties to 'outbid' (Hinrichs 1998: 6) each other with expansionary policy proposals in the run-up to the election in 1972 (Rüb and Nullmeier 1991:443). However, the situation changed considerably in the wake of the first oil price induced recession in the mid-1970s. Reduced employment growth, rising unemployment, earlier entry of retirement pensions, and lower wage levels put considerable pressure on pension funds. The erstwhile expansionary trend came to a halt and, following the general election of 1976, the government made a number of explicit cost-saving proposals. Although not affecting nominal pension rates, the public outrage and sharp criticism against the plans took the government by surprise, also contributing to a 'learning process' within the opposition (Rüb and Nullmeier 1991: 445). Since then both major parties have aimed to keep pension politics out of electoral politics and, if possible, to legislate in conjunction with the respective opposition and social partners in order to share the blame for what were broadly perceived necessary adaptations to changed socio-economic circumstances. In accordance with the notion of the 'new politics of the welfare state' (Pierson 1996, 2001a), the SPD–FDP government employed a strategy of diversification and concealment. For example, the initial plan to switch pension indexation from gross to net earnings was withdrawn and replaced with politically determined ad hoc adaptations and small scale curtailments, such as the delaying of pension indexation, and the introduction of individual contributions by pensioners to health care insurance from 1982 onwards. Other changes, leaving nominal pension replacement rates intact but lowering pension outlays, were introduced in the early 1980s (see Appendix C).

The change of government in 1982 had no impact on either the direction or the pattern of pension policy. The economic recession and high unemployment at the time lowered contributory pension revenue and exerted fiscal pressure on the federal government and the BA respectively who were obliged to pay pension contributions on behalf of unemployed benefit claimants. Using a number of levers, the response was a wide range of small cutbacks, affecting current and future pensioners (see Appendix C). For example, the government ruled that pension contributions for unemployed persons should be based on benefit payment rather than previous earnings. Other measures included a gradual increase in pensioners' contributions to health insurance and a delayed pension indexation. Federal subsidies to public pension funds were lowered, partly brought about by lower pension crediting for persons engaged in military service. Overall, these measures were aimed at curtailing expenditure for both pension insurance funds and the federal government. Cutbacks were justified with reference to the principle that pensions and disposable earnings should rise in equal terms. Largely due to a time lag in pension adjustments, pension levels had risen faster than net earnings in the mid-1970s and early 1980s (see Schmähl 1999: 405).

The SPD refrained from mounting serious objections to these policies, not least since some of the measures had already been planned when the party was in government. Besides, there was a basic cross-party consensus over the need to contain the rise of net pensions vis-à-vis net earnings. More generally, both major parties agreed to uphold the insurance principle and thus merely to adjust the public pension system in accordance with existing parameters (Schmähl 2004). Even more so than in unemployment policy at the time, the social policy wing within the CDU, with Norbert Blüm as their figurehead, set the agenda in pension policymaking during the 1980s. The government's course of 'pension adjustment policy' (Rüb and Nullmeier 1991: 441) was also supported by the trade unions, employers, and other relevant organizations, such as pension funds and their umbrella organization, the VdR (*Verband deutscher Rentenversicherungsträger*). Even the market-liberal FDP was in favour of maintaining existing structures. Of course, within this broad alliance, interests had to be mediated and bargains struck over particular decisions, such as tightening eligibility criteria for disability pensions, for example, which in the first half of the 1980s was by far the most common form of entering retirement, with inflows dropping significantly after 1984 (Bäcker et al. 2003).

Another area of negotiations in the 1980s was prompted by a ruling of the Constitutional Court from 1975, which had obliged the government to equalize pension rights between widows and widowers by 1984. The ensuing debate on how to achieve this extended to a consideration of how to improve the position of women within the German pension system more generally, and to a suggestion of introducing pension credits for child rearing (child credits will be discussed in more detail in Chapter 6). Originating from the 1970s, this proposal was finally legislated in 1986, and credits (for so-called baby years) were subsequently extended. Against a backdrop of fiscal pressure, the problem of how to pay for such credits was eventually solved by further extending ALG entitlements for older unemployed claimants (see Chapter 4 and Appendix A), saving federal expenditure on ALH. As discussed in Chapter 4, this 'shifting yard' policy was feasible due to the fiscal interlocking between different social insurance branches and their tax subsidization by the federal government. The option of (tax) savings due to extended ALG entitlements, in conjunction with political pressure from the SPD and trade unions (but partly also from within the ruling CDU/CSU) and the looming general elections in January 1987, eventually persuaded the government to extend child rearing credits to retired mothers rather than merely new retirees as had originally been planned (Schmähl 2004).

More generally, the first half of the 1980s was characterized by tight budgets of both the federal government and the pension insurance. The response was incremental adjustment as well as frequent increases in pension contributions rates, counterbalanced by lowering contribution rates to unemployment insurance. Tax subsidies as a proportion of total pension expenditure declined during the 1980s (from 15.5 per cent to 14 per cent; VdR 2004). However, increased contribution rates helped to improve revenue, as well as rising employment which raised the numbers of contributors to social insurance after 1984 (growing about 10 per cent in total during the decade; BMGS 2003). At the same time, the proportion of persons over the age of sixty-five dropped slightly (Alber 1998: 211). The combined effect helps to explain that, as a share of GDP, pension payments declined somewhat in the 1980s, before increasing again in the 1990s.

Thus, during the 1980s there was little immediate pressure on pension finances or, put differently, policies responding to pressure in the early 1980s were more than adequate to guarantee fiscal sustainability. Nevertheless a debate about the need for structural reform aimed at reducing costs began against a backdrop of expected longer-term demographic changes and a significant decline in the average pension entry age (Scherer 2001). In contrast to previous instances of far-reaching expansionary reform (1957, 1972), this time the government planned legislation aimed at curbing pension entitlement. Nevertheless, the parliamentary opposition signalled its willingness to cooperate rather than capitalize politically on the government's potentially unpopular policy course. There were several reasons for this.

First, based on a cross-party consensus over adjusting but maintaining basic pension structures, the policy distance between major actors was small. For the SPD, the option of collaboration thus seemed tempting. In addition, the fact that negotiations could be confined to areas beyond the parliamentary arena and media attention allowed constructive negotiations without being seen as failing to take a stance against the political opponent. In addition, contingent and situational factors came into play. In the late 1980s opinion polls indicated a victory for the SPD in the forthcoming general election, creating little incentive to attack the government's pension plans for tactical reasons but to collaborate in order to 'push the reform outcome closer to their own policy preferences' (Schludi 2001: 35). In short, completing legislation before gaining political power seemed more rational than delaying the implementation of retrenchment policies which were perceived as inevitable (Hinrichs 1998: 6).

The pension reform, eventually enacted in 1989 and coming into force in 1992, was prepared in a lengthy process of meetings and negotiations of a relatively small policy network which included the social partners, pension fund organizations, and academic experts (for a detailed account, see Null-meier and Rüb 1993). Within this context, major aims were agreed upon, such as switching formally to indexing pensions in accordance with changes in net rather than gross earnings (Schmähl 1993, 1999: 413). Increasing and fixing the level of federal tax subsidies was another agreement which would allow funding improved child-rearing credits. In an attempt to keep pension reform discussions out of day-to-day politics, deliberations over reform elements were prepared by agencies which also provided social partners with a forum for negotiation. A joint report by the VdR (withheld deliber-ately until after the general election in 1987) was highly influential in this respect, marginalizing radical reform proposals made by individual MPs in favour of lowering the role of public pensions, and paving the way for a corporatist consensus which preceded party compromises. This consensus also included decisions regarding early retirement options.

In the early 1970s access to disability pensions and early retirement for other reasons, such as unemployment, were liberalized. Once unemploy-ment had begun to increase a few years later, large companies in particular made ample use of these options, shedding older and less productive workers, largely at the expense of the unemployment insurance and public pension schemes. The proportion of 55–64-year-olds in employment dropped from around 50 per cent in 1970 to 36 per cent by the mid-1980s, and has remained under 40 per cent since then (Funk 2004). The generosity of social insurance based exit options contributed to a high level of legitim-acy amongst affected workers, while trade unions supported the strategy on the grounds of creating jobs for younger job seekers and lowering registered unemployment amongst older workers, thus avoiding potential pressure on wages. Unemployment and public pension funds, however, were affected by lost revenue and increasing pressure on expenditure.

With hindsight, this trend has been identified as a defining weakness of the German welfare state (Manow and Seils 2000). However, during the 1980s, prevailing party political perspectives were different. In the light of persistent mass unemployment affecting older workers in particular, political parties were reluctant to limit options for early retirement. Attempts to make schemes less attractive were undermined or watered down in the face of a broad alliance of social partners, the economic wing of the CDU/CSU, and the SPD (Mares 2003: 239). In the run-up to the pension reform enacted in 1989, the SPD's (and particularly the trade unions') position was unequivocal. Any suggestions of raising the minimum age for early retirement or of deducting pension payments for those leaving the labour market early were strongly rebuked as long as mass unemployment had not been overcome (Schmähl 2004: 60). At the other end of the spectrum, the FDP pointed out that efforts should be made to raise the average age of pension entry, but not before the mid-1990s. In the end, a compromise was found which postponed making early retirement less attractive until after 2001 with a process of phasing in deductions for early exit and gradually lifting the minimum age for early retirement, to be completed by 2012.

The pension reform eventually agreed to come into force in 1992 entailed a number of changes (see Appendix C) which brought about losses for some groups (those with university degrees and job starters) but improvement for others (improved crediting for child-rearing and carers; see Chapter 6). A complex formula led to the creation of an 'expenditure-oriented revenue policy' (Schmähl 2003a), with the contribution rate as well as the scale of federal tax subsidies determined by expected pension expenditure. However, as a result of this 'self-regulating mechanism' (Hinrichs 1998: 13), rising pension contribution rates would, in turn, reduce the increase in pension payment as a result of the new net wage adjustment system.

Nominal pension levels remained intact, cutbacks were directed at the margins of the labour force (e.g. job starters and unemployed) or affected current pensioners merely to a small extent and were phased in or scheduled to start in the new century (Schmähl 1993). Increases in pension contributions were compensated with lower contributions to unemployment insurance in the typical 'shifting yard' policy discussed in Chapter 4.

By the time the final agreement had been reached in the late 1980s, pension funds had accumulated considerable reserves and their fiscal sustainability seemed secure. Despite a growth in the annual inflow and stock of retirement pensioners, the combined effect of benefit curtailments, rising employment covered by social insurance, and increased contribution rates in the early 1980s resulted in a considerable consolidation effect by the end of the decade. The SPD's social policy speaker asserted what was assumed more widely, that no further corrections would be needed for the next two decades (Schmähl 2004: 78). With hindsight the timing was intriguing. The reform was agreed upon in parliament on 9 November 1989, 'about one hour before the fall of the Berlin wall' (Schmähl 1999: 412). Thus, after years of intricate negotiations within a broadly consensual context, a reform package had been agreed which seemed financially and politically solid for West Germany, but, as became obvious fairly soon, not for unified Germany.

5.3.2 The breakdown of the pension consensus (1990–7)

The 1990s witnessed a complete change both in policy process in and in policy profile. To a considerable extent, this has to do with the impact of reunification as 'the most important factor posing current problems of financing the public pension scheme' (Hinrichs 1998: 7). As a result of the economic 'unification boom' in the west, public pension fund reserves initially increased further, thereby enabling west–east transfers to be funded and pension contribution rates to be lowered. After 1992, however, annual deficits grew rapidly and existing reserves dwindled fast (VdR 2004) due to growing expenditure and decreasing revenue. Between 1992 and 1998 the level of insured employment declined by over two million jobs in the old *Länder* (BMGS 2003: Table 2.6A). This is the background for raising the pension contribution rate after 1992, contributing to the growth of the combined social insurance contribution rate from around 35 per cent in the late 1980s to over 42 per cent by 1997 (see Fig. 3.5).

In addition to employment programmes, the public pension system played a major part in the social cushioning of the collapse of the East German labour market. The previous West German pension system became officially effective in unified Germany in 1992 and special arrangements became applicable to the new *Länder*, such as an early-retirement scheme for workers over the age of fifty-five and a 'social supplement' which was introduced so that pension poverty and recourse to social assistance could be avoided. The number of workers entering retirement in the new *Länder* rose while, in the wake of the economic recession in 1993, early retirement (after unemployment) increased steeply in both parts of the country. During the second half of the 1980s, between 40,000 and 50,000 employees annually entered early retirement due to unemployment, representing about 8 per cent of all pension entrants in West Germany. By the mid-1990s the number had increased to over 130,000, or 15 per cent of all newly retired people (VdR 2004). In the new *Länder*, the trend was even more dramatic, with 169,000 early retirees (after unemployment) in 1995 which was equivalent to 40.5 per cent of all pension entries. Despite a decline since then, early retirement continued to be a prevalent form of labour market exit in both parts of the country (in 2002 representing 14 per cent of all pension entries in the west and 23 per cent in the east; VdR 2004). As a percentage of GDP, pension outlays in the new *Länder* climbed from 15.1 per cent in 1991 to 21.1 per cent in 2001.

These developments had serious political repercussions. Initially, the post-unification economic boom, high pension fund reserves, and the broad perception of successful pension legislation, which came into force in 1992, delayed further reform and contained controversies. As late as 1994, even employer organizations argued that new legislation would not be necessary before the end of the decade, that policies should consolidate rather than alter existing structures, and that change should be brought about in a similarly consensual style as in the 1980s (BDA 1994). Within a couple of years, this position had changed completely. The combination of much more unfavourable economic conditions, a 'more realistic' assessment of the financial costs of unification (Bönker and Wollmann 1999: 522), constraints imposed by the convergence criteria of European Monetary Union (EMU), and rising non-wage labour costs were referred to by employer organizations as justifications for more severe retrenchment in public spending and structural change in pension provision. The government, and increasingly also the SPD, perceived higher contribution rates as counterproductive since payroll taxes came to be interpreted as a major cause of Germany's economic troubles. In the 1980s, much of the successful consolidation of the pension funds had been achieved by increasing revenue. Dismissing the option of higher pension contributions in the 1990s exacerbated the magnitude of savings to be achieved. By the second half of the 1990s the previously 'expenditure-oriented revenue policy' (Schmähl 2003a: 165) had been turned on its head. Maintaining and preferably lowering the pension contribution rate became the overarching policy objective.

In addition, concerns about population ageing, increased longevity, and low fertility rates entered the debate about pension policy more forcefully. Projections of increasingly adverse demographic trends fuelled media discussions about intergenerational equity, with trust in the existing public pension system dropping to 'an all time low' (Hinrichs 1998: 10). Strategically, all these factors provided much impetus for those who had always advocated structural reform, including reduced scope for public and a more important role for private pensions. While in the 1980s, such proposals were easily marginalized by the broad pension consensus, the new socio-economic context created new fault lines not only between the major parties and social partners, but also within them.

Initially, the government attempted to embark on a consensual path. In an effort to bring relevant actors together, an 'alliance for work' was set up in which social partners were invited to address the pension problem. In this context the government enacted a 'part-time work law for older employees' in 1996, which shifted part of the financial consequences for early retirement to employers and also brought forward the planned increase in the age of early retirement. However, the corporatist platform collapsed when the government unilaterally decided to reduce substantially the level of sick pay and the scope of dismissal protection. In addition, a range of cost-cutting measures were planned for 1997 which accelerated the phasing-out of early retirement options and inflicted losses for groups such as students, university graduates, the unemployed, and job starters (see Appendix C). It also brought forward the raising of the standard retirement age for women which became a major point of conflict at a time when unemployment rose faster for women than for men (BMGS 2003).

These measures have to been seen within a context of a shifting corporatist and partisan political landscape. Within industrial relations, persistently high levels of unemployment and increased levels of economic internationalization and capital mobility, improving 'exit options' (Hinrichs 1998: 22), strengthened the structural position of employer organizations vis-à-vis trade unions. After the mid-1990s the FDP increasingly sharpened its market-liberal profile and its influence grew on the back of strong electoral performances in three *Land* elections in 1996. Within the senior government party, the social policy wing's role as dominant agenda setter was waning while the business-oriented wing, worried about the cost of social policy, gained strength (Jochem 2001). Intent on lowering non-wage labour costs, the FDP and the business wing called for unilateral action and a reduction in public pensions (Schludi 2002: 145). Intraparty conflicts over the future of the German pension system began to develop also within the SPD (Egle and Henkes 2003). However, in the absence of government responsibility and the interest of winning the 1998 election, those who acknowledged the necessity for considerable cost savings aligned behind the party's official position, which was to attack the pension cuts announced by the Kohl government (Schludi 2002: 150).

In short, cross-party conflicts over pension policy began to develop more strongly and the policy domain became much more explicitly politicized than it hitherto had been. In the 1980s, electoral considerations favoured a collaboration between the opposition and government. After the mid-1990s a confrontational policy style became a more likely option for the SPD due to both a growing policy distance with the government and because of party competition. Refusing an invitation to participate in the government's pension reform commission and setting up its own commission, the SPD officially revoked the previous cross-party pension consensus in 1996. In turn, the government turned a blind eye to proposals emanating from the SPD commission.

A year later, prompted by the fact that the reforms from 1996 had not prevented a further rise in pension contributions, the government embarked on a new and more far-reaching round of cutbacks and revenue enhancing changes. Since lowering the contribution rate was a consensual goal across parties, some proposals, such as increasing tax subsidies for pension insurance on the back of a higher VAT rate (see Appendix C), were approved by the SPD. Other elements however were fiercely criticized, such as changes affecting the level of pensions and early retirement options for people with disabilities, and the introduction of a so-called 'demographic factor' which was aimed at linking the longevity of particular cohorts with the indexation of pension payments. Intended to dampen the expected pressure on pension expenditure caused by the increase in life expectancy, the measure aimed to limit the increase in the pension contribution rate to 20.5 per cent by 2020 and to 23.5 per cent by 2030 (Schmähl 1999: 415). However, it also implied a (gradual) decrease in the net standard pension level for future pensioners (from 70 to 64 per cent by 2030). This explicit cut in the formal replacement rate became the focal point for reform opponents including the SPD, trade unions, and pensioner organizations (Hinrichs 1998: 18). Having collaborated over retrenchment in the run-up to the general election in 1990, this time the SPD aimed to gain electoral mileage as the proclaimed 'defender of the welfare state' (Bönker and Wollmann 1999: 523). The strategy seems to have paid off. As Schludi (2002: 154) shows, in the general election of 1998 the SPD gained most and the CDU/CSU lost disproportionately amongst older age cohorts.

5.3.3 Incremental change and structural reform (1998–2004)

Chapter 4 identified several phases and policy U-turns within unemployment and labour market policymaking under the red–green government, influenced by intraparty conflicts, changing socio-economic contexts, and electoral considerations. Also within pension policy distinct phases of policymaking can be distinguished, with the pendulum swinging between incremental reform driven by short-term political as well as financial pressure, and structural change aimed at partially departing from traditional pension parameters in order to dampen the expected growth in pension contribution rates.

Honouring election promises, not least to trade unions, the newly formed red–green government in 1998 suspended reforms enacted under the Kohl government which were scheduled to come into force in 1999, that is, the introduction of the demographic factor and curtailments in disability benefits. In addition, people with low earnings and others in atypical forms of employment were included in mandatory pension coverage. A new 'environmental tax' on energy consumption was introduced which was to generate earmarked tax revenue for the pension fund. These revenue-oriented policies enabled the government to lower the combined pension contribution rate from 20.3 per cent in 1998 to 19.1 per cent by 2001.

However, the above measures proved sufficient to deal neither with short-term fiscal pressure on pension funds, nor with their medium-term sustainability in the light of an increasingly adverse demographic dependency ratio (Börsch-Supan et al. 2002: 176). The government thus found itself in a 'dilemma of their own making' (Anderson and Meyer 2003: 34). A projected increase in the combined pension insurance rate to around 24 per cent by 2030 was regarded as both economically 'unsustainable' and violating 'intergenerational equity' (Schmähl 2003*b*: 10). This was also the position of the opposition parties, as well as most commentators in a domestic public policy discourse in which pension reform had become a major focus of attention—very much in contrast with the more technical and less politicized deliberations of the 1980s. And yet a structural reform which would render significant savings, favoured by modernizers within the party including the Chancellor, seemed politically impossible in the face of foreseeable conflicts within the SPD, with the coalition partner, and particularly with the unions. A cross-party consensus with the CDU/CSU seemed also to be no longer an option after the SPD had adopted a confrontational strategy in 1997.

Perhaps surprisingly, the outcome of this impasse was the introduction of the so called *'Riester Rente'* (the Riester pension) in 2001, named after Walter Riester (SPD) who had become the minister of social affairs in the coalition government and who was among those considered as modernizers within the party. In a formal adoption of a 'revenue-oriented expenditure policy', the government plans envisaged capping the contribution rate to 20 per cent by 2020 and to 22 per cent by 2030, to be achieved by a gradual reduction of the (standard) pension replacement rate to 64 per cent within thirty years. This was to be compensated by encouraging employees to pay into private or occupational pension funds, which would attract subsidies in the form of flat-rate benefits or tax breaks. The full tax advantage would become applicable for those who, from 2008 onwards, devoted at least 4 per cent of their earnings to approved non-statutory pension schemes.

This policy implied a break with one of the traditional cornerstones of the German social insurance system, that is, equal contributions from employers and employees. It also anticipated a move from a hitherto 'old age security' focused policy (Hinrichs 2000) towards a partial privatization and a 'multipillar approach' within retirement income policy in Germany (Hinrichs and Kangas 2003). Indeed, despite some changes made to original plans (see later) and the limited scope of the envisaged private element, the reform represents 'undoubtedly an innovation' (Nullmeier 2003: 183) or, put more dramatically, a 'fundamental departure from former policy paradigms and policy beliefs' (Lamping and Rüb 2004: 174). It not only adjusted downwards the public pension replacement rate, but produced a 'goal shift', since the policy suggested that public pensions (on their own) would no longer guarantee status maintenance.

There are several motives which drove the government to adopt such a paradigmatic reform. Only one year after the general election, fiscal pressures within pension policy contributed to a change of course in the government's pension policy with a planned switch of pension indexation (to price increases) for the subsequent two years. Since net wages were rising fast at the time, prospective savings were considerable. Additional proposals to contain pension expenditure included cuts within disability pensions, a more substantial reduction in public pensions for younger age cohorts, the implementation of a needs-based means-tested minimum pension, a new indexation formula, and the earlier mentioned core component of a supplementary pension pillar on a fully funded basis (see Appendix C).

The overarching objective for these proposals was the perceived need of stabilizing contribution rates. As far as the suggestion for a privately funded pension supplement in particular is concerned, Lamping and Rüb (2004: 182) regard this as an act of 'experimental law making' on the part of modernizers within the SPD and the federal chancellery, aimed at creating room for 'politically regulated' welfare markets in pension provision. Indeed, the proposal can be traced to preferences on the part of modernizers who envisaged a social policy which would mesh solidarity with aspects such as economic efficiency and individual self-reliance (Hinrichs 2003). In the context of a much declined level of trust in the existing public pension system, the option of personal savings plan, subsidized by the state, came to be regarded as an appealing feature since it would introduce choice and allow a higher total level of retirement income. Besides, the transition was designed to be gradual. A lower public pension was portrayed as inevitable, necessary cutbacks as being distributed fairly and as improving the sustainability of public pensions.

However, if the proposal of introducing a private pension supplement was a 'deliberate political strategy' (Lamping and Rüb 2004: 181), it was also a risky one (Hinrichs 2003). Its announcement prompted heavy public protest stretching from the parliamentary opposition to the trade unions, MPs within the government parties, and pension fund organizations (see Anderson and Meyer 2003: 37–40; Schludi 2002: 157–61). Social policy experts within the SPD and trade unions opposed the exemptions of employers from the funding of the privatized element, the steepness of the cut of pension benefits, and the resulting prospect of rising pensioner poverty. The CDU/CSU pointed to the heavy burden placed on low wage earners. Except for employer organizations, 'all relevant actors opposed the idea of making private old-age provision obligatory' (Schludi 2002: 160).

Taken aback by the scale and breadth of opposition, and plummeting opinion poll ratings ahead of *Länder* elections, the government withdrew the mandatory character of private pension contribution which the tabloid press had denounced as a step towards a compulsory pension system. Other concessions were made in the direction of the CDU/CSU, including a substantial extension of subsidies and tax relief for those embarking on private pension plans, favouring families with children in particular. Schludi (2002: 161) points to three reasons why the opposition's approval was perceived as politically important. First, sharing the costs of what clearly were unpopular cutbacks in an electorally salient policy field remained an important motive. Second, modernizers hoped that an alliance with the opposition would strengthen the chance of achieving far-reaching reforms by sidelining trade unions and left-wingers within their own party. Finally, some elements within the proposed reform package required the consent of the *Bundesrat* in which the Christian Democratic *Länder* had a majority.

However, despite concessions and a considerable degree of common ground between both major political parties (the need to contain non-wage labour costs and the introduction of a new public-private mix), cross-party negotiations broke down when MPs within the CDU/CSU who opposed a consensual solution for political reasons gained the upper hand. Thus, this time 'it was the Christian Democrats who sought to exploit the pension issue in the electoral arena' (Schludi 2002: 162). As a result, the SPD leadership turned towards left-wing MPs (who threatened to vote against the bill) and trade unions, gaining approval after further concessions had been promised. In addition, the government split the reform package into two parts: one which did not require *Bundesrat* approval, and one for which a majority in the second chamber was achieved after a deal was struck with two CDU-led *Länder* (Schludi 2002: 166).

As the result of this long-winded negotiation process the pension reform of 2001 deviated in several respects from its original design. The overall level of cutbacks was much lower than had been intended, the standard pension replacement rate was to drop by only 3 percentage points (rather than 6) over thirty years, contributions to a fully-funded private pillar became voluntary, and, as a concession to trade unions, collectively agreed pension plans would receive considerable tax incentives and take precedence over private pension plans (Schludi 2001: 36). Also, instead of introducing a minimum floor within pension insurance, a new means-tested pension became part of a 'partial reform of social assistance' (Nullmeier 2003: 176). Thus, in comparison with pension reforms in other countries at the time (Hinrichs 2002) and despite a partial privatization and appreciation of non-statutory pension income sources, the overall scale of restructuring was relatively small. Schludi (2002) explains this with reference to institutional factors located at programme level, channels of political decision-making, and policy legacies. The link between lifetime earnings and pension entitlements had already been very tight in Germany which, in contrast to countries such as Sweden, precluded this 'lever' from achieving substantial savings. As for the second factor, in order to avoid failure or electoral sanctions, reforming German pensions requires negotiations with either the opposition party or trade unions. Political institutions (such as the *Bundesrat*) can, at times offer opponents the chance of blocking or significantly altering legislation. As for policy legacies, despite a loss of trust as to the sustainability of public pensions, the notion of equivalence (linking lifetime earnings to benefit entitlement) remains firmly anchored not only within the pension community, such as the VdR in particular, and also within both major political parties. Unlike in the UK, either party can declare itself a credible welfare state defender and thus gain political weight by opposing retrenchment efforts (Kitschelt 2001). However, if and to what degree these institutional features influence policymakers is also dependent on political conditions, internal party conflicts, and situational contexts which vary over time.

This can be demonstrated with reference to pension policy after 2002. After its implementation in 2001, government seemed convinced that the 'Riester reform' provided sufficient stability for some time to come. However, shortly after the general election in 2002 the red–green coalition responded to short-term financial difficulties in pension funds by raising the contribution rate. A further economic deterioration in 2003 exacerbated pension budget problems. As a consequence the government resorted to yet another round of incremental but wide-ranging short-term cutbacks, including a suspension of pension indexation for 2004 and cost-savings which will negatively affect the pension entitlements of university graduates, job starters, and early retirement options (see Appendix C). In addition, more structural, long-term changes are also to be implemented following the recommendations made by the Rürup commission (after its chairman Bert Rürup). In the wake of Schröder's announcement of the 'Agenda 2010' (see Chapter 4), the commission had been set up to assess options for a financially 'sustainable development' of the public pension (and health and long-term care) insurance. Consisting of academic experts and representatives of relevant organizations and private business (social partners, private insurance companies, employers, and economic consultants), its main recommendations included the introduction of a 'demographic component' within a new pension formula and the gradual increase of the statutory retirement age after 2011 (to sixty-seven years for those born after 1968).

Thus, after having revoked legislation which would have introduced a 'demographic factor' as planned by the previous government, in a complete U-turn the red–green coalition accepted the need to adjust the pension formula in this way by late 2003 and has since introduced legislation which implemented a so-called 'sustainability factor' within pension indexation, taking account of the changing ratio between contributors and pension recipients in each year. While this latest change might improve the fiscal sustainability of the public pension system, the combined impact of further cutbacks is likely to lead to more pensioners having to resort to means-tested benefits which would potentially undermine the insurance character of the public pension scheme (Schmähl 2003a: 178).

In sum, the policy path since 1998 can be described as a sequence of incremental short-term responses to fiscal pressures, interspersed with cautious structural reform, creating room for 'politically regulated welfare markets' in pension provision (Lamping and Rüb 2004: 184) supplementing, not replacing, public pensions. The cross-party consensus and driving motive for this has been to stabilize, and if possible reduce, the pension contribution rate. This, however, proved difficult in a context of periodically declining revenue and fiscal pressure which is forecast to grow as a result of demographic change. While the policy style might have changed from resting on cross-party consensus to conflict, policymaking has not become any easier due to new intraparty conflicts, the need to negotiate with organizations of the traditional pension policy network, trade unions, and the political opposition. In such a situation, pension policy under the red–green government has not been guided by a clear and coherent strategy but resembled a 'permanent *muddling through* without conceptual orientation' (Nullmeier 2003: 184; emphasis in original). Nevertheless, ever since the late 1990s, German pension reforms have gathered speed with pragmatic incremental cost-containment changes followed by unprecedented structural change in recent years. In some respects, the trajectory in the UK has been the reverse.

5.4 REFORMING BRITISH PENSIONS

5.4.1 Freezing the basic state pension and scaling down of SERPS (1979–90)

As discussed in Chapter 4, before winning the general election in 1979, the Conservative Party had made no specific plans as to the future shape of most social policy areas during its time in opposition. This also applied to pensions. And yet, a major change was announced in 1980 with the switch to indexing the value of the BSP in line with inflation—as opposed to pegging its value to the higher of inflation or the increase in average earnings, as had been practised before. Such a move appeared in line with the government's plan of reducing the scale of public spending, which was regarded as hampering economic prosperity. Social spending was the largest part of government outlay, and within it pension expenditure the biggest single item by far. Pension cuts were therefore to be expected. On the other hand, in its first term of office, the government was cautious and carefully chose areas for explicit cutbacks which were regarded as electorally less harmful, such as unemployment benefits (see Chapter 4).

Besides, changing the indexation of the basic pension could not be expected to yield major financial gains in the short term. In the long run, however, the effect was significant. Because earnings grew faster than prices, without the switch in indexation the extra costs would have amounted to £43 billion between 1980 and 1992 (Timmins 2001: 374). What is more, freezing public pension entitlement can be regarded as a process of gradual and 'implicit privatization' (Pierson 1994: 59) since economic growth and raising real earnings would be translated into growing scope for non-statutory provision. In short, there were sound economic and ideological reasons for a move which seemed incremental but represented a substantial form of retrenchment in the long run. How was such a policy feasible?

First, except for its scale the policy was consensual within government. The Treasury had intended to increase pensions even below the level of inflation. However, this was successfully resisted by Patrick Jenkin, then Secretary of State at the Department for Health and Social Security (DHSS) who was prepared to accept reductions in benefit spending in return for a pledge of avoiding cuts in the NHS budget for three years (Timmins 2001: 373). Due to fears of electoral retribution, Margaret Thatcher repeatedly promised to maintain the purchasing power of pensions, which was important since inflation stood well above 10 per cent.

Second, at the time the impression was given that the change was not irreversible but a temporary cutback due to tight economic circumstances. By implication, the BSP would 'at least occasionally be subject to a higher uprating' (Nesbitt 1995: 36). Third, opposition against a change in indexation lacked force. The pensioner lobby was relatively weak and the criticism made by the Labour Party stood on shaky ground. It accused the government of breaking with the convention of keeping pension income up with changes in earnings. In response, the government pointed out that this practice was not a traditional feature of British pension policy. Indeed, the favourable indexation of pensions (to the higher of earnings or price inflation) had formally been implemented only by the previous government. Last but not least, the nature of the reform itself, that is, a small change with little impact, made it difficult for opponents to portray it as 'a major assault on state provision' (Pierson 1994: 59).

The general election of 1983 provided the government with a much stronger parliamentary majority (see Table 3.1), making a more explicit and structural change in public pension policy politically more feasible. The dominant objective after the election was to sustain the economic upturn, to control the exchange rate, and to keep interest rates as low as possible (Gamble 1988). This was to be achieved by denationalizing state-owned industries, further labour market and employment deregulation, and containing public expenditure (Deakin and Wilkinson 1994). Social security was the largest and fastest growing part of public spending (Deakin 1994; Robinson 1986), making it a prime target for the perceived need for cutbacks. In addition, enhancing the gap between wages and benefits and introducing private elements in welfare provision remained important ideological policy priorities. These factors led to a review which was heralded by Norman Fowler, the Secretary of State for Social Services, as the most 'substantial examination of the social security system since the Beveridge Report forty years ago' (HCD, 2 April 1985, c.653).

The implicit assumption for the review was to identify savings which could be converted into future tax cuts. However, this objective was expected to create public discontent in the light of opinion polls which indicated strong public resentment towards reductions in welfare spending even if, as a consequence, taxes were to be reduced (Taylor-Gooby 1987). In order to enhance the legitimacy of proposals which had not been announced in the election manifesto, consultation from interested groups outside parliament was thus encouraged (Adler 1988). However, the vast majority of comments were critical and expressed concerns about the 'zero-cost' condition upon which the review was premised and which led to the Social Security Act 1986, implemented in 1988 (Dilnot and Webb 1988).

One of the major components of the review process was the reform of secondary pensions. Fowler favoured the phasing out of SERPS in order to strengthen the role of private pensions, to be achieved by introducing portable personal pension plans (Timmins 2001: 371). It was hoped that the latter would deal with the so-called 'early leaver' problem, that is, the loss or reduction of pension entitlement for employees who left an occupational pension scheme before retirement because of redundancy or changing jobs. But pension policy was also driven by a debate about the future cost of SERPS, fuelled by new demographic projections and an unexpected increase in SERPS membership due to redundancies, compared with stagnating membership in occupational pension schemes (Nesbitt 1995: 42). In 1983, the CPRS (Central Policy Review Staff), a conservative think tank, had published a report in which the long-term cost of SERPS was regarded as insupportable and hence recommended its phasing out and replacement with private pensions. After the general election the government began to take up this suggestion. Official publications in 1984 pointed to the advantage of personal pensions which, because of their funded character, were not regarded as representing a burden on future generations. However, Thatcher was fearful of potential electoral repercussions as a consequence of simply abolishing SERPS, and thus favoured its replacement with a compulsory private scheme. She was also somewhat hesitant of formulating policy in a field which was expected to affect a future rather than the current government (Timmins 2001: 395). Nevertheless, the Prime Minister agreed to the inclusion of SERPS in the review process, not least because of the attraction of widening private 'pension ownership', which, in addition to home and share ownership, would strengthen 'popular capitalism' in the UK and reinforce the Conservative Party's social base (Bonoli 2000: 71).

Thus, the reform of SERPS has to be seen as not merely, and probably not primarily, driven by cost-saving but also by electoral and ideological motives. One of those latter aspects was Fowler's assertion that earnings-related benefits, that is, transfers which are more generous to the better-off, were not in accordance with the conservative's notion of targeting state support to those who needed it most. This position seemed a departure from the Conservative Party which had supported the implementation of SERPS as formulated in the Social Security Act 1975, and developed its own earnings-related pension plan in the early 1970s. However, the latter owed much to the prevailing economic climate at the time, was much more modest than SERPS, and was intended to function only as a 'reserve' scheme rather than one which would be a competitor to occupational schemes (Nesbitt 1995: 20). By the mid-1980s the government had returned to its original stance of encouraging private secondary pension provision with the state merely providing a flat-rate first safety net.

However, the proposed phasing out of SERPS was heavily criticized from a 'significant and probably unexpectedly high number of actors' (Bonoli 2000: 71). These included the Labour Party, trade unions, and lobby groups such as Age Concern and the CPAG (Child Poverty Action Group), which remained sidelined however because of the wide gap in policy preferences. For example, the Trade Union Congress (TUC) demanded an increase of the BSP to half average earnings. The Labour Party favoured restoring its link with earnings and rejected any changes to SERPS. Such positions were too distant from the government's proposals, rendering any potential cross-party negotiations over elements of the re-form fruitless. Of more relevance were misgivings on the part of the Treasury and reservations expressed by groups sympathetic to the government. Once he had worked out what the costs of tax relief for private provision would be, Nigel Lawson turned against the idea of replacing SERPS with compulsory personal pensions (Timmins 2001: 400). Employ-ers and representatives of occupational pension funds argued that personal plans should merely represent a voluntary third pension tier so as not to undermine occupational pension schemes which were regarded as an im-portant instrument of personnel management. In addition, expressing the classic 'double payment' problem inherent in switching from a pay-as-you-go to a funded scheme, the Confederation of British Industry (CBI) pointed out that employers (and employees) would have to fund both SERPS entitlements of current pensioners as well as making mandatory contribu-tions to private schemes for future retirees. Thus, rather than the abolition of SERPS, the CBI and others advocated its modification, which included a change in the benefit formula with pensions based on lifetime earnings rather than the 'best twenty years' (Nesbitt 1995: 89).

The magnitude of such criticism led to Norman Fowler abandoning the idea of phasing out SERPS in favour of changing its benefit formula which rendered the scheme financially much less attractive (see Appendix D), in turn making private provision more attractive. In addition, new personal pensions were introduced and take-up supported by offering an additional 'special bonus' over and above the existing NIF rebate for opting out of SERPS. However, heeding reservations from employers, these incentives were restricted to those leaving SERPS for personal pensions, rather than also to existing members of occupational pension schemes. As a whole, the changes amounted to a considerable scale of retrenchment. The combined effect, in addition to a smaller change introduced in 1995 (see below), was to 'reduce the value of SERPS benefits by around two-thirds' (Blake 2003: 23). Those less able or willing to transfer out of SERPS into private provision lost out, that is, particularly those with lower earnings and less continuous work careers and also older workers with limited time to build up new entitlements. How was the government capable of imposing such a high degree of welfare loss and what were the motives?

Emmerson and Johnson (2002: 303) point to the 'failure of original architects' to estimate the long-term costs of SERPS. However, there was no immediate pressure on spending since demographic change had yet to have an effect. Instead, the more important motive was ideological. Disregarding the conflict between the Treasury and DHSS, there was strong backing within the government in favour of expanding private pensions and reducing the scale of public provision. A large majority after 1983 allowed the government to be bolder than in its first period in office and to override objections from political opponents in the House of Commons more easily. However, the government underestimated the complexities and consequences of its ideological drive to phase out SERPS. The result was not a U-turn or retreat, even if it appeared so if measured against Norman Fowler's original plans. Instead, once concessions were made, the government proceeded with scaling down public provision in favour of expanding personal pensions. This was facilitated by institutional parameters. SERPS had only been established a few years earlier and few people were drawing the pension. For those paying into the system, changes were introduced with a considerable time lag (see Appendix D). Changes clearly disadvantaged those who remained within the system, that is, mainly the low paid who had relatively little political influence. By contrast, the reform left the position of occupational pension members unchanged and offered considerable incentives to those prepared to switch to personal pensions. The enormous take-up of personal pensions after 1988 confirms that the reform cannot be categorized as unpopular welfare retrenchment which might have required skilful political tactics. Instead, rather than 'blame avoidance', 'claiming credit' seems a more plausible motive for policymaking. Offering what at the time seemed more favourable pension prospects for a sufficiently large number of people can be regarded as on a par with the sale of council houses to sting tenants a few years earlier.

5.4.2 Dealing with policy failure and further retrenchment (1990–7)

The popularity of the SERPS legislation exceeded government's expectations, with about 25 per cent of the workforce opting to purchase personal pensions (Disney et al. 2004). This trend was driven by additional financial incentives attached to 'contracting out' and a heavy advertising campaign by both the government and the insurance industry (Bonoli 2000: 80). However, the unexpected increase in take-up also increased the costs for the

Exchequer as a result of the considerable tax breaks attached to personal pension plans, at a time when the country entered a new economic recession. Another, and for those affected more immediate, problem was the often poor quality of the advice given by salespersons of personal pensions. Prospective buyers were enticed into leaving SERPS or exit occupational pension schemes even though personal pension plans were often less favourable because of high commission charges, rebates which could not be fully made use of, and the absence of employers' contributions. Indeed, as many as 90 per cent of the 500,000 employees who transferred their assets from occupational pension schemes to personal pension plans had been given inappropriate advice (Blake 2003: 24) and as many as three million people were sold private pensions when they would have been better off staying in SERPS (A. Walker 1999: 515). This 'mis-selling' scandal influenced policymaking during the 1990s, aimed at tightening the regulatory framework for private pensions and forcing pension companies to compensate those who had been given inappropriate advice to a total of over £2.6 billion by 1999 (Disney et al. 2004).

Even before the mis-selling scandal erupted in late 1993, private pensions had become a major public issue. After the death of the media tycoon Robert Maxwell in 1991 it was revealed that about £400 million had been taken out of his companies' pension funds and placed into insecure investments. This transaction had resulted in a massive loss of pensions entitlements which were only marginally compensated by a relief fund set up by the Department of Social Security (DSS, the successor of the DHSS). The Maxwell scandal led the government to set up a committee which included the pensions industry and academic experts. In its report from 1993 the committee recommended stronger safeguards against fraud, restrictions on withdrawal of occupational pension surpluses, and changes to the structure in which trustees are appointed (Nesbitt 1995). These recommendations directly influenced the Social Security Act 1995 which introduced stricter regulations of trustees' actions, more accountability towards fund members, and a regulatory body for occupational pensions.

The 1995 reform also implemented further cost-saving measures, one of which was the decision to raise the retirement age for women from sixty to sixty-five, to be phased in between 2010 and 2020, coupled with an increase in required contributions for eligibility to a full BSP. Although an equalization of pension ages between men and women was required by EU legislation, it was left to individual member states to decide how to achieve this. After initial discussions about flexible forms of retirement, the British government eventually settled for raising the female retirement age to sixty-five because this made 'sound financial sense', according to Peter Lilley, the

Secretary of State, who pointed to the need for fiscal sustainability in the public pension system (DSS, Press release, 20/7/1995).

Even though its long-term viability was not under threat, the Social Security Act 1995 introduced a new calculation method for SERPS which generated further savings (Pension Policy Institute 2003: 31). The measures reduced public spending by a third of what, at the time, was forecast to be the cost for the scheme by 2030 (Banks and Emmerson 2000). Also further privatization was encouraged via the introduction of new age-related rebates to National Insurance contributions which 'should make it worthwhile for people to stay contracted-out' (Lilley, DSS, Press release, 20/7/1995). Finally, the government deregulated the contracting out of SERPS into occupational pensions. Before the 1995 changes, occupational pensions had been required to at least match the pension benefit accrued within SERPS had employees not contracted out. In addition, employers had to index the level of the occupational pension in line with inflation up to a maximum of 3 per cent, with the state covering the cost should inflation rise above this level. The abolition of this requirement saved public expenditure and made offering occupational pension provision more attractive to employers.

How was it possible significantly to retrench SERPS further without much criticism? Two factors appear to be important. First, as the 1995 reform focused on solving problems and improving the security of (private) provision, attention seems to have been deflected from elements which implemented cutbacks. Second, the nature of such cutbacks might have been difficult to gauge because of the complexity of the alterations made to SERPS. Both of these considerations resonate elements of the 'new politics' thesis of welfare retrenchment (Pierson 2001*b*) which points to the need obscuring negative distributive reform impacts and combining welfare losses with gains within the same reform package (Bonoli 2000).

However, two other factors are perhaps more relevant. First, as a self-reinforcing mechanism, the retrenchment of SERPS implemented in the 1980s had made further cutbacks more feasible. The massive take-up of private pensions after 1988, the exodus from SERPS of more than five million people by 1993, and hence the decline of SERPS coverage from more than half of the workforce in 1987 to about a quarter by the early 1990s (Schmid 1997; Emmerson and Johnson 2002: 303) lowered the potential for resistance considerably. In turn, the size of the electorate either not affected by the reform or that gained as a result of new incentives for private provision had grown considerably, as underlined by the increase in the coverage of occupational pensions after 1994 (Disney et al. 2001: 75).

The second reason relates to a process of reorientation within the Labour Party as to the role of public and private pensions which began in earnest after the unexpected defeat at the general election of 1992. Until that time the party had objected to the scaling down of SERPS, demanded a significant rise in the level of the BSP, and pledged to restore its link to average earnings. However, already in the late 1980s Labour implicitly acknowledged the popular appeal of contracted-out pensions and their reversal as 'extremely impractical' (Bonoli 2000: 77). A policy document in 1996 (Security in Retirement) indicated that the Labour Party was no longer willing to restore the BSP in line with earnings or to reverse the cuts made to SERPS, but to improve the level of means-tested support and to introduce secondary type pensions for low earners (A. Walker 1999: 517). Despite fierce protests from within the party and from pensioner lobby groups, these plans were not abandoned but fed into pension plans which were finally revealed in late 1998. It made clear that, like their conservative predecessors, the new government had become intent on shifting the balance of pension provision further in the direction of private sources and the responsibility for retirement income onto individuals. However, in other respects there were also signs of policy discontinuity.

5.4.3 Targeting public provision and expanding private sources of retirement income (1997–2003)

One of the Labour Party's core election campaign issues was its intention to reform substantially the welfare state. As discussed in Chapter 3, the party pledged to 'think the unthinkable' and introduce new measures, guided by an ideology of citizenship which would rebalance rights and responsibilities (DSS 1998a). Within the field of unemployment and labour market policy, plans were fairly advanced by the time Labour entered office, and New Deal programmes started less than a year into the new government. This was not the case for pensions where merely the overall policy direction had been agreed upon. Despite the promise of early legislation, it took until December 1998 before a Green Paper finally emerged with policy proposals (DSS 1998b). It announced that the BSP, while remaining a 'building block of the pension system', would continue to be indexed to prices. A new means-tested minimum guarantee (MIG) would supplement the BSP for those on low income. Compared with existing benefit rates, MIG set a higher income threshold below which pensioners with no or few savings should not fall. In 2003 the scheme was replaced with the Pension Credit (PC) which addressed the problem of creating disincentives to savings inherent in a strict means-test (Appendix D). Labour's departure from a preference for reviving contributory-based provision in old age to embracing a means-tested public minimum was underlined by the fact that MIG (PC) was to be indexed in line with earnings, widening the gap with the BSP which remained linked to prices. Prospectively this means that the share of means-tested state pension transfers will grow substantially over the forthcoming decades, from currently 10 per cent of all public spending on retirement income to 30 per cent by 2050 (Attanasio et al. 2004).

The Green Paper also announced the replacement of SERPS with a new state second pension (S2P) in 2002. The S2P continued to provide earnings-related entitlements, but will become a flat-rate benefit in 2007 (Appendix D). The system is targeted particularly at low earners (less than about half average earnings), and even those with up to average earnings are better off with S2P than under the post-1995 SERPS system (Pensions Policy Institute 2003: 35). However, the Labour government clearly favours private forms of retirement income over statutory provision. This design of S2P after 2007 (earnings-related contributions for a low flat-rate benefit) provides yet another incentive for contracting out of state secondary pension provision. In addition, further rebates have been provided for workers without occupational pensions or suitable private pensions to opt into a new form of regulated funded schemes, the so-called 'stakeholder pensions'. Provided by employers, mutual organizations, trade unions, banks, or private insurance companies, these are defined contribution schemes similar to personal pensions, but simplified and closely regulated regarding charges, the level of minimum contributions, and the flexibility and transferability of funds. Stakeholder pension schemes are voluntary, but since October 2001 employers with more than five employees have been required to provide access to such a scheme, unless they offer occupational pension provision. It can be assumed that this requirement has, after a very slow start, contributed to a considerable increase in take-up in recent years (Cebulla and Reyes de-Beaman 2004).

In sum, the direction of pension policy under the Labour government has been to reduce the role of public provision and to foster private sources of pension income. A declared objective is to reverse the current ratio of 40 per cent private to 60 per cent public pension income within the coming decades. Public pension support has become more redistributive than under the previous government, but also more dominated by means-testing. Since the minimum income guarantee (PC) is set at a higher rate than previously and there is a less rapid rate of withdrawal for those with income and savings, the net of means-testing has been cast more widely, beyond those with average earnings. On the other hand, currently even a small non-statutory (or statutory second) pension is enough to remove entitlement to the PC. In other words, 'the extension of means-testing is potentially wide, but quite shallow' (Hills 2003: 20). However, since the PC is linked to average earnings, the private (second) pension income required to remain outside the PC entitlement has been calculated to grow steadily from currently about 12 per cent of average earnings to 27 per cent by 2027 (Clark and Emmerson 2003: 81). Thus, the proportion of pensioners entitled to means-tested support is expected to grow. At the same time, as a component of total public pension transfers, the BSP will be reduced to a third or less. Politically, Labour's reinforcement of the trend towards personal responsibility and the restructuring of the remaining public support presents a stark departure from its policy preferences in the early 1990s. What was the political logic behind this outcome and how was it achieved?

The answer to the second question is fairly straightforward. As in 1983, the (even larger) parliamentary majority in 1997 helped the government to ignore the dissenting voices of Labour backbenchers or criticism levelled from the parliamentary opposition. Little attention was paid to the pension lobby favouring higher contributory pensions (A. Walker 1999). Once settled, the government's position on pension policy was only seriously threatened at one point when the idea of restoring the link between BSP and average earnings emerged more forcefully. Brought about as a result of low inflation, the derisory increase of BSP in April 1999 (of 75 pence per week) attracted major criticism from within the party, trade unions, and the pensioner lobby, and led to a defeat for the party leadership at the annual conference. However, protests subsided once the Chancellor signalled a strong increase of BSP in the next round of indexation. Besides, since Labour's initiatives (second pension, MIG, PC, stakeholder pensions) have favoured the lower paid, trade unions have found it difficult to mount serious attacks on the government's pension policy.

The answer to the question of what motivated Labour to break with traditional policy objectives is more multifaceted. Emerging gradually after the election defeat in 1992, new party preferences were shaped by electoral considerations, by intraparty conflicts, and by cost considerations. Last but not least, policy priorities changed in accordance with the landscape of British pensions which had altered considerably since the late 1970s. As to the first point, the unexpected defeat of the 1992 general election represented a turning point for Labour. It triggered a search for policies which would improve the prospect of gaining political power, most of all the idea of shedding the image of a party which was intent on increasing taxation, a theme which had been effectively exploited by the Conservative Party in its 1992 election campaign. Indeed, not raising existing income tax levels became a dominant pledge in Labour's campaign five years later, as well as sticking to the Conservative government's spending plans for the first two years in office.

Having taken over the party leadership from Neil Kinnock, John Smith set up a 'Commission on Social Justice' in 1992. The Commission's report, launched by Tony Blair three months into his leadership in 1994, included the recommendation of dropping the long-standing pledge to index the BSP in line with prices and creating a new earnings-linked but means-tested minimum income for pensioners. The report attracted criticism from the left of the party but failed to 'ignite outrage' (Timmins 2001: 533) across the party seemingly prepared to accept new policies in order to gain electoral appeal after four consecutive defeats. Labour's Treasury spokesman, Gordon Brown, also favoured the idea of a means-tested pensioner guarantee. Modelled on US experience, Brown sympathized with the notion of tax credits as incentives for working age people to take up low-paid jobs and to save for retirement (Hewitt 2002). Raising the level of BSP would have required substantial resources which would have been channelled to people perceived as not needing them, whereas means-tested support in the form of tax credits would limit public spending and target state support on lower earners. However, in the mid-1990s there was a rival vision within the party as to the future of public pensions, and the character of social security more generally. This was most prominently advocated by Frank Field who had effectively attacked the conservative government for presiding over an unprecedented increase in means-testing. Unlike Brown, Field opposed means-testing as undermining incentives to work and save, and having a corrosive impact on personal responsibility and self-esteem. His idea was to revive the notion of comprehensive compulsory social insurance, albeit one which involved non-statutory providers such as friendly societies or a new national insurance corporation, with the state making contributions on behalf of those who could not do so themselves.

Sympathizing with some of his plans, and urging him to contemplate a radical overhaul of welfare state structures, Tony Blair promoted Frank Field to the position of Minister for Welfare Reform in 1997. However, it soon became obvious that Field's ideas were regarded as too radical, requiring a major restructuring of public sector finances and, initially at least, higher public spending. The magnitude of the latter and the absence of detailed policy proposals delayed progress in pension policy formulation. In addition, Gordon Brown introduced policies which undermined Field's ideas. For example, in November 1998 'winter fuel payments' for pensioners were introduced which were higher for those on means-tested benefit. The Chancellor also signalled replacing in-work benefit payments for families on low earnings with tax credits which, since they went up much higher in the income scale, increased the number of people covered by means-tested public support.

The conflict between Field and Brown (and also between Field and Harriet Harman, the Secretary of State at the DSS) was finally resolved in a Cabinet reshuffle in July 1999 in which Field was offered a post in another department but resigned. Harriet Harman was replaced with Alistair Darling, who had previously been chief secretary to the Treasury and who shared Brown's preference for targeted public support. Subsequent speeches and policy decisions, that is, introducing a means-test for contributory funded disability benefits, indicated that the erosion of National Insurance benefits within the architecture of British social policy was not going to be reversed but fostered under a Labour government (Clasen 2001).

An array of subsequent legislation transformed social security benefits into tax credits (Hewitt 2002) which, by implication, provided the Treasury with an increasingly powerful position in social policy formation. In fact, after having made the Bank of England independent, it can be argued that the Treasury's main role has shifted from macro-economics to driving domestic welfare reform, rather than merely funding (Timmins 2001: 560). In addition, successive Secretaries of State in the Department for Work and Pensions (DWP, the successor of the DSS since 2001) had previously been in the Treasury, facilitating a closer understanding between the two ministries.

Finally, the decision to shift from contributory to means-tested pension support has been influenced not only by cost-saving motives and ideological preferences but also by pragmatic considerations. As outlined earlier, the Labour Party had already begun to acknowledge the popularity of private pensions in the late 1980s. During the 1990s private pensions contributed to incomes for average pensioners rising faster than average real earnings, and to a declining share of pensioners having to resort to means-tested support (see Table 5.2). At the 2000 Labour Party conference Jeff Rooker (Pensions Minister at the time) justified the departure from Labour's earlier position regarding BSP with reference to the these trends and pointed to the increasing dispersion of pensioners' income. Restoring the earnings link of BSP would have benefited a considerably larger share of pensioners who were not really in need of extra state support in 2000 compared with 1980, he argued. Besides, the effect would be to increase rather than decrease income inequality amongst pensioners (Timmins 2001: 600–1).

Indeed, pension policy has become more redistributive since 1997 (Brewer et al. 2002), with poorer pensioners having gained as a consequence of the government's strategy of switching from a traditional comprehensive to a targeted approach and increasing the means-tested minimum. The risks involved, such as creating disincentives to save and adding further complexity to public pension provision, have been acknowledged by the government (Emmerson and Wakefield 2003). There is also the risk of cementing social bifurcation between a minority of those who entirely or dominantly rely on state support and a majority in receipt of predominantly private pension income (some of which is increasingly insecure as a result of the trend of closing down final salary occupational schemes). While the gap between pensioner income and those in work has declined, inequality has grown within the group of pensioners (Disney et al. 2004) and can be expected to increase further, leading even more to 'two nations in old age' (Titmuss 1958: 74).

Thus, public pension provision in the UK has not become more sustainable. On the contrary, with the majority of future pensioners likely to depend on means-tested public support, the system has a considerable in-built economic irrationality in terms of having created disincentives for many people to save for the future. In addition, lower fertility and longer life expectancy also affect the UK and will thus increase the pressure for more wide-ranging reform, possibly raising the pension age, lowering public benefits in old age, or raising taxes. Ironically, in stark contradiction to its policies of the early 1980s, the conservative opposition is now calling for less means-testing of retirement income, a stronger profile of the BSP, and linking its value to increases in average earnings. The Labour government meanwhile has engaged in 'commission politics', the outcome of which has yet to be seen (Pensions Commission 2004).

5.5 COMPARATIVE CONCLUSIONS

The discussion has shown that, on the whole, public pensions in both countries have been subjected to a considerable degree of retrenchment. As a proportion of average earnings, the British state pension has steadily declined since the early 1980s and, applying legislative parameters as they existed in the late 1970s, the cumulative long-term effect of cost-containment measures implemented in both countries over the past two decades has been substantial, lowering the level of pension payments as a proportion of average earnings for future retirees. However, as outlined in Chapter 2, retrenchment remains limited if used as a sole concept for social policy change. Core indicators, such as the level of wage replacement of a standard pension, remain fairly meaningless if they are not observed over a long timespan. Moreover, they tell little about the generosity of a public pension system in a society in which employment patterns are rapidly changing. Moreover, calculating the scale of retrenchment with reference to the amount of cost-savings depends on long time frames of developments in prices, average earnings, and so on, as well as taking account of functional equivalents to public pension outlays, such as social insurance rebates or tax allowances for private provision, which can be considerable. More theoretically, under conditions of 'fiscal austerity' the thesis of the 'new politics of the welfare state' (Pierson 1996) has a tendency to regard retrenchment as the main motivation for pensions policymaking. However, as has been shown, some cutbacks in public pension programmes were driven by motives of credit claiming rather than blame avoidance, such as the 1986 reforms in the UK. In short, the 'architecture' of pension provision within a particular country might change considerably not only because of retrenchment but due to restructuring, impinging on the balance between public and private provision.

While following broadly the same policy direction, the scope of re-trenchment and the policy profile of restructuring differed in the countries under observation. In the UK, public pensions were subjected to a more immediate and stronger degree of curtailment than in Germany. This affected both the BSP and SERPS, with cuts imposing losses to all claim-ants of either scheme. By contrast, during the 1980s and much of the 1990s, the curtailment of German public pension programmes tended to be selective and followed a more incremental policy pattern. As assumed earlier (see Section 5.2) losses remained relatively concealed, phased in, or postponed. A general reduction in the formal pension level, affecting all future retirees, was introduced only recently, as well as structural reform which will gradually lead to a new balance between public and private income sources in old age, albeit one which will remain biased towards public pensions. First and foremost these differences in policy patterns have to be related to differences in structure and scope of existing public pension arrangements, resulting in different (degrees) of challenges such as demographic ageing or changes in employment careers (Bonoli 2003*a*). As in unemployment support policy, policy preferences, contingent opportun-ities for policymaking, and different institutional settings help to account for reform directions and profiles. However, the discussion has shown that national programme-specific institutional parameters, changes therein, and their impact on the dynamics on party policy preferences were most relevant in this respect.

5.5.1 Institutional factors as policy legacies

As discussed in Chapter 3, there are few formal barriers or institutional veto points for British governments with sufficiently large majorities. Indeed, internal conflicts of interest and the position of employers and private pension providers were the more relevant influences on pension policy formation. By contrast, as discussed, in Germany both the partisan and the corporatist arena are significant locations for negotiations over more than incremental change. Both the political sensitivity of public pensions as well as the need to overcome the *Bundesrat* as a veto point made the government seek a broad political consensus. At times, policy impulses come from other actors, most importantly the Constitutional Court, which required governments to improve gender equality (survivors' pension) or pension rights for parents (see Chapter 6).

From a comparative perspective aimed at capturing differences in profiles of pension restructuring, programme-specific characteristics (or policy legacies) are the more important variable for explaining variations in national reform patterns in the two countries. As outlined (Section 5.1), Germany is a prime example of a social insurance pension country, whereas the UK has one of the most developed multipillar pension systems in Europe. As a corollary, there are significant differences regarding the role of public pensions as a source of income during retirement, their organization, the involvement of collective actors, and the notion of wage replacement. Equally, significant differences in the prevalence and scope of private pensions create a very different context for policymaking. In short, programme-specific features and differences in the scope of private provision provide different opportunities for reforming public pension schemes (see also Bonoli 2003*a*).

The discussion on reform processes has shown that many of Pierson's (1994: 71–2) arguments regarding the impact of 'policy legacies' on pension policy in the UK and the USA can thus be extended to the two countries under investigation here. The already significant scale of private provision and programme-specific features of the latter allowed British governments to expand private pensions at the expense of public provision by adjusting the financial attractiveness of each option. Although their cumulative effect over time was considerable, the nature of some of those adjustments appeared initially of little significance (e.g. the indexation of BSP). Even before the 1986 reform the architecture of SERPS was only moderately based on wage replacement principles and the scheme had only been introduced in the late 1970s. The build-up of entitlements had not advanced much, thereby providing options for retrenchment compensated by incentives to expand private pension coverage. By contrast, the German pension landscape is dominated by mature public schemes which did not allow for opting out. Public pensions represent the most important form of pensioners' income for the vast majority of retired persons. Entitlements are legally strongly codified and indexed in line with earnings. Such schemes face difficulties of structural reform for technical reasons (such as the double payment problem), but do not rule out reform in the form of, for example, grafting new schemes on top of existing ones.

It should be pointed out that this chapter has aimed to demonstrate the dynamic nature of policy legacies. This has been most obvious in the UK, where the scaling down of public pensions was facilitated by inducements to switch to (what sometimes merely appeared to be) more favourable private alternatives. As discussed, the popularity of this policy changed the pensions landscape considerably which, in turn, facilitated a further curtailment of SERPS in the mid-1990s. The same process also contributed to a gradual reformulation of pension policy preferences within the Labour Party (see below). Equally, institutional features of the German pension system do not rule out far-reaching change, but shape the type and scale of restructuring. The partial privatization and the amendments made to the original Riester pension, as well as the fate of the 'demographic' (later 'sustainability') factor are good cases in point.

Chapter 4 highlighted the link between unemployment suppport and other aspects of national political economies as a structural influence on reform profiles. This also applies to some areas of pension policy. For example, Ebbinghaus (2001) has shown how different pathways into early retirement have been shaped by interdependencies between pension pro-grammes on the one hand and national production regimes and industrial relations systems on the other. In the UK the scale of public early retire-ment options, such as the Job Release Scheme in the 1980s, were financially of little appeal and had thus a low take-up rate (Casey and Wood 1994). More important were disability benefits on the one hand, and private and occupational pensions on the other, because these can be drawn before reaching the statutory retirement age, unlike the BSP. Accordingly, responding to short-term changes in the business cycle and aiming to downsize workforces, companies enticed older workers to retire early with the prospect of redundancy payments and occupational pension plans, without much collaboration with trade union representation who have little influence on company pension policy.

By contrast, as discussed, the institutional design of German public pensions offers several options for early retirement, often in conjunction with long entitlement to unemployment benefit for older workers (see Chapter 4). As discussed in Chapter 3, in Germany's 'coordinated market economy' (Hall and Soskice 2001*b*) large employers are not solely driven by cost minimization but by recruiting, maintaining, and adapting skills re-quired for 'diversified quality production'. Ever since the 1970s, companies have been able to make use of welfare state programmes as vehicles which would facilitate circumventing the 'rigid dismissal laws' and shedding 'elderly workers at a relatively low cost' (Mares 2003: 257). The welfare state has thus been instrumental in workforce restructuring in a socially acceptable way, honouring lengthy employment contracts, seniority pay rules, and career trajectories 'irrespective of the business cycle' (Ebbin-ghaus 2001: 90). Trade unions 'colluded' (Ebbinghaus ibid.) in the externalization of the costs of this practice to pension (and unemployment) insurance, protecting the position of those with long service and long social insurance records, that is, groups who tended to be trade union members. By comparison, if UK employers colluded in anything, it was the erosion of social insurance as one instrument of weakening organized labour and lowering production costs (Wood 2001*b*).

In short, as in unemployment protection, a degree of 'institutional complementarity' can be identified between the public pension arrangement and Germany's production regime and industrial relations system, providing an incentive structure for collective actors and policymakers which contributed to one of the lowest employment rates of older workers in Europe (Funk 2004). Of course, such institutional interdependencies between policy domains do not determine pension reform processes, nor do they impact on all aspects of pension policy equally. Nevertheless, they represent an important element in the interpretation of diverse policy profiles.

5.5.2 Policy preferences and contingent factors

Given their large financial scope, their wide coverage, and their inherent promises to provide an income in retirement, institutional features of public pension systems can be expected to exert an even stronger influence on the dynamics of policy preferences than unemployment support systems. In addition, the respective balance of public and private pension provision has no equivalent in unemployment support. Not surprisingly, governments in the two countries differed considerably regarding policy priorities. Successive conservative administrations in the UK were driven by an ideology which envisaged a smaller role for public and stronger role for private pension, coupled with the general aim of reducing public expenditure and the notion that state support should be restricted to lower income earners. These objectives were highly influential on changing the indexation of BSP and the downgrading of SERPS which had originally been intended to be phased out. Even though the government continued to make reference to the problem of sustaining the fiscal viability of public pensions, the decisions taken in the 1980s reduced the costs considerably which, despite population ageing, resulted in a very different policymaking context than in Germany. Rather than merely cost-saving, both the Conservative and Labour governments have been more concerned with trying to increase the coverage of private pension provision. The policy reversal of the Labour Party in the mid-1990s can, as discussed, be regarded as the outcome of a process of policy learning, triggered by the defeat in the general elections in 1992 and reinforced by the growth and popularity of private pensions since the late 1980s.

At times, differences in policy priorities between the relevant spending departments on the one hand, and the Treasury on the other, influenced the scale of curtailment or delayed reform, for example, after 1997. Instances of shaping policy profiles, like the retreat from phasing out SERPS, remained rare. More generally, once often merely marginal disagreements had been solved, there were no further serious conflicts of interest which might have jeopardized major pieces of legislation which were introduced on the strength of large parliamentary majorities. The interests of employers and private pension companies contributed at times to the eventual shape of policy reforms, such as in 1986. Reinforcing the shift to private provision and concentrating public provision on those with or no little private pension coverage has remained a common feature of British pension policy, with the Treasury gaining control due to the switch to a modified version of means-tested (tax credit) support.

The situation could hardly have been more different in Germany. Both the SPD and CDU/CSU have portrayed themselves as welfare state centrist parties. In the 1980s and most of the 1990s policymaking was pragmatic rather than ideological, with both parties interested in adjusting institutional parameters in order to maintain traditional pension structures. As in unemployment insurance, much policymaking has been short-term adaptation in response to deficits in an earmarked fund. The menu of options was wide, ranging from lifting contribution rates and cost shifting to other social insurance branches, to implementing cutbacks at the margins or phasing in curtailment over a long time horizons. The political risk associated with unilateral action remained high due to the political salience of the public pension system. German governments have thus typically sought to organize some form of 'consensus over pension reform either in the partisan or in the corporatist arena' (Schludi 2001: 19). Having learned from the backlash against explicit proposals for cuts in the 1970s, each party rightly feared high political costs for imposing welfare losses (Kitschelt 2001). The strategy was thus to coopt the opposition party which, depending on the political constellation at the time, had often been possible both at times of expansion as well as retrenchment due to the small distance between the major parties on pension policy.

Finally, government party interests and policy preferences were, as discussed, dynamic and in part influenced by changes in contexts or contingent factors. In the UK, this can be illustrated with reference to the miss-selling scandal of private pensions in the early 1990s, as well as Labour's defeat in the 1992 election which contributed to a process of policy reorientation within the party. In Germany, unification had a major impact on the distribution of power relations between traditional wings of the major political parties and the formation of new policy preferences during the 1990s. As discussed, the long-term economic impact of massive transfers of public resources to the east, exacerbated by a severe recession and a changed macro-economic context (EMU, economic internationalization of product, and capital markets), generated a new consensus regarding the diagnosis of Germany's investment problems, that is, high non-wage labour costs. Within pension legislation this led to the direction of revenue-oriented policy during the 1990s. Removing higher contribution rates from the menu of adjustment levers perceived as feasible limited the options of how to respond to demographic change and growing fiscal pressure. In turn, this weakened traditional orientations and added to intraparty conflicts of interest. After the mid-1990s, the proximity to the general election contributed to the former traditional cross-party consensus collapsing and turning into conflict. Overall, the policy path since the mid-1990s is evidence of the absence of a coherent set of policy preferences and a much more uneven reform trajectory determined by changes in short-term economic conditions, long-term demographic pressure, and electoral politics.

6

Family policy: charting new waters

Public pensions and unemployment support programmes were introduced in response to the consequences of industrialization and the creation of a landless working class, with early schemes reaching back to the late nineteenth and early twentieth centuries (Flora 1986; Flora and Heidenheimer 1981). By contrast, family policy is not a traditional welfare state area and family benefits are a post-Second World War phenomenon. Moreover, family support has remained a fairly diverse and less discrete policy field. In fact, much of what can broadly be considered family policy might be subsumed under other types of public intervention. In the context of this chapter, this includes wage subsidies for parents in low-paid employment (a form of labour-market policy) or public support to parents engaged in child raising (e.g. pension credits).

Kaufmann (1993, 2002) distinguishes four types of family policy. 'Legal' interventions define the status of family members (marriage, divorce, parenthood); 'ecological' interventions provide infrastructural opportunities for families and children (including housing, child care, etc.); 'personal' interventions restore or improve the capacities of individuals (via health care, education, counselling for parents, etc.); and 'economic' interventions affect the material situation of family households, not only via benefits and taxation but also by other means, such as employment policies which might be geared towards, for example, women. Even remaining within one of these four categories, empirical research has illustrated a large degree of policy variation across countries. For example, evaluating the impact of transfers which help with the cost of raising children, Bradshaw et al. (1993; also Bradshaw and Finch 2002) identified national 'child support packages' with different emphases put on cash transfers, taxation, housing, education, and health, and national policies targeting particular groups or making use of certain policy instruments. Focusing on the two countries under investigation here, prominent policy measures in the UK have included targeted support for lone parents, free prescriptions for children, and in-work benefits for low-paid families. In Germany the tax system has played a more important role (favouring not only parents but also married couples, families who build their own homes, children in education, and so on), as well as privileges for spouses and parents within social insurance (e.g. the free inclusion of family members within employee health insurance). In fact, the total expenditure devoted to these types of programmes is actually higher than for 'classic' family transfers such as child benefit and child tax allowances (Bäcker et al. 2000: table VII.11).

Compared with other countries, such as France, family policy in both the UK and Germany has been portrayed as traditionally weak in national political debates, largely symbolic, and lacking coherence (e.g. Kaufmann 2002). This might, however, be contested. For example, both countries have traditionally and consistently promoted policies favouring gender divisions in paid and unpaid care. A range of policies (see below) have put a high premium on married women in West Germany to opt for child care at home rather than employment. More by default and lack of public support, British governments have long pursued similar objectives. There are thus important differences in motives driving family and gender policy, even though the aims might be similar (see Daly 2000).

However, Kaufmann (2002: 425) provides a useful categorization in the latter respect. He distinguishes typical arguments made in support for families as influenced by 'institutional motives' (supporting the family 'as a value in itself'), 'natalist motives' (concentrating on demographic aspects), 'eugenic motives' (e.g. racist population policy in Nazi Germany), 'economic motives' (preserving and improving human capital over generations), 'societal motives' (upholding the family as a constitutive element within society), 'socio-political motives' (compensating parents for taking on family responsibilities), 'women's issues motives' (addressing gender inequalities in paid and unpaid work), and 'children's welfare motives' (focusing on the well-being and socialization of children). After the Second World War, West German family policy was predominantly guided by 'societal motives', that is oriented towards safeguarding the institution of marriage and the family. 'Socio-political motives', compensating parents for the costs of children, as well as 'economic motives', gained prominence in the 1970s, albeit remaining oriented towards the 'breadwinner–housewife' model (Kaufmann 2002: 465). Not for reasons of child welfare but related to the 'abortion struggle' (see Section 6.3), 'women's issue' (perhaps better termed 'gender equality') motives entered the political arena more forcefully in the 1990s, eventually providing the impetus for 'ecological interventions', such as child care provision, which took off only fairly recently. In the UK, a traditionally stronger general restraint of policy intervention into what is regarded a private sphere has left equally little room for ecological interventions. Apart from concerns over 'children's welfare', the 'dominating motive' (Kaufmann 2002: 473) has been poverty alleviation and a targeted approach to supporting families and children in need, reinforced during the 1980s by a neo-liberal government intent on reducing the role of the state and fostering self-reliance. As in Germany, gender equality and economic motives (particularly regarding the labour-market integration of mothers) have become more pronounced in recent years within a more general work-focused social policy context.

The fact that British policy has not been guided by 'societal motives' towards the family per se has been regarded as an indication of an 'implicit' family policy, typical for Anglo-Saxon countries which are devoid of a discourse centred on the family (Kaufmann 1993; 2002). Another indicator for this might be the absence of a government department in charge of the family. Indeed, the UK has no ministry for the family or family affairs, but Ministers for Women (or responsibilities for women's issues) have existed for some time, located initially within the Home Office, then the Department of Social Security, and currently represented by the Secretary of State for Trade and Industry. There is also ministerial responsibility for children (with a focus on child protection, social services for children, and children in care), currently attached to the Department of Education and Skills.

By contrast, a discourse which expresses support for the family in society as well as a dedicated government department makes Germany a country with an 'explicit' family policy (Kaufmann 2002; critically, Barbier 1990). A Ministry for Family Affairs (*Familienfragen*) was installed as early as 1953 in West Germany, but has since been restructured six times, over the years adding responsibilities for young people, senior citizens, and health, the latter of which was separated out again in 1991 when two ministries were created which both incorporated the term 'family' in their title. Since 1994 the responsible department has been the Ministry for the Family, Senior Citizens, Women, and Youth (BMFSFJ). These frequent organizational and ministerial changes (between 1982 and 1998 there were eight Ministers in charge of family affairs) suggest a policy domain which is more dynamic but potentially less prominent than pensions or labour-market policies. As discussed (Chapter 4), for most of the post-war era the latter two domains brought the two major political parties and social partners together and these areas remained located within a single Ministry and headed by the same Minister during the entire sixteen years of the Kohl government.

Apart from a weak institutionalization of family policy in both countries, other aspects make (some aspects of) family support potentially more directly amenable to political intervention by central governments than pension or unemployment protection. For example, unlike in other European countries or other transfers in the UK and Germany, child benefits and child tax allowances are not indexed, that is, pegged to developments in wages or prices. This puts governments bent on making savings in social spending in a potentially more favourable position since the latter can be achieved via 'non-action', that is, freezing nominal benefit levels. More generally, family policy is institutionally less entrenched than unemployment or pension policy. This applies to Germany in particular because of the absence of earmarked contributions, separate funds, wage-related transfers, or the involvement of social partners, indicating lower potential for political mobilization. On the other hand, other areas of family policy are less open to central political steering. In Germany, the responsibility for childcare provision and education, for example, rests with *Länder* and municipalities rather than the federal government.

For reasons of cross-national compatibility, recent political salience, and analytical interest in policy expansion (Meyer 2003*a*), this chapter is restricted to two overlapping areas of family support in both countries. First, policy changes in monetary support linked to children and to child raising will be investigated; and second, measures aimed at reconciling family life and paid employment. Apart from child benefits and child tax allowances, the first domain also covers maternity and parental benefits, indicating that a clear dividing line between the two policy areas cannot be drawn. Parental leave, to which benefits are attached, can be regarded as both compensation for child care provided, as well as a measure which improves the compatibility between participation in paid work and family life. Other aspects to be covered within the second field are in-work benefits and tax credits for parents (characteristic of reforms in the UK) and child raising credits within pension insurance (a focus of policy change in Germany).

As in Chapters 4 and 5, the aim here is to discuss and seek explanations for both policy direction and policy patterns. More than in unemployment support or pension policy, it might be assumed that gradual changes in the socio-economic and labour-market context have influenced policymaking in a less immediate but potentially more sustained fashion. For example, the growth of female employment and changes in household formation can be expected to have put pressure in favour of the expansion of child care facilities, potentially fostering cross-party alliances (e.g. of women MPs) or strengthening non-parliamentary interest groups, such as family and other lobby organizations. However, a point of departure is the assumption that family policies are rarely based on a clear diagnosis of existing problems, needs, demands, interests, and attitudes of families or children. Instead, as Ostner (2002) argues, demographic, labour market, or household developments are often portrayed in certain ways and used as a platform for policy advocacy, at times amalgamating diverse aims and instruments. For example, the introduction of wage supplements for low-income earning parents can be justified as either family or employment policy, or both. More generous family transfers and parental leave benefits can be promoted with reference to the need to combat child poverty, to compensate parents for the cost of raising children (including the opportunity costs of lost earnings), to reduce labour supply, to address low birth rates, or to promote a more balanced gender division of paid and unpaid work within families. Indeed, in Germany more and better provision of child care facilities have long been demanded by groups striving for greater gender equality. More recent interest in the beneficial impact of early childhood education has provided more, and arguably more effective, political support (Ostner 2002: 261). In the UK, calls for achieving equal opportunities and gender equality have recently gained influence due to a more strongly employment-oriented policy agenda.

The chapter starts with a discussion of contextual trends in both countries which are assumed to have influenced (and, in turn, were influenced by) family policy. This includes normative orientations towards gender roles, changes in household structures and of female and particularly mothers' employment, fertility rates, and child poverty (Section 6.1). Section 6.2 sketches respective patterns of change, followed by separate discussions on policy formulation in Germany (Section 6.3) and the UK (Section 6.4). The final section (6.5) provides an assessment and an account of common direction but different national profiles of policy change.

6.1 SIMILARITIES AND DIFFERENCES IN TWO 'STRONG MALE BREADWINNER' COUNTRIES

Focusing on gender divisions, Lewis (1992) has categorized modern welfare states by the degree to which national social policies influence the position of women as wives, mothers, or workers (see also Lewis and Ostner 1994; Ostner 1995). Given that the design of benefits and services can strengthen or weaken women's dependence on male earners, welfare states can ideal-typically be distinguished as 'strong', 'weak', or 'moderate' male breadwinner models. From such a vantage point countries such as France and Germany which, according to Esping-Andersen (1990), firmly belong to the same type of conservative–corporatist welfare state, represent different paradigms. The more comprehensive provision of child care and array of family benefits suggests that motherhood in France has come to be regarded in part a public responsibility and employment not a predominantly male affair (see also Hantrais 1994). In contrast, in its post-Second

World War heyday the West German welfare state assumed and promoted continuous male full-time employment which would provide both a family wage and entitlement to core social provision for married women and children (health care and pension income in particular) derived from husbands' social contributions. The UK has equally been classified as a traditionally 'strong male breadwinner' country, treating married women as dependent wives for social policy purposes, assuming male employment as the basis for family support, and leaving child care responsibilities to families, and thus women (Land and Lewis 1998; Lister 1994). Hence, in the 1950s and 1960s, the normative orientation fostered by governments in both countries was for women to leave paid employment after marriage, returning to the labour market not before the youngest child reached school age. As a consequence, employment patterns for mothers were much more discontinuous than in many other European countries, such as France, Belgium, or the Nordic countries. Even by the mid-1990s, three-quarters of West German mothers who re-entered employment after parental leave had taken time off work for three or more years (Ostner 1998: 128).

Subsequent research has elaborated the impact of national social policies on gender relations, taking account of differences in care provision and marital status, for example (Sainsbury 1996), and conceptually refined the categorization of welfare states (e.g. Hobson et al. 2002). More specifically, Daly's (2000) in-depth exploration of the British and the German welfare states and their impact on gender divisions illustrates that the common emphasis on family care has been more influenced by an 'anti-poverty orientation' in the UK (Daly 2000: 85), as well as by concerns over maintaining work incentives. Moreover, there has been a stronger readiness to intervene in intra-familial affairs (e.g. by directing benefits to mothers or granting social entitlements to carers). The latter approach (also so-called 'family member' policy; Dienel 2002) was only adopted in West Germany in the 1970s and remained contested thereafter (see below).

Influenced by the Basic Law (Article 6) from 1949, post-Second World War West German policies were strongly oriented towards upholding and protecting both the family and marriage as core social institutions. Due to a potential conflict with Article 3 (equal rights for men and women), this stipulation has created ample work for the Constitutional Court in subsequent decades. Influenced by Catholic thinking, a division between a private sphere of family life with responsibility for child raising, and a public responsibility for education, became firmly institutionalized in West German society (Bird and Gottschall 2004). Compared with the UK, the larger financial scale of policies in support of the family, as well as the ways in which relevant services were organized (e.g. short opening hours for kindergartens and schools), illustrate a comparatively stronger family-centred approach, with predetermined gender roles especially for married mothers (Ostner 1993). For example, the spouse-based income tax splitting system, which was introduced in West Germany in 1958, continues to provide a strong fiscal advantage to married spouses (rather than parents) and a considerable disincentive against (full-time) employment for married women (Dingeldey 2001a, 2002). Cross-national differences in the development towards gender equality might be illustrated with reference to legislative change in the late 1970s. In the UK the 'married women's option', that is, opting out (or paying a reduced rate) of National Insurance in return for diminished benefit entitlement, was abolished in 1977 (Wikeley et al. 2002: 118). In the same year a prerogative was finally dropped which had allowed German husbands to stop their wives from taking up paid employment if they considered this to be detrimental to family life (Ostner 1993: 99). Normative orientations towards married women in employment changed more slowly in West Germany than in the UK. Opinion surveys in seven West European countries in the mid-1980s show that the traditional gender division of labour, with married women remaining out of the labour market, was most strongly supported in West Germany, but least favoured in Denmark and the UK (Becker 1989).

To some extent these cross-national differences are reflected in broad changes in social structures which have started to converge only in recent years. Since the 1960s, as in other Western countries, the UK and West Germany have witnessed trends of greater plurality of family and household structures in the wake of rising female employment, a growth in divorce, and a decline in childbirth (Castles 1998). However, the scope of change has been more pronounced in the UK. For example, since the 1970s lone parenthood increased in both countries, but much more steeply in the UK which has the highest rate of single parent households in the EU (twice the rate of Germany) and, with about 25 per cent, also by far the highest number of children growing up in such households (BMFSFJ 2003; Brüderl 2003). Moreover, while employment of married mothers increased in the 1980s, rates fell for lone parents in conjunction with a growing reliance on means-tested state support (Millar 2003a). Since then benefit dependence amongst lone parents has declined and employment increased (to 53 per cent by 2002; Gregg and Harkness 2003). These trends have influenced British policymaking, particularly in the 1990s.

Remaining fairly stable during the 1960s and 1970s, West German women began to enter the labour market more forcefully only in the 1980s. However, recent increases have lifted female labour force participation rates (for Germany as a whole) above the EU average and narrowed the gap to British rates (see Table 6.1). In fact, remaining cross-national differences in female employment can be attributed to higher labour force

Table 6.1. Female labour force participation (LFP) (15–64) and part-time employment rate (PTE) of women (15–64), UK and Germany

	LFP 1980	LFP 2000	PTE 1983	PTE 2003
UK	58.3	67.7	40.1	40.1
Germany	52.8	63.7	31.2	36.3

Source: OECD (2004*b*).

participation rates amongst both younger and older British women, whereas German women aged twenty-five to fifty-four are now even more integrated in the labour market than their British counterparts. The prevalence of women working part-time has also converged (Table 6.1). Of course, a more detailed analysis would need to distinguish between the number of women working part-time and the actual numbers of hours worked per person. For Germany, this would show that more women participate in the labour market but that the average number of hours per part-time working woman has declined (Beckmann 2003). In comparison with the EU average, a high but since the mid-1980s decreasing proportion of British women work fewer than twenty hours, while the trend has been the reverse in Germany (OECD 1998), indicating further convergence of part-time working hours in the two countries (Van Bastelaer and Vaguer 2004). As for families with children, the one-(male)-earner model has ceased to be the norm in either country, but remains more prevalent in Germany (40 per cent) than in the UK (30 per cent). While both parents working full-time is not unusual (26 per cent in Germany, 29 per cent in the UK), this configuration is less widespread than in any other EU country barring the Netherlands and Ireland (Franco and Winqvist 2002). More common are combinations of male full-time and female part-time employment.

However, to some extent the convergence between the two countries is an artefact resulting from aggregating what are still significant differences between East and West Germany. For example, only 15 per cent of West German parents both work full-time, compared with 45 per cent in the East (Ludwig and Schlevogt 2002). In the 1960s and 1970s the GDR developed comprehensive supervision for nursery, pre-school, and school-aged children outside of school hours, but also leave arrangements for parents in order to foster female employment which reached levels almost on a par with male employment (Gerlach 1996). In 1990, female labour force participation in the East was 82 per cent, compared with 56 per cent in the West. The respective rates for mothers in paid work (aged 25–35) in 1991 were 97 per cent in the new *Länder* and 51 per cent in the territory of the old West Germany (Roloff 1993).

However, during the 1990s there was a steep increase of female employment in the old *Länder*, whereas women in East Germany dropped out of the labour force at both ends of the age spectrum, mainly due to increases in participation rates in education and early retirement. Married East German women of core working age (30–55), however, continue to be as strongly integrated in the labour market as they were in the early 1990s (with rates above 90 per cent). Thus, despite considerable increases in the west (Spieß 2003), married West German women of the same age group trail up to 20 percentage points behind the labour force participation of their East German counterparts (Fuchs and Weber 2004). By contrast, a higher proportion of women of core working age (25–45) without children are in work in the West than in the East (85 to 77 per cent in 2003; Notz 2004).

These differences are often associated with the more comprehensive level of child care provision in the East, an argument which is strengthened if employment patterns of parents with young children are compared (Table 6.2). The East German network of public child care facilities continues to be more comprehensive than in the West, both in terms of coverage and structure. While the supply of places for the youngest age group (see Table 6.3) is well below the level of demand which has been estimated to be about 20 per cent in the West (Sell 2002), the provision has remained considerably better in the new *Länder*. For children of kindergarten age (3–6), coverage in the West has improved but remains below the supply in the East, which surpasses demand (Table 6.3). Moreover, kindergarten places in the new *Länder* are generally offered on a full-day basis, compared with only 19 per cent full-time places in the West (Büchel and Spieß 2002: 78). Finally, about 95 per cent of schools in Germany are half-day (with significant variation across *Länder*) and, on average, just over 3

Table 6.2. Employment rates of mothers by age of youngest child (West and East Germany, 1991 and 2000)

		1991	2000
Under 3	West	37	48
	East	76	52
3–5	West	48	56
	East	83	64
6–14	West	59	68
	East	87	73

Source: Klammer and Klenner (2004).

Table 6.3. Supply of public child care places by
age of children (Germany)

Germany	1980	2002
Under 3	1.5	2.7 (37)
3–6.5	69*	88 (105)
6–14	1.6*	3.1 (22)

Note: available places as a proportion of children in age
group (figures in brackets are for east Germany)
Source: for 1980: Bahle 1995; * figures for 1986: BMFSFJ
1998; for 2002: own calculations based on Statistisches
Bundesamt (2004b; Table A 3.2).

per cent of school age children have a place in publicly provided after-school
care in the West (once again with considerable differences across *Länder*; see
Statistisches Bundesamt 2000b). Not surprisingly, particularly West
German working mothers rely heavily on informal child care provided by
relatives. By comparison, the use of paid childminders is very low and the
care provided exclusively by parents for the under three-year-olds high, at
around 60 per cent in both parts of the country (Büchel and Spieß 2002: 78).

The educational system in the UK, with children starting school earlier
(four or five) and school-days lasting longer, is comparatively more conducive to female employment. However, successive Conservative and Labour
governments have been unwilling to invest in nursery provision. The
'official view was that it was better for the health and well-being of young
children that their mothers stayed at home and looked after them' (Land and
Lewis 1998: 66), followed by part-time employment for mothers once
children reached school age. During the 1980s, the supply of local authority
child care places actually declined, while private provision (mainly by
childminders) grew. By the late 1980s, publicly funded and provided day-
nursery places were available for less than 1 per cent of children under five in
England and Wales, with another five per cent were being looked after by
publicly regulated childminders (Randall 2002). During the 1990s non-
statutory child care provision surged (Land and Lewis 1998) but a clear
shift in policy direction towards a more explicit and extensive promotion of
child care occurred only after 1997, characterized by the continued reliance
on (improved) financial subsidies for meeting the cost of child care targeted
primarily on low-income parents, and lone parents in particular, coupled
with 'supply-side' subsidies for different types of providers (Lewis 2003).
The Labour government also guaranteed free child care for three- and four-
year-olds, but only on a part-time basis (usually 2.5 hours per day) while
subsidies (tax credits) tend to cover merely a fraction of what is often

expensive private provision. As a result, British mothers, especially as 'second earners', continue to be faced with substantial barriers to employment, or continue to rely on informal child care (Millar 2003*b*). In short, despite a recent increase in employment of mothers with young children in both the UK and Germany as a whole, the gap in employment rates between mothers with younger and those with school-age children has remained considerable (Table 6.4).

Of course, employment of mothers is not only influenced by the availability, affordability, and quality of public child care, but also by labour demand, as well as cultural patterns, perceptions, and attitudes towards public and family child care provision (Sims-Schouten 2000: 280). However, given that the gap between the employment rate of mothers compared with women without children is much lower in countries with more comprehensive child care provision (Franco and Winqvist 2002), it can be assumed that better infrastructure of public child care would increase German and British mothers' labour supply. For West Germany, surveys provide strong support for this argument (Engelbrech and Jungkunst 2001; Spieß 2003). What is more, recent German panel data analyses indicate that there is a positive effect of the availability of day care for children on birth rates (Hank et al. 2004).

These employment related aspects have influenced family policy debates in Germany and the UK in the 1990s. By contrast, demographic factors played a role in Germany but not in the UK. To some extent this might be linked to the more drastic decline in fertility in Germany and to the impact of German unification. As mentioned, in contrast to the non-interventionist stance in the west, the GDR improved child care facilities in the early 1970s, and introduced leave arrangements to look after sick children or cope with housework and granted parents a shorter working week (Gerlach 1996: 240). These explicitly pro-natalist policies contributed to the reversal of the decline of the number of childbirths in the late 1960s, with fertility rates in the 1970s and 1980s remaining well above West German levels (see Table 6.5). However, precipitated by the collapse of the East German

Table 6.4. Employment rates of mothers by age of youngest child (UK and Germany, 1996, and 2000)

Germany	1996	2000	UK	1996	2000
< 3	43	48	< 2	44	51
3–5	51	57	2–3	52	54
6–14	67	70	8–16	73	74

Source: BMFSFJ (2003: 107); Robinson (2003: 236)

Table 6.5. Fertility rates (average number of births per woman), Germany and the UK, 1960–2001

	West Germany (East Germany)	Germany	UK
1960	2.36 (2.32)	—	2.69
1975	1.44 (1.54)	—	1.81
1980	1.44 (1.94)	—	1.82*
1989	1.39 (1.57)	—	1.82*
1993	1.39 (0.77)	1.28	1.76
1998	1.41 (1.09)	1.35	1.72
2001	—	1.29	1.63

Source: Herden and Münch 2000; Castles 1998; Eurostat 2004; Office for National Statistics, Population trends, various years; total fertility rates
*rates for 1981 and 1991.

economy and the massive increase in unemployment amongst women after unification, fertility rates in the east halved within only a few years.

In the UK fertility rates also declined but not to the same level, and played no role in policy debates. Instead, in addition to normative ideas (e.g. about motherhood), aspects such as the cost of social spending, the growth of the number of lone parents dependent on social security, concerns over work incentives, and, particularly in the 1990s, the extent of child poverty, informed British policy formation. In the light of differences in the incidence of child poverty this does not seem surprising.

Across all family household types in Germany poverty rates remained fairly stable between 1985 and 1998, with single parents and large families experiencing a higher risk than others (Bäcker 2003: 299). On the other hand, over the entire period under investigation there has been a large increase in the number of children (up to fifteen years of age) dependent on social assistance, from 2 per cent in 1980 to about 7 per cent in 2002 (Bäcker et al. 2003), and the amalgamation between the social and unemployment assistance in 2005 (see Chapter 4) is expected to lead to a further increase, with about 10 per cent of all German children to become dependent on means-tested benefit income. By contrast, in the mid-1990s close to one-third of British children grew up in households in receipt of means-tested income. Accordingly, the scale of child poverty is much higher in the UK than in Germany. In the mid-1990s, 10.6 per cent of German children grew up in households with less than 50 per cent of median income, which was 1 percentage point above the average for thirteen EU countries, but well below the rate for the UK of 18.6 per cent (Förster 2000; see also

Unicef 2000). Panel data covering the period from 1991 to 1998 indicate higher persistent child poverty in the UK (affecting 7 per cent of all British and 2 per cent of West German children), and a higher proportion of British children growing up in poor lone-parent households (15 to 9 per cent) and in lone parent households with no income from paid work (10 to 4 per cent). Overall, 18 per cent of British children who are poor grew up in households with no adult in work, compared to 6 per cent in Germany (Jenkins et al. 2002). However, in recent years the problem of child poverty in Germany has gained policy prominence and not least due to the publication of national reports issued by trade unions and social welfare organizations (Butterwege 2000; Huster 2003), as well as the first ever official 'poverty and wealth' report by a German government (Bundesregierung 2001).

In sum, despite broad similarities in terms of a reluctance to interfere in family affairs, as shown with regard to the provision of public child care, for example, traditional family policy interventions have been guided by different motives in the two countries. Support for the family (and marriage) as a constitutive institution in German society contrasts with a stronger emphasis on targeted public support directed at children's welfare and poverty alleviation in the UK. These contrasing orientations influenced policymaking, as well as other differences, such as the scale of child poverty or fertility decline. However, family policy orientations within government parties themselves were highly dynamic over the past twenty-five years or so, to some extent adjusting to growing levels and changing patterns of female employment. However, before embarking on a discussion on policy processes in each country, the direction and the patterns of change need to be established.

6.2 POLICY EXPANSION AND POLICY CHANGE

Applying several indicators within the two areas of family policy covered here, an overall expansionary policy trend can be identified between the early 1980s and recent years in both countries. For example, according to Eurostat data (Abramovici 2003), the real level of cash family benefits increased in Germany by about 80 per cent and in the UK by about 20 per cent between 1991 and 2000. However, such figures need to be treated with caution. Because of a wide spread over a wide range of programmes, calculations of the level of family expenditure are rather complex (the earlier figures do not include 'tax benefits', for example) and their value for comparative purposes is therefore limited (see also Barbier 1990). Resorting to national statistics, consistently measured figures can at least indicate trends over time. Such data show that in Germany expenditure on family related transfers (which includes tax subsidies for marriage) has remained rather stable between 1980 and 2001 (albeit well below rates for the 1960s and the mid-1970s). The same applies to family related transfers as a proportion of total social spending (Table 6.6). National statistics also reveal that the scale of the 'married couples tax splitting' (see above) has remained very significant, amounting to about €22 billion in the year 2000 compared with €32 billion spent on child benefit in total (BMAS 2001).

However, Table 6.6. conceals the fact that state support was declining in the 1980s, and thus ignores the steady increase in absolute and relative spending since the mid-1990s. Since then annual growth rates have been consistently higher for family related transfers than for any of the other major aggregate sectors of social expenditure (health, employment,

Table 6.6. Major indicators of change in family policy, Germany

	1980	2003
1. Expenditure on family transfers (% of GDP)	4.9	4.8 (2001)
2. Expenditure on family transfers (% of the 'social budget')	16	14.9 (2001)
3. Child benefit per child (as % of average gross wages)	1.6 (first), 3.3 (second); 6.6 (third and subsequent)	5.6; 6.7 (fourth and subsequent)
4. Relative tax advantage of families (%)	6.1	22.5 (2002)
5. Child related pension credits	No	Yes (worth up to €140 per month and child)
Maternity/parental leave	Maternity, contributory (6 months)	Maternity and parental; 3 years in total (until child reaches age 8)
Maternity/parental benefit	Maternity, wage-related (6 months)	Maternity and parental (flat-rate 6 months; income-tested 18 months)
Entitlement to child care place	No	Yes (children 3 and older)

Source: 1. and 2. BMAS (2001)—figures include tax subsidies for marriage; 3. BMGS 2003: 3; own calculation based on Tables 5c and 8.17); 4. Tax advantage of family household (couple with two children) over single person household (both on average male industrial wage), values for 1979 and 2002 (Hofäcker 2004: 267); 5. Child raising credit for three years plus credits for a working parent (with 60% of average gross earnings) for the time when the child is between four and ten years old (Veil 2004).

pensions). To some extent, these trends have more to do with demographics than with policy. The number of children in receipt of child benefit or tax allowances declined in West Germany from 12.5 million in 1980 to 10.2 million in 1990, but rose in unified Germany, from 12.7 million in 1991 to 15.1 million in 2002 (BMGS 2004). In short, because of a growth in the number of children, rising total expenditure does not undermine the criticisms of family support failing to keep pace with the actual costs of bringing up children (Lampert 1996). However, since 1999 the real level of child benefit and its share of average earnings has increased considerably (Table 6.6). Also the tax position of parents (over a single person with the same earnings) has substantially improved, even if the figure now includes child benefits which have been incorporated with child tax allowances since 1996. Finally, as will be discussed later, there have been real improvements for parents with regard to parental leave and benefit, pension credits, and entitlement to child care.

Due to various additions which apply to the more prevalent types of means-tested benefits in the UK, calculations of the level of child and family-related spending over time are even more complex than in Germany. Defined as all transfers that otherwise equivalent households without children would not receive, Adam and Brewer (2004) show that the total amount spent on child-contingent support grew substantially in real terms and also as a share of public expenditure (Table 6.7). Stagnating during the 1980s, some of this growth occurred between 1990 to 1994 and most of it since 1999 (Adam and Brewer 2004). The fact that this was a policy- rather than demand-driven expansion is illustrated by the fact that the number of children in receipt of child benefit was only very slightly higher in 1980 than in 2003 (13 million).

Within this growth there has been a shift towards both means-tested transfers and, especially since 1998, a strong surge in tax credit support for families (Adam and Brewer 2004). In contrast, the relevance of universal child benefit diminished both relative to overall family support and in terms of its real value (Table 6.7). Once again a closer look reveals that most of the decline occurred during the 1980s (the value of child benefit reached a low of 2.9 per cent of average wages by 1991). Subsequent increases during the Major government marginally improved the value (to 3.0 per cent), with a larger increase observable under the Labour government, not least due to a historic 26 per cent benefit rise in 1999 (DWP 2004*b*). The introduction of child tax allowances in 2001 also helped improve the tax position of parents with children (Table 6.7).

Another indicator of the overall upward trend and the shift in the type of support for families are subsidies payable to parents in paid work. In 1970 the Conservative government introduced the so-called Family Income

Table 6.7. Major indicators of change in family policy, UK

	1980	2003
1. Expenditure on child contingent support (% of GDP)	1.5	2
2. Expenditure on child-contingent support (% of public spending)	3.4	4.7
3. Value of child benefit (% of average gross wage)	4.4 (7.2 for lone parents)	3.4 (first child); 2.4 (subsequent children)
4. Relative tax advantage of family (%)	3.9	5.6
5. Expenditure on family related wage subsidies (FIS, FC, WFTC) (% of social security budget)	Below 1	7
Child tax allowance	No	Yes
Maternity/parental leave	Maternity (effectively 40 weeks right to return to job)	Maternity (26; plus 26 weeks unpaid); parental (13 weeks); (until child reaches age 5); 2 weeks paternity
Maternity/parental benefit	Contributory; 6 weeks (90%); flat-rate (12 weeks)	Maternity: 6 weeks (90%); flat-rate or proportionately (20 weeks); 2 weeks paternity leave (flat-rate)
Entitlement to pre-school child care place	No	Yes; for all 4-year-olds (2001); all 3-year-olds (2004)

Source: 1. and 2. Adam and Brewer (2004); 3. and 4. DSS (Social Security Statistics various years), DWP (2004*a*; 2004*b*) and New Earnings Survey (weekly full-time adult earnings), own calculation (1£=1.52€); 4. (see Table 6.6; 4) values for 1979 and 2002; Hofäcker (2004: 267); 5. Family Income Supplement, Family Credit (since 1988), Working Family Tax Credits (since 1999) (DSS Social Security Statistics, DWP 2000*a*), own calculations.

Supplement (FIS) which was a means-tested in-work benefit (wage subsidy) for parents working at least thirty hours per week (twenty-four hours for lone parents). The rather blunt form of means-testing and low levels of support offered can be assumed to have contributed to a low take-up of around 50 per cent (Wikely et al. 2002: 384). The real level of FIS was considerably raised in 1980 (see below) and its successor, Family Credit (FC), lowered marginal tax rates on additional earnings in 1988. As a result, claimant numbers increased steeply, and spending rose from less than 1 per cent of all social security spending in 1991 to 2.5 per cent in 1996. Once replaced by various tax credits restricted to parents in work, expenditure grew from 4.3 per cent in 2000 to 7 per cent in 2003, which was due to both a larger number of claimants and an increase in the average wage subsidy received.

Finally, in a clear policy change towards a more explicit family policy, the Labour government guaranteed a free (albeit part-time) child care place for all four-year-olds (by 2001) and three-year-olds (by 2004). As in Germany, maternity leave arrangements and benefits were improved, and extended to parental leave. However, the total leave (one year) is shorter than in Germany (three years) and offers less flexibility (see Appendix F). In addition, the maternity/parental benefit for the first six months in Germany is a universal payment followed by a means-tested benefit for another eighteen months. By contrast, in the UK maternity pay is earnings-related (for six weeks) and subsequently flat-rate (wage-related for low earners) for another twenty weeks, conditional on a contributory or earnings record (albeit a fairly lenient one; see Appendix F). Interestingly, these cross-national differences do not correspond with the traditionally more employment-centred German versus the more means-tested oriented British welfare state in core social security fields, such as pensions or unemployment compensation. As the discussion demonstrates, this is yet another indication of the need to investigate social policy reform at the programme-specific level. More generally, within a similarly expansionary trend and a common turn towards an 'employment-centred' family policy (Warth 2004) in both countries in the 1990s, the latter has been more pronounced in the UK, whereas in Germany a work-focused reform course has emerged alongside a family (compensation) approach, both of which have expanded.

6.3 REFORMING FAMILY POLICY IN GERMANY

6.3.1 *The appreciation of child care work within families (1982–9)*

Before the change in government in 1982, the profile of family policy in West Germany had started to change. Whereas previous government policy had been firmly oriented to upholding marriage and supporting the traditional (or 'modern'; Ostner 2002) family as a core institution providing social cohesion (Dienel 2002), the SPD–FDP centre–left coalition of the 1970s began to support individual family members and improving opportunities for children in disadvantaged families (Bleses 2003*a*). Examples of this included the introduction of education grants, the replacement of regressive child tax allowances with more generous child benefits, strengthening the legal position of children and women, and supporting working mothers. In the latter respect, however, the government position at the time was not devoid of ambivalence. For example, official reports indicated that the government regarded paid work of married women as potentially hampering the socialization of young children (Opielka 2002: 23). Nevertheless, with an eye to improving the situation for mothers in the labour market, the SPD–FDP coalition introduced four months' maternity leave (previously two) coupled with the receipt of an earnings-related maternity benefit in 1979. Criticized as unduly disadvantaging mothers not in employment, the CDU/CSU advocated the alternative of a 'family benefit' payable to all mothers for (eventually) three years (Kolbe 2002). In addition to representing a more equitable scheme, it would allow mothers in paid employment to take extended leave for looking after young children, which was regarded as the most appropriate form of care for the child's development (Bleses and Rose 1998: 251).

However, the position of the CDU/CSU towards family policy was also in the process of change. By the late 1970s the Christian Democrats had started to acknowledge secular changes in employment, family, and household structures and began to emphasize equality between mothers in paid work and those who provided unpaid care work at home (Bleses and Rose 1998: 249). This notion had been developed within a broader context of a 'reorientation' of social policy in the late 1970s, which included a stronger profile of family policy. In its Mannheim Party Programme from 1976, the CDU demanded a shift in focus towards the 'really' underprivileged and insufficiently protected in modern society (Anthes 1984). Industrial workers had become successfully integrated in society as a result of social legislation. In the meantime, new inequalities and disadvantages had been permitted to emerge, affecting groups such as older people, immigrants, single parents, and women. Heiner Geißler (CDU), who later became the first Minister responsible for the family within the Kohl government, emphasized the 'difficult position of women, faced by an often insufferable multiple burden of paid work, child rearing and work in the household' (Geißler 1976: 2).

Some of these diagnoses informed subsequent policy formulation geared towards tackling material disadvantages on the part of families, but also to socially upgrading unpaid care work, while fertility rates can be considered as an additional influence (Münch 2005: 10). Ideologically, the conservative government pointed to a 'new partnership' between men and women and openly rejected ideas which predetermined gender roles and the division of tasks within families. On the other hand, improving options which would allow women to interrupt employment for long periods were favoured because this was regarded, particularly within the CSU, as most beneficial for the development of children.

The breakdown of the SPD–FDP coalition in 1982 did not, however, lead to an immediate change of policy. On the contrary, within the context of a severe economic recession and tight public budgets the CDU/CSU–FDP coalition continued with cost-containment policies that its predecessor had started in 1982 (see Appendix E). Most importantly, the Kohl government did not restore cuts in child benefits but implemented a means-test for the receipt of transfers for the second and subsequent children, albeit guaranteeing a minimum (non-means-tested) element for all children. The Ministry of Finance had originally envisaged the introduction of a means-test also affecting the first child. Resistance by the Family Ministry however led to a compromise which exempted first children from any cutbacks at the cost of lowering the minimum guarantee payable to subsequent children (Münch 2005: 26).

This form of retrenchment was portrayed as guided by principles of selectivity and focusing scarce public resources on families most in need. By contrast, the return to a 'dual system' of child support, that is, child tax allowances alongside child benefits, was justified with reference to achieving a more equitable tax system. Whereas SPD politicians pointed to the need of achieving more vertical redistribution in favour of low-income families, and therefore rejected child tax allowances which favoured families with a higher income within a progressive tax system, the government argued that policy should be geared towards securing a socio-cultural minimum for children as well as producing greater equity between families with children and those without in each income group. In other words, the reintroduction of child tax allowance was justified with reference to achieving greater horizontal redistribution.

The phase of cutbacks came to an end in 1984 and was succeeded by a series of 'in part spectacular benefit improvements or innovations' (Bleses and Rose 1998: 149). However, the magnitude of the improvement of some measures needs to be put in context. The considerable increase of tax allowances in 1986 and subsequent years, alongside a child benefit top-up for parents unable to make (full) use of tax advantages (see Appendix E), was accompanied by the abolition or reduction of other schemes, such as child-related tax allowances for education. Nevertheless, on the whole, family support was subject to both strong expansion and innovation in the mid-1980s. The most significant reforms affected the maternity leave scheme and the introduction of pension credits for child rearing (the so-called 'baby years'), both of which came into force in 1986. In order to assess the reasons behind these reforms, it seems appropriate to discuss them separately.

Replacing maternity leave and allowance with child raising leave and benefit
The above mentioned call by the CDU/CSU in favour of an extended 'family benefit' for all mothers of newly born babies can be traced back to the 1970s. After the return to power in 1982, legislation was delayed because of tight finances. Indeed, prompted by fiscal problems and initiated by the Finance Ministry in 1983, the level of existing maternity allowance was envisaged to be cut for 1984. This was strongly criticized by pressure and advocacy groups, such as the German Council of Women (*Frauenrat*) and the Youth Institute. More importantly, some conservative-led *Länder* (especially Bavaria) threatened to vote against this proposal in the *Bundesrat*. In the light of this pressure the government decided to implement the new child raising (i.e. parental rather than maternity) scheme earlier and to extend individual benefit entitlement to all mothers. The planned cut in maternity (now parental) pay was not averted but made less severe, with now universal flat-rate benefits payable (for six months) at a level about 30 per cent below the maximum rate of previous contributory earnings-related maternity pay.

Universal maternity allowances had already existed in some conservative *Länder* and the Family Minister Heiner Geißler exploited this experience for the development of a federal scheme (Münch 2005: 17). The guiding idea was to improve the social recognition of care work provided within families with universal child raising benefit and an extended leave option (initially ten months) which would make the choice of providing child care at home more attractive. Within government the most disputed aspects were the level of the income ceilings for the benefit applicable after six months of universal benefit, and particularly the scope of the envisaged 'employment guarantee' attached to the scheme. Supported by employer organizations and the FDP, the CDU/CSU's business wing warned that a job guarantee for one year would represent too heavy a burden for small- and medium-sized companies. The Family Ministry and the CDU's social policy wing, however, supported by the CDU women's association, demanded a full guarantee of a return to the same job. Parental leave without an employment guarantee would resemble a 'birth premium' and would induce windfall effects, the Family Minister argued (Münch 2005). In the end, a compromise exempted companies with up to five employees from the return-to-work guarantee. In addition, instead of a right to take up the same job, parents could merely insist on a return to the same employer and the same level of pay.

The parliamentary opposition criticized the new (reduced) level of child raising benefit and argued that the nominally gender neutral scheme would lead to predominantly women leaving employment because of, on average, the higher wages and full-time employment of their male partners. The legislation would thus not make work and family life more compatible or foster a reorientation of the division of unpaid work within families, an issue which was also at the forefront of demands made by women's organizations, as well as the Family Ministry. The concern was well founded given that only 1.5 per cent of parental leave recipients turned out to be men. This low take-up influenced the Family Ministry in 1988 to advocate extending the leave and allowances up to kindergarten age (three) as the 'most urgent requirement within family policy' (cited in Münch 2005: 24). While this aim was, in principle, backed by Helmut Kohl, budgetary concerns in 1989, most vehemently expressed by the FDP, prevented a more rapid expansion beyond initially a further three and later six months (see Appendix E). However, most conservative *Länder* governments already provided their own so-called 'family' or 'baby' allowances, often as programmes which extended the entitlement to the federal parental benefit scheme.

The introduction of child raising credits in pension insurance
The introduction of credits for child rearing within pension insurance (see Appendix E) has to be set in the context of a ruling by the Constitutional Court from 1975 which required the government to legislate in favour of equal treatment between widows' and widowers' entitlement to a survivor's pension by the end of 1984. The ruling can be considered as a necessary ingredient which led to policy implementation in 1986. In principle, pension credits for mothers had been favoured by both major parties for more than fifteen years, but previous policy moves had been blocked by fiscal problems on the one hand and cross-party differences over the type of funding and eligibility criteria on the other. Basically, the CDU/CSU favoured a tax funded and universal provision for all mothers in contrast to the SPD which advocated labour-centred contributory and eligibility principles. For example, in 1972 the SPD intended to pay mothers a pension supplement (equivalent to one year crediting) to be funded by contributions and, consequently, restricted to women in insured employment. These conditions led the CDU/CSU to use its majority in the *Bundesrat* to block the proposal, whilst agreeing to other expansionary policies at the time (Schmähl 1999: 410). In the second half of the 1970s the CDU revisited the idea. This time the proposal of pension credits for mothers was rejected by the ruling SPD with reference to budgetary constraints. The plan reappeared for the third time under the SPD–FDP

coalition in 1982 when draft legislation was prepared by the Ministry for Social Affairs (BMA). However, once again with reference to problems of funding, plans were delayed.

A year later it had become difficult for the new conservative–liberal government to postpone policy implementation yet again for several reasons. First, due to the requirement to adjust the survivor's pensions in accordance with the ruling of the Constitutional Court, a broad pension debate had ensued. Although the Court's ruling in favour of gender equality was intended to benefit men, leaving the position of female pensioners untouched would have been politically extremely difficult. By the early 1980s a broad agreement had emerged about a design flaw in the German pension system, structurally disadvantaging women due to their, on average, lower lifetime earnings and shorter insurance records (see Chapter 5). Second, simply ignoring the opportunity of introducing the long-standing and principally consensual policy in favour of child raising credits would have been politically risky in the light of demands made most vociferously by women from all political parties. Finally, the overall pro-family policy profile claimed by the centre–right government, as well as a demographic debate which began to link the decline of fertility with the sustainability of the pension system, provided further ammunition for the introduction of pension credits for child raising (Rüb and Nullmeier 1991: 450).

Despite a general consensus, cross-party disagreements remained and echoed discussions over maternity leave and pay. The centre–right government introduced credits for mothers for each child, equivalent to one year' employment based on 75 per cent of average earnings. However, full credits were restricted to mothers not in paid work during a child's first year of life. The justification was the aim to compensate mothers who gave up paid work in order to look after children. The SPD portrayed this as unduly discriminating between mothers and disadvantaging women who managed the double burden of employment and raising children. The SPD thus demanded child credits to be added to actual financial pension contributions made by mothers who continued in paid work (the so-called additive calculation). In short, although positions within both major parties were slowly changing (see below), the employment-centred social democratic discourse was clearly distinguishable from a Christian Democratic focus on compensating (traditional) families.

Over time the popularity of child raising leave and benefit led the SPD to alter reluctantly its prior wage-labour focus, implicitly agreeing with the government that benefits should be universal. However, policy positions also cut across party lines. For example, when the issue of child credits resurfaced again during 1988 and 1989 within the context of discussions over the pension reform (see Chapter 5), female MPs from all parties, supported by female government Ministers (the then Minister for the Family, Rita Süssmuth, CDU, and Irmgard Adam-Schwätzer, FDP) demanded the crediting of a further two years per child and the introduction of the additive calculation method. Concerned about financial outlays, the government eventually reached a compromise with the introduction of credits for two additional years applicable to mothers with children born after 1991, not 1986 as had been demanded by the Family Ministry and others (Schmähl 2004: 69). The Pension Reform Act implemented in 1992 (see Chapter 5) thus extended child raising credits to a maximum of three years per child, without switching to the additive calculation. Moreover, up to ten years spent caring for a child could be used for fulfilling the waiting period for pension eligibility. According to the government, these measures improved pension entitlements for 80 per cent of women at a rate of 5.4 per cent on average (Schmid 1997: 80).

Finally, within the broadly expansionary policy direction, there were also instances of retrenchment and cost-containment, largely concealed in the form of non-decisions. For example, child benefit for the first child remained at the nominal level from 1975. This decline in real value was one of the concerns expressed by pressure groups, as well as the scientific council advising the Family Ministry in 1988. During the election campaign in 1987, the re-elected centre–right coalition indicated its intention of responding to these demands within a context of improving family support more generally. However, budgetary concerns served as justification for the more modest extensions of child raising leave in 1989 and 1990, and merely small improvements in child benefit for the second child, initially planned for 1992 and later brought forward to 1990 at a lower rate than originally envisaged (see Appendix E).

6.3.2 German unification and the role of the Constitutional Court (1990–8)

German unification proved to exert a considerable influence on the development of family policy, albeit one which functioned as a catalyst, accelerating change rather than altering overall policy direction. Unification required policy adaptation which, in family policy, was a considerable task due to large differences in household structures and employment patterns in the two parts of the new country (see Section 6.1). Marriage and divorce rates, as well as the proportion of lone parents, were lower in West Germany than in the former GDR, where dual breadwinner couples were the norm. As discussed, facilitated by a comprehensive network of child care facilities, a much higher rate of East German mothers were in (often full-time) employment than their West German counterparts.

German unification thus put pressure on expanding measures which would help reconcile family life and employment. Some forms of provision were relatively quickly harmonized, such as employment leave for parents looking after sick children or means-tested payments to lone parents where the absent parent did not make any (or insufficient) contributions (see Appendix E). In other fields, unification added impetus to demands for further extension of child raising leave and benefit. The Family Ministry argued that improvements were needed in order to address the gender bias of the scheme, with parental leave almost exclusively made use of by mothers. The parliamentary opposition suggested a significant extension of the leave period, as well as improved pay and extended leave for lone parents. Once again, employer organizations pointed to financial problems which would arise for small and medium-sized companies. The government eventually settled the debate by extending parental leave to three years and (means-tested) child raising benefit to two years from 1992 onwards, albeit without altering its level (see Appendix E).

Apart from unification, family policy decisions in the early 1990s were made in the context of an at times heated debate about the reform of the abortion law. Originally this issue was triggered by the Constitutional Court in 1975, which nullified the then SPD–FDP government's legalization of abortions within the first twelve weeks of pregnancy. The Court regarded the latter as in breach with the Basic Law and ruled abortions to be permissible only for women in precarious social circumstances and after having had counselling. In addition, the Court had ordered the government to complement any future reform of the abortion law with measures which would help mothers and parents decide in favour of having and raising children. One response to this ruling was a government proposal from 1979 which would have granted children between the age of three and the start of school a place in a kindergarten. However, the CDU/CSU majority in the *Bundesrat* rejected the proposal with reference to the significance of the family for the development of young children.

At the time the idea of a guaranteed kindergarten place was guided by concerns about child development rather than gender equality or the issue of reconciling work and family life (Auth 2002: 241). However, the latter issues slowly gained prominence during the 1980s, with longer and more flexible opening hours of kindergartens advocated by the opposition, pressure groups, and the Family Ministry (Kolbe 2002: 372). On the whole, however, child care policy remained a marginal issue compared with maternity leave, child pension credits, and child transfers. In part, this bias can be linked to policy preferences on the part of the coalition partners. However, child care policy is also more difficult to influence since financial and policy responsibility rests with the *Länder* not the federal government.

Policy compliance on the part of *Länder* would have thus required a considerable financial inducement. This was apparent in 1990, for example. In principle supported by all parties (Auth 2002), a federal government initiative of a guaranteed kindergarten place was blocked by the *Länder* on the grounds of insufficient financial contributions offered by the federal government for such a scheme.

German unification presented an opportunity to overcome this political deadlock. The unification treaty required a common framework to be created by 1992 and abortions within the first twelve weeks of pregnancy had been legal in the GDR. In the context of legalizing abortion within the first three months, the coalition introduced the entitlement for a place in a kindergarten for all children between three and school age. This and previous improvements of child care provision were, as Ostner (1998: 131) put it, 'defined as protective measures for mothers and their (unborn) children. No mother should have an abortion for non-medical reasons, such as anticipated difficulties in combining work and child care'. The implementation of the measure was initially planned for 1996, but the nationwide introduction was delayed until 1999 due to some *Länder* which continued to regard the financial contribution of the federal government (brought about via a change in tax revenue sharing) as insufficient.

Other substantial reforms during the 1990s can be linked even more directly to the influence of the Constitutional Court. In 1996 child transfers were significantly increased, the partial means-testing of child benefit abolished, and the dual (child benefit and child tax allowance) system replaced with an integrated scheme (see Appendix E). The impetus for these changes stemmed from 1990 when the Court interpreted child transfer policies which had been introduced in 1986 as not in accordance with the Constitution. In particular, the latter requires both horizontal (tax) equity (between parents and persons without children in the same income bracket), as well as the guarantee of a tax-free socio-cultural subsistence minimum for each member of a family. In order to comply with the Basic Law, the Court decided that the government would have to increase the level of tax-free child support considerably. After protracted debates, the government eventually responded with higher child support levels and the abolition of the dual system (child benefit and child tax allowance) in favour of an integrated scheme, which reduced somewhat the advantages accruing to parents with high earnings (Dingeldey 2001*b*).

Further decisions by the Constitutional Court prompted governments to legislate in favour of parents, and sometimes single parents in particular, in tax law and in the pension system (for details, see Gerlach 2000). In the context of this chapter, the most significant aspect was the Court's deliberations over the government's decision (in 1986) to treat working and non-working mothers differently regarding child raising credits within pension insurance. This, the Court decided, was a breach with the 'principle of equality' since child care provided within the family was considered as constitutive for the sustainability of the pension system as financial contributions from employment. The government's decision in 1997 to raise the value of child raising credit and to switch to 'additive calculation' (see Appendix E) has thus to be seen as a direct response to the Court's ruling (Gerlach 2000: 29–30). In this instance, therefore, the Court's influence affected not only the scale of improvements but also the pattern of policy by requiring the government to change eligibility conditions and thus the character of existing family support.

Finally, as in the previous decade, within an overall expansionary policy context, the tight fiscal situation in the mid-1990s induced some concealed cost-containment in family related fields. This included the failure to uprate child benefit (until 1996 for second and subsequent children) or child raising benefit (unchanged since its introduction and thus diminishing the proportion of parents remaining eligible after six months). More directly, the child raising benefit became means-tested also for the first six months in 1994. However, since fairly generous income limits applied (see Appendix E), only very few parents lost out completely (Bleses and Seeleib-Kaiser 2004: 83).

6.3.3 Reconciling work and family life slowly moving centre-stage (1998– 2003)

During sixteen years of opposition, family policy orientations within the SPD had shifted significantly. Already during the 1980s the erstwhile employment-oriented emphasis, illustrated by maternity legislation from 1979, was abandoned in favour of the government's universal model. The previous focus on individual 'family member policy' (Dienel 2002) was gradually replaced by an emphasis on the positive role of the family for individual development and for society as a whole (Bleses 2003a: 201). The difference to the CDU/CSU was a call for more rapid expansion of existing provision and a more explicit normative neutrality to family forms. Accordingly, the direction of family policy remained initially unaltered under the SPD–Green government, but the pace accelerated in the form of increased levels of cash support, as well as further child raising crediting for parents within pension insurance.

In 1998 the Constitutional Court ruled the restriction of child care tax allowances to single parents as a breach of the Basic Law, and also developed a new definition of a tax-free minimum for each child, which included expenditure on subsistence, on care (either within the family or within an institution), and for educational purposes. The government responded with a number of improvements which significantly increased the generosity of child benefit and child-related tax allowances (see Appendix E), and removed any tax advantages which previously had been granted to single parents only. Once again then, family policy was strongly influenced by the Constitutional Court. However, it should be pointed out that this time the impact affected more the scale and the timing of policy-making than the overall policy direction. Improvements of public support and compensation for child care provided by families had already been indicated in election campaigns and coalition agreements between the SPD and the Green Party.

Within a general expansion of child transfers, most of the gains accrued to better paid parents. In 2002 the total monthly tax allowances per child for top income earners increased to €230, compared with the alternative of child benefit which increased to €154 (Schratzenstaller 2002: 129). More-over, the proportion of families which gained from tax allowances rather than the alternative child benefits increased from below 4 per cent to 16 per cent in the year 2000 (Dingeldey 2001*b*). On the other hand, as a result of a tax reform in 1999, the gains accruing from the married tax splitting system diminished somewhat, albeit not to the extent which had been announced in the coalition agreement of 1998 (Dingeldey 2001*b*: 218). Finally, the new government also raised income limits for the receipt of child raising benefits, making more than good the erosion of the real value of benefit levels since 1986 (see Appendix E).

Overall, the above measures indicate the government's initial further expansion of traditional 'family-centred' state support rather than a shift towards a 'work-centred' focus (Warth 2004). Gradually, this was to change with the government beginning to emphasize expanding child care, coupled with the promotion of part-time work for parents of young chil-dren. This policy shift can be illustrated with legislation introduced in 2001 and 2002, which, apart from further improving pension credits for parents, provided a stronger financial incentive for shorter parental leave and made leave more compatible with (longer) part-time work (see Appendix E). All these policies were guided by the explicit aim of better reconciliation of family life with employment for both partners.

In January 2002 Family Minister Christine Bergmann announced the government's intention of providing family support in the form of better 'infrastructure' for child care, that is, public provision for under three-year-olds, rather than better child benefits. Chancellor Schröder echoed this with the claim that 'within family policy there is nothing more important than stepping up the expansion of child care provision' (*Das Parlament, 17,*

2002). Despite tight fiscal conditions at the time, which led to cutbacks in other policy fields, the government pledged to set aside federal subsidies amounting to €1.5 billion annually (from 2005) for *Länder* for the expansion of all-day child care facilities for children under the age of three (aimed at providing places for 20 per cent of this age group). Well below the existing level in the new *Länder* (see Table 6.1), this nevertheless implied a significant increase for West Germany (Spieß and Frick 2002). In addition, another €4 billion was set aside for helping *Länder* and municipalities convert traditional half-day to full-day schools in the period 2003 to 2007. Starting from a very low level of 5 per cent of schools which also teach in the afternoons, latest government figures show a high uptake of the federal subsidies and the number of full-day schools rising by 64 per cent between May 2003 and June 2004 (BBF 2004). In addition, the promotion of child care within companies became another policy focus.

In short, after initially simply expanding previous transfer-oriented family policy, the expansion of child care provision has figured more prominently since the general election in 2002. Moreover, with growing employment orientation, family policy moved from a traditionally marginal position closer to the centre of policymaking within the senior government party. Making work and family life more compatible was a central topic at the 2001 SPD annual conference, and all-day child care options for children of all groups was identified as an important instrument (Opielka 2002: 25). How can what the government called a 'paradigm shift' towards child care (Bundesregierung 2004) be explained?

One factor seems to be popular demand. Opinion polls in 2001 and early 2002 indicated both the relevance of family policy on the one hand and disappointment about the lack of government initiatives on the other (Mackroth and Ristau 2002). Trying to take advantage, the CDU/CSU responded with the suggestion of a 'family benefit' which would significantly improve existing transfers as part of an integrated allowance to be used by parents either for providing child care within the family or for the purchase of services. Even though the proportion of parental leave taken by men was rising, in about 95 per cent of all cases it was women rather than men who interrupted employment for reasons of child care (BMFSFJ 2004). The strategy of 'making children more affordable' (Engelbrech 2002: 140) via improved transfers for parental leave would thus have been unlikely to achieve greater gender equality in paid and unpaid work. Politically, the opposition's proposal widened the gap to the government which began to favour the expansion of public child care provision rather than compensation for family care. Apparently, this strategy had positive electoral effects (Ristau 2003; Roth and Jung 2002). Government sponsored opinion polls suggested that expanding child care corresponded with a demand by parents who favoured public provision for educational reasons as well as a measure which would help to combine family life and employment more easily.

Second, there were economic incentives to expand child care. Improved provision became regarded as an appropriate strategy help increase the employment of mothers, both in the short term and in the context of an expected decline in labour supply after 2010, especially in the service sector. The link between child care and female employment was strengthened by references to experiences in other countries with extensive child care infrastructures, such as Sweden (see *Frankfurter Allgemeine Zeitung*, 28 October 2004). However, domestic developments too provided policy support. There is evidence that the guaranteed kindergarten place since 1996 has contributed to the increase in employment amongst mothers with children aged three to five at a rate which was considerably higher than the growth of employment amongst mothers generally (BMFSFJ 2003: 107). This outcome might be regarded as an example of the influence of policy feedback. Once implemented, increased child care options generated a further impetus for expansion and also contributed to a normative reorientation, in this case towards 're-casting mothers as part-time workers' (Ostner 1998: 132).

Third, the government began to link concerns about low fertility rates an inadequate supply of child care facilities. Whereas expenditure on families in Germany is relatively high in the international context, other European countries were held up as evidence that sufficient all-day child care provision for younger children facilitated both higher female employment and comparatively higher birth rates.

A fourth factor was the influence of a debate which ensued after the publication of an international assessment of educational achievement amongst fifteen-year-olds in December 2001 (the PISA study; see OECD 2000). Germany's poor ranking in the study triggered a major public and political debate on structural problems of the education system and education policy (see Allmendinger and Leibfried 2003; Schmidt 2003*a*). More specifically, the research indicated a positive relationship between the level of public child care provision, the cognitive development of children, and educational standards. The study has become a standard reference point in government declarations in favour of expansion of especially early childhood care and education (e.g. www.ganztagsschulen.org).

In short, the recent turn towards the expansion of child care (at the expense of further compensation for family care) was based on economic incentives, strengthened by policy feedback and facilitated by contextual influences, such as popular demand and the debate on early childhood education. The example illustrates that institutional impediments (in this case *Länder* responsibility) can be overcome or weakened by strong political motives and a favourable context. Furthermore, it suggests that institutional settings seem less influential in family policy than in other social policy fields, because of both less entrenched and solidified policymaking structures and a broad policy direction of expansion rather than retrenchment.

6.4. THE UNITED KINGDOM

6.4.1 Ambiguities, impediments, and avoiding burdens on employers (1979–90)

British family policies after 1979 were formulated within a context of reducing public spending, directing state support to those deemed most in need, and lowering financial burdens on employers. Ideologically, Conservative governments kept stressing basic themes such as personal responsibility, independence, individual freedom, and self-reliance. However, in the first years of the 1980s, the 'real imperative was simply to save money' (Timmins 2001: 374) since public spending was regarded as impeding economic growth. The retrenchment strategy was not radical but consisted of reductions at the margin: delaying benefit upratings, trimming entitlements, focusing on social security fraud and abuse, and targeting public support at those in greatest need, a 'user-friendly modern euphemism for means-testing' (Lister 1989a: 117). Partly because of rising unemployment, but also as a result of emphasizing needs-based support, the number of social assistance claimants (Supplementary Benefit until 1988, then Income Support) almost doubled between 1979 and 1987.

Convened by the Prime Minister's personal adviser, a 'family policy group' was briefed to collect proposals which would help to 'restore the family to a central role in social policy' (Deakin 1994: 103). However, albeit critical towards certain family structures (lone parenthood in particular), the group was less concerned with advocating traditional gender roles than with ways of transferring responsibility for social protection from the state to the family (Willets 1989: 266). Policy areas included education (advocating more parental choice), pensions (more private provision), and social security, exemplified by the introduction of lower (means-tested) benefit rates for under twenty-five-year-old unemployed people and the abolition of cash transfers for practically all claimants under eighteen. Other fields of public policy relevant for families, such as child care services, offered little scope for retrenchment because of the minimal role of public provision (Randall 2002). Ideologically, the government remained suspicious of state support which was seen as inferior to child care provided by mothers. John Patten, minister with responsibility for women in 1989, stated: 'I don't think the State should step in to help the working mother unless her life has collapsed' (cited in Lister 2000: 78). Policy formation was not devoid of ideological ambivalence or free from constraints, however. This can be illustrated with reference to changes in three areas: child benefit, in-work benefits aimed at helping low-paid families, and reforms in the area of maternity pay and leave arrangements.

Child benefit
In 1977 previous family allowances and tax exemptions had been replaced by child benefit which, for the first time, also provided universal cash support for the first child. The incoming Conservative government in 1979 was torn between the value of this benefit, which was highly popular, but at the same threatened to undermine core objectives of cost-containment and directing scarce public resources to those in greatest need. Government think tanks advocated the abolition or means-testing of the scheme and Margaret Thatcher herself was 'deeply sceptical about the value of a universal child benefit' (Deakin 1994: 123). However, a sizeable number of Conservative MPs, including the Conservative Women's Committee, supported its non-means-tested character and its role as anti-poverty family benefit paid directly to the carer (mainly the mother). Tensions within the party led eventually to the decision to retain the benefit but increase its value well below the rate of inflation in 1980 (DWP 2004*b*).

Fostered by the lack of a 'coherent approach to means-testing or incentives' (Timmins 2001: 375) in the early 1980s, the ambiguity over what to do with child benefit led to a stop-and-go policy. The government acknowledged that a benefit reduction, while saving public expenditure, might exacerbate work disincentives because the gap between disposable income of people in work and those on means-tested benefits would diminish. This point was repeatedly made by the poverty lobby led by the CPAG (Child Poverty Action Group) in its campaign to 'save' child benefit and to restore its original value. This, in conjunction with party internal pressure, contributed to the government making good the shortfall before the 1983 elections (DWP 2004*b*).

In the context of the major review of social security (see Chapter 4), discrepancies between the Treasury and the DHSS over child benefit became apparent in the mid-1980s (Timmins 2001: 398). As a most explicit devotee of greater targeting, the Treasury fuelled suggestions of abolishing means-testing or taxing child benefit. Resisting such proposals, Norman Fowler, then Secretary of State at the DHSS, enlisted the support from the CPAG and about seventy other pressure groups and organizations, including some trade unions, of the so-called 'Coalition for Child Benefit'. But the government was also wary of embarking on radical change because of fear of a middle-class backlash and protests from within the party. Once again the political outcome had the air of a compromise: maintaining the universal character of child benefit but decreasing its real value in 1985, inflation linking it in subsequent years but keeping the scheme 'constantly under review' (Lister 1989*b*: 216).

Wage subsidies for parents

Cuts in the value of child benefit were routinely justified by claiming that resources were thereby freed for families in greatest need, and working parents in particular (Willets 1989: 271). In 1970 the then Conservative government had introduced Family Income Supplement (FIS), a means-tested in-work benefit for low-paid parents. As discussed (Section 6.2), its low value and interaction with the tax system and other benefits created high marginal tax rates and reduced take-up. As early as 1980 the government signalled its intention of addressing this problem, increasing the value of FIS well above inflation. However, the take-up rate (of about 50 per cent) stagnated and the overall number of claimants rose much more slowly than the number of families in receipt of out-of-work means-tested benefits (Walker and Howard 2000: 191–2). This trend contributed to replacing FIS with the more generous Family Credit (FC). Coming into force in 1988, FC was designed to ameliorate the work disincentive problem (see Appendix F). It doubled the proportion of parents eligible to a wage subsidy (Dilnot and Webb 1988), which became the government's explicit strategy to tackle family poverty in the second half of the 1980s (Willets 1989). However, the reform was also motivated by its potential effect of dampening pay demands of low-paid male workers (Bennett 1987: 125; Lister 2000: 77) since, unlike its predecessor, FC was no longer to be paid as a social security benefit to the caring parent but initially planned as reducing the liability for income tax or addition to gross pay respectively (tax credit), to be paid directly by employers into the claimant's pay packet.

This plan met with strong resistance inside and outside parliament. A considerable number of Conservative backbenchers agreed with the poverty lobby (including some trade unions) and women's groups which argued that the scheme should primarily be about limiting child poverty and thus continue to be paid to the carer (mainly mother) and not the earner. This coalition of interest was joined by representatives from small businesses who resisted the additional administrative burden which the new benefit would have created. Eventually, this 'unholy alliance' (Bennett 1987: 125) led to an 'unexpected climb-down on the payment of family credit through the pay-packet' (Lister 1989*b*: 209).

Maternity allowance and leave

Payable since the introduction of National Insurance in 1946, modest contributory maternity allowances (payable for thirteen weeks) had been reformed as part of the 1975 Employment Protection Act, which selectively improved financial support during maternity leave and introduced a job guarantee. Restricted to women with a continuous employment record of at least two years, the legislation obliged employers to pay a supplement to the flat-rate maternity allowance, so that the total gross wage replacement amounted to 90 per cent for six weeks, and to guarantee a return to her previous job within twenty-nine weeks of confinement. In return, employers were entitled to a rebate from the Maternity Pay Fund (which later merged with the National Insurance Fund).

During the 1980s, provisions became less generous due to retrenchment and restructuring in the sense of changing eligibility conditions. Already in 1980 the new government weakened the right to return to the previous job, affecting women working in small firms with up to six employees in particular (Ringen 1997: 51). Reflecting core policy objectives of containing public spending and shifting responsibility for social protection to non-statutory sources, a new scheme (Statutory Maternity Benefit, SMP) was introduced in 1986 which maintained the earnings-related character (for six weeks) for women with longer employment records but reduced the value of the (subsequent) lower flat-rate benefit (Lonsdale and Byrne 1988: 146). Eligibility to SMP became linked to an earnings threshold and a sufficient continuous employment biography, thus overcoming the situation 'whereby a woman could claim maternity allowance on the basis of past contributions, even if she was not in paid employment at that point in time' (Lonsdale and Byrne 1988: 152). The introduction of SMP made employers liable for administering (but not necessarily paying) maternity benefit in the large majority of cases.

The new scheme illustrates conflicting policy objectives at the time. Reducing administrative burdens for employers, an explicit aim of employment deregulation (HMSO 1985), was in this case apparently subordinated to the intention of limiting public responsibility for social protection and curbing social expenditure. This can be exemplified also with the fate of a one-off maternity grant. Following a review of all forms of maternity support in 1980 (DHSS 1980), the government first abolished its contributory condition, making all expectant mothers eligible to receive the grant in 1982 (Wikeley et al. 2002: 557). What seems like an act of expansion and restructuring (from contributory to universal support) was at the same time a very inexpensive policy since the grant's level of £25 (unaltered since 1969) was left untouched. A further decline in real value over subsequent years facilitated its eventual conversion into a more generous but means-tested benefit in 1987, a move which caused 'barely a stir' (Timmins 2001: 402).

6.4.2 Continuity and modest pragmatic expansion (1990–7)

Under John Major as Prime Minister, family policy changed direction from retrenchment to hesitant expansion in some areas (child benefit and maternity leave/pay) and strong expansion in another (Family Credit). In the light of dramatic socio-economic trends affecting families, this might not seem surprising. The proportion of children living in poor households (less than half average income) trebled between 1979 and 1992 (to about 30 per cent; DSS 1994). During the 1980s the share of lone parents participating in the labour market diminished (Gregg and Harkness 2003: 100) and benefit receipt grew accordingly (Millar 2003a). By contrast the proportion of married mothers in paid employment rose steadily (by over 10 per cent), and more so for mothers with children under the age of five. However, neither child poverty nor a growing demand for child care affected the government's broad policy approach, with arrangements for child care, for example, continuing to be regarded as an essentially private matter (Randall 2002: 230). Instead, Conservative politicians turned to 'family issues' with a moralizing public discourse, making state provision partly responsible for the breakdown of traditional families and absent fathers for problems of childhood development, juvenile crime, and other social ills (Pascall 1997; Lister 1997). This was the context in which the controversial Child Support Agency, charged with making absent parents (usually fathers) pay child maintenance, was introduced (Ford and Millar 1998).

The Prime Minister dissociated himself from the more aggressive rhetoric towards lone parents employed by some of his Cabinet colleagues. Ideologically more pragmatic than his predecessor, John Major avoided an explicit antipathy towards working mothers, without abandoning voluntarism as the government's preferred policy position (Lewis 2003). As in the late 1980s, largely unsuccessful appeals were made to employers to provide day nurseries and modest financial inducements were offered to the voluntary sector for more pre-school and after-school care places. A more direct strategy of making family life and employment more compatible was pursued with the help of FC, changing its design by including the introduction of a child care allowance, for example (Appendix F). Other improvements to the scheme contributed to higher take-up rates and the doubling of claimant numbers between 1989 and 1997 (McKay and Rowlingson 1999: 113; Millar 2003b: 127). Heralded as a great success by the government in the mid-1990s, these reforms indicated a growing relevance of subsidizing wages for low-paid parents in an increasingly deregulated labour market.

Other initiatives also indicated a hesitant move towards helping parents reconcile family and work, such as a nursery voucher scheme for parents of four-year-old children which was introduced in 1996 as a means of fostering choice and competition between public, private, and voluntary providers of child care. However, with the Treasury 'alarmed over the cost' (Timmins 2001: 546), a stronger expansion remained subordinated to the objective of curbing public spending and avoiding legal and financial burdens on employers. The value of the voucher was thus relatively low, while recouping resources from local education authority budgets proved partly detrimental to existing nursery provision and expenditure on primary schools (Lewis 2003: 224).

There were also considerable external steers in favour of employment-oriented family policy in the form of EC directives on maternity and parental leave. Initiatives in the late 1980s were blocked or watered down by the UK government (Falkner and Treib 2003), which regarded such regulations as representing disincentives for employers to hire women of child-bearing age (Ringen 1997: 53). Driven by a free market ideology and an ambiguity towards lone mothers in paid work (Lewis 1999), the government's strategy remained voluntarist and hesitant. Tackling benefit dependency was not easily reconcilable with the prevailing preference for mothers providing care as best for the development of young children.

However, the EC Pregnant Workers' Directive in 1992 (Levin 1997) was binding also for the UK since it was introduced under the heading of 'health and safety'. It stipulated a minimum of fourteen weeks maternity leave for all working mothers, irrespective of length of employment, a job guarantee, and a level of social security support at least equivalent to sick pay (Wikeley et al. 2002: 559). Due to UK intervention the directive became less extensive than had originally been intended. Nevertheless, it made modest British maternity benefits more generous for women who had resort only to the lower rate of SMP. Indirectly the directive was also responsible for easing access to the higher rate of SMP (see Appendix F), but only because this was the administratively simplest option of complying with EC law (Wikeley et al. 2002). Equally, the subsequent alignment of maternity allowance (for those not eligible to SMP) was largely due to administrative simplification rather than purposeful policy expansion.

In short, a modest extension of maternity benefits required external (European) influence while improvements in FC, progressively functioning as a form of labour-market policy for low-paid parents, can be regarded as in accordance with the ongoing deregulation of the labour market and the expansion of a low-paid sector. By contrast, a clear turn of policy direction can be observed in the area of child benefit. After the general election of 1987, John Moore, the new Secretary of State at the DHSS, decided to freeze its value for 1988 and 1989 as a way of, in the words of Conservative MP Sir George Young, 'marking time' before a decision would be made in which direction to move (cited in Lister 1989*a*: 120). Moore's subsequent suggestions of taxing or income testing child benefit contradicted earlier Conservative election pledges (Timmins 2001: 447). Besides, political obstacles for such reforms had become stronger since John Major had been appointed Chief Secretary to the Treasury in 1987. Major recognized the popularity of the benefit's universal character and, once he became Prime Minister, finally settled the government's policy ambiguity. Over-ruling his Chancellor, he pledged to preserve its universal character, to restore its 1987 value by 1992, and to index it in line with inflation. While these decisions marked a clear shift in policy direction, cost-containment remained an important government priority. Benefit improvements and inflation indexation applied to first born children only. In short, in the context of expansion, the government also restructured child benefit, creating a two-tier scheme with lower increases for second and subsequent children, failing to make good the benefit shortfall since 1987 for larger families.

6.4.3 New Labour: tackling child poverty and employment as the 'best family policy of all' (1998–2003)

The development of family policy under New Labour illustrates that parties 'matter' on the one hand, and underlines the dynamic nature of party policy on the other. After the lost election of 1992, the Labour Party slowly began to adopt many Conservative policy positions, most poignantly the overriding objectives of maintaining labour-market flexibility, contain-ing public spending, and fostering non-statutory means of social protec-tion. In the context of family policy, Labour's departure from a traditional opposition to means-testing was particularly relevant. However, in many other respects, under the new government a policy direction became visible which was clearly distinguishable from previous Conservative policy. This applies to a more active role of the state in general, and a 'commitment to an explicit "family policy" ' (Lewis 2003: 221) in particular, with a range of activities, innovations, and investment in areas such as early education, child care, and family support becoming increasingly coherent over time.

An early consultation paper (Home Office 1998) indicated an explicit emphasis on family policy under the new government, and also a broad approach with policies to address problems such as family breakdown by 'strengthening marriage' (e.g. with 'pre-nuptial' written agreements) or providing services in support of new parents (e.g. courses in parenthood education). The latter more normative aspects proved contentious, however, and were subsequently dropped. By contrast, indicating a clear policy intention and direction, most other measures announced in the consultation document and other early official texts (e.g. HM Treasury 1999*b*) were subsequently introduced and extended during Labour's first and second term in office. These included programmes providing support for 'serious family problems' (e.g. addressing youth offending or teenage pregnancy), targeted support for families and children in deprived areas (through Sure Start and other programmes; see Millar and Ridge 2002), as well as more general policies aimed at improving 'financial support to families' (including child benefit, tax credits, and subsidies for child care costs) and helping families 'balance work and home' (e.g. via a National Childcare Strategy and improved maternity and parental benefit, and leave).

Two main objectives connect these areas and guided policy formation: tackling child poverty and increasing the labour-market participation of working age benefit claimants, including mothers with young children and lone parents in particular. These ambitions were informed by dramatic socio-economic developments and growing fiscal pressure due to expenditure on social security, which continued to rise even after the economic and labour-market improvement had begun in 1993 (DWP 2004*a*). By the mid-1990s there had been a further rise in the proportion of children living in poor households (to about a third; DSS 2000) and more children were growing up in a larger share of households with no adult in work (Gregg and Wadsworth 2003). Many of the latter were lone parent households and the proportion of lone parents in receipt of out-of-work benefits had risen further. In addition, labour-market inactivity amongst prime working-age men continued to increase even after unemployment declined and employment rates started to rise after 1993 (Faggio and Nickel 2003; Clasen et al. 2004).

Labour's response was to make welfare provision more focused and conditional upon paid employment. The origins of this approach can be traced back to debates following the lost election in 1992, with prominent MPs, such as Bryan Gould, questioning the party's traditional commitment to universalism and calling for targeted policies geared to helping women into paid work. Malcolm Wicks, a prominent Labour MP and expert on family policy, proclaimed employment as 'the best family policy of all' and advocated more efforts in child care provision but also restrictions, for example, preventing lone parents staying on benefit until their youngest child was sixteen years old, which arguably impeded transition into work (Wicks 1995). By 1997 such work-focused family policy had become mainstream within the new government. The abolition of the 'one parent' benefit premium, for example, (Timmins 2001: 567) was justified with reference to equality (between couples and single parents) and the need for switching state support to measures which would assist transitions from 'welfare-to-work' (DSS 1998*a*: 57). This was to be achieved by increasing the financial return from employment (introducing a minimum wage and topping up low wages), launching employment programmes such as the New Deal tailored for specific groups (see Chapter 4), and making benefit receipt generally more conditional, thereby creating a 'need to define legitimate reasons for not undertaking paid work' (Rake 2001: 211).

The link between this employment-based policy agenda and combating child poverty was not immediately recognizable within Labour's agenda before their return to power in May 1997. However, the promotion of paid work soon became explicitly coupled with poverty reduction and the intention of eradicating child poverty 'within a generation' in particular. Characterized as 'clever politics as well as high ambition' (Timmins 2001: 590), the latter signalled an adherence to traditional Labour Party aspirations to critics on the left, while making redistrubutive policies by helping low-income parents into employment more palatable to middle-class voters. In the same vein, finding new mechanisms for channelling resources to lower-income families via the tax system can be seen as a strategic choice of instruments in the pursuit of an interventionist and redistributive family policy with the connected aims of employment promotion and tackling the 'scarring nature of childhood poverty' (HM Treasury 1999*b*).

Child poverty was to be tackled by an array of support programmes largely directed at low-income families (Ridge 2003), but also including universal child benefit. At first glance, this seems to go against Labour's new turn towards targeted state support at the expense of its traditional position in favour of universal provision. Before the 1992 general election the Labour Party had promised they would increase the value of child benefit and maintain its universal character (Bennett 1992). Five years later, the Shadow Chancellor Gordon Brown publicly contemplated taxing the benefit for higher earners (Timmins 2001: 562), a plan which figured in the government's early proposals for welfare reform (DSS 1998*a*). Means-testing the benefit for parents with children aged over sixteen at school or college was another suggestion made by the Chancellor (Hewitt 1999). In the end, the government not only preserved the universal character of child benefit but increased its value by a historic 26 per cent (for the oldest child) in April 1999 (DWP 2004*a*). Although child-related elements within means-tested programmes were raised to a similar and subsequently even greater magnitude, maintaining the design of child benefit seems at odds with the new emphasis on selective support for the poor. Arguably, planned retrenchment was prevented due to populist motives. As discussed, Conservative governments in the 1980s refrained from cutbacks in the face of public opinion, with Labour lending support to the vociferous defence of the benefit's universal character. After 1997, the positions were reversed with the Conservative opposition joining protests against plans for reforming the benefit (*Guardian*, 1 June 2001). However, there seem to have been additional reasons for Labour's change of mind, not least a realization of only marginal financial gains. The Treasury's plan of taxing child benefit for higher rate income earners would have added administrative complexity in return for a relatively small reduction of public spending.

Thus, rather than curbing child benefit the Labour government increased its value by an unprecedented amount. This move was explicitly related to the reduction in the value of the Married Couple's Tax Allowance. In turn, the subsequent replacement of the latter and its transformation into the Children's Tax Credit in 2001 (see Appendix F) was legitimized as switching resources from married couples to couples with children. However, just as with child benefit, it seems that assumed middle-class resentment stopped a more redistributive policy. Since the Married Couple's Allowance was available to taxpayers irrespective of the level of earnings, simply replacing it with a means-tested child tax credit was regarded as politically difficult. Nevertheless, the government moved in this direction via the introduction of a 'light touch' income test which progressively reduced the new allowance for people in the top income tax bracket. Thus, although children's tax credits (and now the 'family element' of Child Tax Credit; see below) stretch to families with well above average earnings, it is in accordance with Labour's preference for 'progressive universalism' (HM Treasury 2002), that is, support for all parents but with an emphasis on disadvantaged families.

Labour's programmatic reorientation in general, and its pursuit of improved but employment-based and targeted family policy provision in particular, can best be illustrated with the replacement of FC by Working Families Tax Credit (WFTC) in 1999. Traditionally critical of in-work benefits (Timmins 2001: 544), as late as the early 1990s the Labour Party vociferously opposed public subsidies for low paid employment as preserving inequalities and rewarding stingy employers (Wood 2001*a*). By the mid-1990s, however, the party's leadership had accepted the argument that a flexible and deregulated labour market represented a constitutive comparative advantage for the British economy. In addition, motivated by the aim of halting and reversing the growth of benefit dependency amongst working-age persons (see Chapter 4), Labour began to regard wage subsidies as a central policy instrument in its welfare-to-work agenda. Thus, after initially making FC more generous and allowing for a substantial rise in disregarded child care costs (Appendix F), Chancellor Brown subsequently replaced the scheme with the more encompassing WFTC. Motivated by a perception of work disincentives inherent in FC, the reform aimed to raise the take-up rate by decoupling the new scheme from the social security system and associating it more explicitly within the context of paid employment (McLaughlin et al. 2001: 166). In addition, it widened the gap between out-of-work benefits and transfers for people in work, which signalled a 'rejigging (of) the less eligibility principle in a way appropriate for an enlarged low-waged sector' (Hewitt 1999: 166). These changes accelerated the growth in the number of parents in receipt of wage subsidies under the Labour government, doubling within six years (to 1.4 million families in February 2003; Inland Revenue 2003).

The switch to a tax credit scheme in favour of low-paid families is illustrative of the Labour government's general policy preferences, its ability to gain sufficient support by making modest concessions and combining policy aims, and its creation of increasingly coherent family policy through the transfer of political power to the Treasury. First, WFTC represented a cheaper and administratively simpler system, but also a transfer of family support from the (largely female) child carer to the (more often male) income earner. As already discussed, a similar plan met with considerable opposition in the 1980s, forcing the Conservative government to abort its reform. Labour faced similar protests from interest groups (Rake 2001: 218). Less effective this time, the government nevertheless relented to some extent by allowing claimants to opt actively to have the credit paid to the non-earner parent. Subsequent revisions of WFTC and its split into the Working Tax Credit (payable also to low earners without children) and the Child Tax Credit (integrating various types of tax and benefit child support; see Appendix F) confirmed Labour's growing enthusiasm with means-testing (or targeting) as the central mechanism for family support. The strategy allowed the party to keep their election pledge to contain public expenditure, while at the same time engaging in less explicit but effective redistributive policies in favour of particularly low-income and lone parent families (Brewer and Gregg 2003). Politically, the introduction WFTC and the creation of the new Child Tax Credit implied a considerable increase of control exerted by the Inland Revenue (and thus the Treasury) at the expense of the DSS and its predecessor, the DWP. With the Inland Revenue also responsible for child benefit, the financial support for families has become increasingly centralized, coherent, and coordinated (if complex; see Ridge 2003). Politically this process concentrated more power in the hands of the Treasury which has established itself as the dominant driver of welfare reform (Deakin and Parry

2000), assisted by institutional changes in the implementation of public policy (Carmel and Papadopoulos 2003).

Last but not least, the area of maternity and parental leave and also child care marked a change of policy direction after 1997 and thus an alignment with other aspects of family policy, particularly with regard to Labour's work focus. Driven by the motivation to create more 'family-friendly' employment policies (DTI 1998) the government implemented an EU directive which extended the period of minimum maternity leave and allowed for unpaid parental leave (Appendix F). While this was certainly the 'minimum necessary for compliance with the Directive' (Wikeley et al. 2002: 560) and current arrangements in the UK continue to lag behind more extensive and generous arrangements in many other EU countries (Falkner and Treib 2003), subsequent reforms in maternity and parental leave and pay have contributed towards a record of substantial policy expansion (see Bennett 2004; Appendix F). Moreover, improvements in maternity pay and leave were explicit election pledges in the run-up to the 2001 election (Maclean 2002) and the government has since signalled its intent on further expansion (HM Treasury and DTI 2003).

Child care policy too has figured strongly in Labour's employment-centred agenda (Randall 2002). In recognition of the cost of child care as a main barrier to paid work, the government set up a national Childcare Strategy aimed at improving the supply and quality of child day-care. Reflecting the government's commitment to a 'mixed economy of child care' (Lewis 2003), the strategy envisaged local 'partnerships' between public bodies and private and voluntary agencies, subsidizing providers and making the cost of formal provision more affordable for parents via improved child care tax credits. It also guaranteed free half-day (two and a half hours) places for all four-year-olds, and subsequently three-year-olds, creating a total of 1.6 million new child care places by 2004. Geographical variations in provision remain important, informal care continues to be relevant, and demand continues to outstrip supply. Nevertheless, there has been considerable progress since 1997, from one child care place available for every nine children under eight years in 1997 to one place for every four by the end of 2003 (Daycare Trust 2004). Recent research (Gregg et al. 2003) has shown that both better maternity rights and child care provision have contributed to a stronger labour-market attachment of mothers, albeit with mixed and sometimes merely modest impacts on earnings due to the prevalence of (generally lower paid) part-time work.

In sum, British family policy under the Labour government has become more interventionist, coordinated, and increasingly coherent, with the explicit aims of reducing child poverty and fostering the employment of parents. Previous ambiguity, over the role of lone mothers in particular, has been replaced by a commitment to a policy aimed at labour-market integration as a principal goal. An erstwhile traditional Labour Party commitment to universalism has been replaced by a targeted, employment-focused, and 'obligation-oriented' approach to citizenship (Plant 2003), coupled with an implicit redistributive agenda in favour of low-income families. The instruments applied were partly innovative (child tax credits, tailored New Deal programmes), partly inherited (e.g. tax subsidies for working parents) but restructured and made more comprehensive, indicating a clear change in policy direction in some areas of family support, such as child care. The final section (6.5) of the chapter assesses the causes of policy expansion and factors shaping national patterns of reform.

6.5 COMPARATIVE CONCLUSIONS

Over the entire period under investigation, family policies expanded, in part strongly, albeit with cross-national differences. In Germany the process started in the mid-1980s, with further improvements in the 1990s and a stronger push after 1998. By contrast British governments of the 1980s engaged in a strategy of cost-containment and retrenchment, followed by modest expansion during the first half of the 1990s and more pronounced improvements under the Labour government. In addition to expansion there were instances of policy innovation in both countries. In Germany child raising pension credits were different from other types of credits (say, for time spent in education) in the sense that bringing up at least two children became sufficient for establishing eligibility for a pension payment without ever having been in paid employment (Bleses 2003a: 196). New forms of provision (child credits in particular, but also universal maternity benefits) represented 'a considerable change of direction of family policy' (Schmidt 1998:71). In the UK, improved wage subsidies for parents can be regarded as an instance of policy expansion, the adoption of an employment-centred policy for mothers with young children represented a policy U-turn, and the introduction of guaranteed child care places for pre-school children was without precedent.

In short, despite periodic cutbacks, common trends of expansion can be identified, with differences both in timing and in national policy profiles. What is more, shared normative positions prompted different policy patterns at times. As discussed, traditional policy orientations favoured family care over public provision in both countries. However, in the 1980s the UK government remained indifferent to growing female employment in the sense that the problem of balancing child care and paid work was left to families and mothers. By contrast, the conservative government in Germany responded in a more interventionist fashion, improving the material situation and social entitlement of mothers and thereby reducing the opportunity cost of providing child care at home. In other words, two actors with broadly similar normative orientations adopted different policies in order to pursue similar public policy goals characterized by a bias towards domestic child care.

Another example of variation within common trends of expansion is the growing focus on employment-centred family policy, and the promotion of public child care in particular. Until very recently, improvements in this field were not on the policy agenda either in the UK or in Germany. Instead, leaving aside differences in starting points, timing, and scale of expansion, both countries preferred improvements in family-related cash transfers, as well as maternity or parental benefits and leave arrangements. This changed only under centre–left governments which put public child care policy at the core of what became increasingly employment-oriented family policy. New Labour embarked on such a trajectory earlier and with more vigour than the red–green German government. Besides, while the 'work-centred approach' (Warth 2004) has become dominant in the UK, supplemented by a complementary strategy of social inclusion, the German version emerged only recently and has yet to be firmly established alongside a 'family-centred' approach. As in Chapters 4 and 5, this concluding section assesses causes for these similarities and differences in policy direction and national policy profiles, addressing motives and preferences on the part of government parties first, before turning to the other two sets of impacts, institutional influences and situational or contingent conditions.

6.5.1 Changing motives and preferences

Despite some signs of party convergence and dynamic normative positions (e.g. towards the role of mothers) in both countries, it is obvious that party differences and their policy preferences matter in family policy. This is best exemplified with the turn towards a less residual and decidedly more employment-centred policy under centre–left governments in both countries. As discussed, such a strategy had already been advocated within the Labour Party in the early 1990s, became established within the party leadership before the 1997 election, and has strongly guided policy since (Lewis 2002: 336). By contrast, a clear divergence between the previous centre–right government in Germany and the subsequent red–green coalition can be observed only after the general election in 2002, heralding a more explicit employment-centred approach also in family policy (Bleses 2003a: 206). Recently the CDU/CSU, too, began to advocate the expansion of public child care provision, albeit subject to federal financial support for *Länder*.

Looking back over the period under investigation, policy preferences have been shown to be dynamic and family policy subject to internal conflicts within government parties in both countries. This was most obvious between the finance ministries on the one hand and the family ministry (Germany) or DSS (UK) on the other, with spending ministries often being supported by interest groups within and across parties (e.g. female MPs), as well as non-parliamentary lobby groups. These interest coalitions had some impact on policy formation. Maintaining FC as a cash benefit rather than tax credit in 1988 is a case in point in the UK. However, rather than altering policy direction or policy profile, the influence was often more limited in the sense of weakening the scale of cutbacks envisaged by finance ministries or accelerating planned expansion. Lifting other areas onto the policy agenda was largely beyond the power of such interest coalitions, however. This was most evident in the area of child care in both countries. In the UK, there was an explicit government stance against public provision for ideological reasons in the 1980s. In Germany, demands from the opposition, female MPs, and the family ministry for more initiatives in this field were, until recently, either ignored or deflected with reference to improvements in other forms of family support.

In short, government party preferences and interest were highly influential on the direction and profile of policy, but at the same time dynamic in nature, undergoing considerable change from the late 1970s and early 1980s onwards. In Germany, both major parties made the case for stronger public support for families and linked this to changes in household structures and employment patterns. The latter influenced the CDU/CSU's adoption of formal neutrality to family types and gender roles. Nevertheless, improving compensation for all mothers providing care at home reflected the adherences to traditional Christian democratic preferences for family over institutional care for young children. The SPD for their part had to acknowledge that the government's rhetoric on choice and fairness (entitlements for mothers who opt for child care instead of employment) proved highly popular. In turn this contributed to the SPD shedding its previously strong wage-labour focus, exemplified by the maternity benefit legislation in 1979.

Over time, the aim of improving the compatibility between family life and employment slowly gained policy prominence within conservative governments in both countries. And yet, better provision of public child care was kept out of the policymaking arena. In Germany, the extension of parental leave and improved child raising credits were the CDU/CSU's preferred alternative to publicly provided or supported child care. Demanding more public child care provision, there was a prevailing opinion also within the SPD that child raising was ideally best left to families, a position which was reiterated as late as 1988 (Münch 2005: 12). Partly out of 'societal motives' (Kaufmann 2002), that is, upholding the family as a constitutive element of society, partly by a disposition towards limiting public intervention into what was considered to be a private matter, a similar absence of expanding public child care prevailed also in the UK for the entire period of Conservative Party rule. More generally, British family policy in the 1980s was driven by a strong neo-liberal ideology—the intention of cutting down public expenditure and concentrating state support on targeted poverty alleviation. At times these aims were in conflict with each other, not consensual within the ruling party or regarded as unpopular and thus as politically damaging. As a result, a clear policy direction was not always evident, best exemplified by developments with child benefit. At other times, the ideological preference for non-statutory policy provision and cost-containment overruled other objectives, such as lowering the burden on business (e.g. the introduction of SMP).

Preferences which influenced policy in the 1980s remained relevant under the Major-led government, albeit pursued within a more pragmatic context, a less ambivalent approach towards child benefit and a slow and moderate alignment of labour market and family policy via wage subsidies, and the reluctant expansion of maternity pay and leave, the latter pushed by the EU. A more explicit expansion of pre-school child care provision was blocked by concerns over public expenditure and the avoidance of financial and legal burdens on employers. After 1997, the Labour government's explicit promotion of child care provision and improved family transfers targeted at low-income parents is evidence of the party's policy reorientation (see Chapter 3) and the adoption of an employment-based and targeted policy regime.

In Germany, family policy during the 1990s did not change direction, but the expansion accelerated. To a considerable extent, this was less due to government plans, and more strongly influenced by the impact of unification and the increasingly prominent role played by the Constitutional Court (see below). The latter also impacted on family policy under the red–green government, thereby accelerating improvements which the government had planned. As discussed, there are several factors that contributed to a change of party policy preferences, initially supplementing the traditional 'family-centred' (Warth 2004) approach and recently complementing and even superseding it with an explicit employment-oriented policy profile.

6.5.2 Institutional factors

Family policy is less institutionally entrenched than pension or labour-market policy. Strategies, boundaries, and preferences, as well as the interface with other policy fields, are more fluid. Within a context of expansion, and despite national differences in traditional emphases on the role of families discussed earlier, it left governments more of an 'open field' and thus choice for designing new types of public intervention and deciding on their scope. This applies to all three areas of institutional influences, that is, formal policymaking structures, programme-specific parameters, and the connection between family policies and national political economies.

As for programme-specific settings, compared with pension policy in particular (Chapter 5) family policy has much less of a 'policy legacy' to guide reform. Instead, the absence of corporate actors in policy adminis-tration, of earmarked contributory funding, or even of benefit indexation makes a government more directly accountable, but at the same time allows a relatively wide scope for manoeuvre. It means that family policy is less influenced by sudden changes in economic or labour-market contexts. For example, instead of pressure exerted by annual deficits in earmarked budgets, less immediate policy influences, such as slow socio-economic and cultural changes in society and labour markets, tended to challenge traditional normative positions (on gender divisions, privacy of the family) and gradually impacted on changes in policy direction. However, under-lining the difficulty of separating out family policy from other policymak-ing domains, an important aspect of German family policy since the 1980s has been its connection with the sustainability of the public pension system.

Almost by definition, because of its less discrete policy domain, pro-gramme-specific characteristics impinge less on policy formation affecting families than unemployed or retired persons, at least in Germany. This does not apply to formal policymaking structures. As discussed, the *Bun-desrat* blocked early legislation for kindergarten guarantees in the late 1980s, apparently making expansionary child care policy difficult because of the *Länder's* prerogative in the area. However, these were not insurmountable structural obstacles but, at times, resembled convenient excuses for not taking on unwelcome tasks. For example, improved financial subsidies would have arguably paved the way for earlier legislation in the field of pre-school child care guarantees. Thus, fiscal concerns more than institu-tional constraints prevented policymaking.

As in the other policy domains, therefore, it is relevant to investigate empirically the influence of veto actors rather than merely stipulating the policy constraining influence of formal veto points (Jochem 2003). In Germany, this applies to the Constitutional Court in particular which, as a formal institutional influence, impacted on family policy in two ways. As discussed, it acted as a policy catalyst by determining the timing and scale of expansion, particularly during the 1990s (see also Meyer 2003*a*). How-ever, at times the Court also determined the pattern and profile of policy, for example, by ruling out the government's decision on child care credits which initially discriminated against working mothers. In short, the Court's rulings had a strong impact on family policy in the 1990s in general, and on the further expansion of family support within the tax system and appreciation of family child care work within the pension system in particular. In turn, the extent to which the Court's dynamic interpretations of the Basic Law (on gender equality, support and protection of families, tax equity, and so on) were influenced by changes in family forms, household patterns, and societal norms over time has yet to be subjected to more in-depth analysis (see Gerlach 2000, 2005).

In the UK there is no equivalent to the German Constitutional Court. To some extent the EU might be seen as an exogenous institutional influence in the sense that some directives have directly impacted on British policy. As a direct consequence of EU legislation in the early 1990s, maternity and parental leave arrangements were improved. At the time this was not the case in Germany because standards had already been above the minimum required. Also in recent years British policymaking in this area has been influenced by EU directives. However, this is attributable more to the congruence between Labour's policy preferences and the EU's agenda, rather than to the growing power of the EU at the expense of the British national government. Of course, this does not imply that the EU's influence has been negligible or that it is unlikely to gain a more direct policymaking role in the future.

Finally, the link between social policy programmes and wider national political economies in which schemes were embedded were found to be an important third set of institutional influences on policymaking in the two previous domains of pensions and unemployment support. This is less the case in family policy, although some instances have been identified, especially in the UK. The creation of FC in the late 1980s, as well as the programme's subsequent expansion, was partly motivated by tackling poverty in the UK, but also by dampening the pay demands of low-paid male workers. The more recent expansion of wage subsidies for low-paid parents illustrates the Labour government's broader strategy of 'making work pay', that is, of publicly subsidizing and thus promoting low-wage economic sectors within a flexible labour market. Other measures, including recent policies introduced in Germany, illustrate a growing significance of making family policies more compatible with economic policy generally and employment integration in particular.

6.5.3 Contextual influences

Not only motives and institutions but also contingent contextual aspects proved somewhat different in family policy than in the two other policy domains. There are examples of relatively sudden contextual changes impacting on policymaking. However, periodic and relatively direct policy pressures, such as those resulting from business cycle effects on unemployment and social insurance reserves, play little role in family policy. Instead, relatively slow processes of socio-economic and cultural change regarding household structures, labour-market patterns, or gender roles have influenced policy debates and normative positions and thus, over time, impacted on family policy. Low fertility rates, rising child poverty, and growing dependency on social transfers are other issues which proved to be policy relevant. There was certainly no simple correlation between the scale of social problems and the political importance attached to them. It has been observed that family policy did not follow functionalist patterns in either country (also Meyer 2003a). However, contextual changes impacted on the careers of some policies. A good example for this might be the guaranteed kindergarten place in Germany, a policy which was rejected by the government in the early 1980s out of 'societal motives' (Kaufmann 2002), that is, preserving the role of the family. Subsequently it was gradually accepted for 'socio-economic' reasons (making family life and employment more compatible), before becoming advocated in recent years with reference to economic considerations (human capital formation) and as a measure which would improve children's welfare (the role of early childhood education for the development of children). This example serves as an illustration of the complexity and dynamism of family policy, with policy legitimacy being fed by multiple motives, the relevance of which can change over time.

More immediate influences, equivalent to 'windows of opportunities' in unemployment policy (Chapter 4), remained rare. In part, this might be because of differences in policy direction. Public scandals, for examples, can be exploited for the purposes of policy retrenchment, or enhance legitimacy for changes in policy direction, but are somewhat less relevant in the context of policy expansion. However, the timing and speed of policy expansion might well be influenced by a sudden and profound change in circumstances. In family policy, this was best exemplified by German unification. As discussed, unification provided a new impetus for the debate on abortion, broke the political deadlock over guaranteed child care for pre-school children, and created more pressure on developing policies which would help reconcile work and family life.

In sum, in family policy too, motives (preferences), means (institutional capacities), and opportunities are important ingredients for understanding policy direction and national policy profiles. However, their relevance was somewhat different in family policy compared with each of the previous two policy fields. Albeit influenced by different traditional norms and policies towards families, motives of policymakers proved more dynamic over time and differences in party policy remained pronounced, whereas the link between family support and national political economies (as in unemployment support), or the role of programme-specific institutional features and policy legacies (as in pension policy), proved relatively less influential. Gradual shifts in policy debates and proposals reflected secular developments in household and employment patterns. Changes in policy contexts can thus be regarded as having exerted a strong albeit less immediate impact than in the other two policy domains.

7

Conclusion

Discussions and findings presented in previous chapters have aimed to underline three aspects of cross-national research into welfare state reform: the need to investigate relatively long time frames, the relevance of systematic empirical and contextualized comparisons, and the usefulness of comparing welfare states at programme level. In addition, in order to provide more robust explanatory accounts of reform paths over time, earlier chapters have emphasized the need for empirical clarity with regard to the 'dependent variable'. Longer time frames facilitate a more adequate assessment of reform outcomes. The change to the indexation of the British BSP is a good case in point. At the time a relatively innocuous and seemingly technical matter, its considerable effect on the generosity of public pensions became more noticeable only years after the rule had been introduced. Equally, some changes in political or economic conditions can have major short- or medium-term effects on reform profiles. German unification initially delayed reform but later provided considerable leverage for actors interested in more than incremental retrenchment. Secular changes in female employment and household patterns influenced government policy preferences in both countries.

A longer time frame also draws attention to changes in contexts which can influence power relations or alter party policy preferences, or improve options for policy reform. As discussed in Chapter 3, economic circumstances have changed considerably since the early 1980s, bringing about a 'role reversal' of the two countries regarding labour market conditions and public finances. Successive electoral failure shaped the programmatic shift of social policy priorities within the Labour Party after 1992. If occurring at the 'right' time, changes in public opinion or public scandals (such as the false job placement figures in Germany in 2002) can open windows of opportunity for reform minded actors. Finally, policy outcomes can influence the direction of further rounds of policymaking. Legislative change during the 1980s had a major impact on the British public and private pension landscape of the 1990s. In turn, this influenced decision-making processes and policy preferences within the Labour Party. This type of feedback mechanism has been aptly described as 'when effect becomes cause' by Pierson (1993).

The analyses presented in Chapters 4–6 are premised on the fact that welfare states as a whole are ill-suited for comparisons of reform dynamics since actors and institutional settings vary across welfare state programmes within a country. At the same time, ostensibly covering the same risks and providing support for the same clientele, the characteristics of social policy domains differ across countries. By implication, the strategy for empirical investigations of welfare state reforms in this book consisted of three types of comparisons. First, diachronic comparisons contrasted programme features of the early 1980s with those applying in recent years. Second, analyses of reform sequences and processes unfolding over time highlighted the roles played by actors as well as respective institutional parameters across diverse programmes within the same country. Third, comparisons of supposedly functionally equivalent policy programmes revealed significant cross-national differences in all three areas, such as the notion of the 'social wage' in unemployment support, the public/private mix of national pension provision, and traditionally different motives for public interventions in family policy.

Adopting a programme-specific perspective also highlights the fact that some instances of contemporary welfare state reform are indeed inadequately interpreted as retrenchment, such as activation policies, partial pension privatization, or child raising credits which were innovative within German (but not British) social insurance. By implication, this suggests two analytical dimensions of reform, retrenchment (or expansion) and restructuring, with the aim of capturing both changes in policy direction as well as policy profiles, as outlined in Chapter 2. Finally, programme-level perspectives underline the relevance of multi-causal explanations. As discussed, policy preferences, institutional variables, but also contingent factors have impinged on the direction of policy change and shaped diverse national reform profiles. However, their respective relevance has varied across programmes. Different institutional characteristics of public schemes (policy legacies) and the respective balance between private and public forms of retirement income have influenced pension reform processes, suggesting that the concept of 'path dependence' is particularly instructive in this policy field. Differences in programme structures and their role within the wider national political economy proved to be most relevant for the understanding of changes in unemployment support policy. The traditionally tight connection between the latter and the German industrial relations system contributed to a selective retrenchment pattern. By contrast, global retrenchment, early and more prescriptive activation policies, have brought about a greater alignment between unemployment support and flexible and deregulated labour markets in the UK. The Labour government's endorsement of the latter influenced reform paths in family policy, too, thereby indicating both the relevance of party competition and also the dynamic nature of party policy preferences. The same applies to German family policy, although additional factors also proved relevant, such as the role played by the Constitutional Court and traditionally more active public intervention in the field guided by the notion of upholding the value of the family as constitutive of society.

No doubt the perspective adopted in this book, that is, programme-level comparisons of policy directions and policy profiles, and the analytical framework involving three interrelated sets of variables—with the institutional dimension consisting of three separate aspects—lends itself to at times complex assessments of reform processes and outcomes. However, more generalized accounts of welfare state change over time can easily be reductionist. Applying social spending as the only indicator of change is liable to miss modifications to the 'architecture' of national welfare state programmes which might become manifest only after some time. 'Social rights' indicators (such changes in entitlement and eligibility rules) are more likely to capture such changes, but need to be robustly conceptualized and operationalized, as well as complemented by 'volume' indicators such as spending or beneficiary rates. Abstracting from programme-specific institutional factors, purely actor-centred explanations of welfare state change tend to be of limited value for comparative research. At the same time, structural–functionalist versions of reform processes unduly disregard the relevance of party competition, changes in power relations, and the dynamics of preference formation. More generally, often neglected or ignored within comparative welfare state research, preceding chapters have aimed to underline the influence of contingent and contextual conditions on the timing, scale, and sometimes also type of reform introduced.

Thus, as the empirical analysis illustrated, the answers to questions posed in the Chapter 1 (regarding convergence and divergence and the relevance of party competition) have to be put in programme-specific contexts and be based on multicausal accounts of reform processes. For example, Chapter 4 has shown that national unemployment support policies have converged to some degree. Looking back over the past two decades, a general trend of policy retrenchment has been observed. Current benefit rates are less generous than they were in the early 1980s, the role of means-tested support has increased, and contributory-based entitlement has waned in both countries. However, differences in the scope and speed of retrenchment were noticeable, as were instances of expansion in Germany but not in the UK. Moreover, the type of retrenchment differed, homogenizing benefit provision in the UK but maintaining the division of unemployment support in Germany, with a shrinking core of a relatively better protected clientele. Moreover, until recently, there had been more restructuring in the UK than in Germany, most evident in the area of activation, which started earlier and became more encompassing. Only very recent legislation in Germany has accelerated the same trend.

As discussed, these variations were influenced by programme-specific parameters, such as funding structures or the relevance of earnings-related versus flat-rate benefits, and also the link between unemployment support and other aspects of national political economies. The notion of a 'social wage' and the 'tight coupling' between unemployment support and German industrial relations influenced the particular policy profile of retrenchment. This also implies that policy restructuring, notably the recent introduction of ALG II, has potentially far-reaching consequences for the German political economy, such as possibly widening the extent of low-wage employment and thus the degree of wage dispersion. As a consequence, the policy path continues to be more stony than in the UK. By contrast, the Labour Party's new found preference for liberal market economy structures allowed it to accept basic policy structures created by conservative governments and to pursue a more coherent policy course, aligning unemployment support more closely with employment structures.

In the field of retirement pensions, there has been little convergence. While Germany has adopted some British-style pension elements, the UK has accelerated its shift away from social insurance based structures. Germany has departed from the erstwhile narrow focus on linking entitlement to monetary contributions by defining 'work' more broadly, thereby providing new or improved credits for care work in the family or child raising. This softening of 'Bismarckian' principles can also be observed with regard to the increase in taxation subsidies for the public pension system. Moreover, the recent part-privatization is a modest step towards a multipillar approach which has been common in the UK for some time. And yet, the gap between the two countries has widened due to British reforms in the 1980s and 1990s which reduced the role of the first-tier public pension, abolished German-type earnings-related elements, and increased the scope of non-statutory pension provision. As a result, retirement income from occupational and private sources has become more important, while the already larger role of means-testing within public support is expected to increase further provided current structures remain unchanged.

As discussed, the concept of path dependency as applied in previous explanations of pension policy (Myles and Pierson 2001) proved instructive for explaining pension reforms in Germany and the UK. At the start of the period under investigation, the two countries represented distinct models of public pensions (Bonoli 2003*a*) and their respective scale vis-à-vis private provision varied considerably. In addition to different government party preferences during the 1980s, programme-specific attributes shaped diverse policy paths in the context of adverse demographic developments and fiscal pressure. During the 1990s, unification and economic recession exacerbated fiscal pressures and triggered the breakdown of the hitherto broad partisan and corporatist pension consensus in Germany. Since then policymaking has lacked a clear direction but developed in a stop-go fashion, punctuated by short-term retrenchment efforts to balance annual budget deficits and medium-term structural reform. Both major parties became caught between fiscal pressure and the principal willingness to engage in structural reform on the one hand, and strategic electoral considerations on the other. In the UK, the Labour government's policy priorities have not differed considerably from its predecessor regarding the role of the basic pension or the concentration of public support on pensioners with insufficient occupational or private retirement income. However, despite a clear set of priorities, a potential worsening of pensioner poverty and the impact of mass means-testing on savings shows that policymaking has failed to create a sustainable public pension structure.

Within family policy, recent changes in particular indicate cross-national convergence rather than divergence. Both countries have been described as traditional 'male breadwinner countries' (Lewis 1992), and yet the ways in which the division of gender roles in paid and unpaid work were publicly reinforced differed. A stronger regulatory and financial intervention in favour of safeguarding the societal role of traditional families in West Germany contrasted with the more hands-off and poverty-oriented state support in the UK. During the 1980s and early 1990s the latter approach became even more pronounced, accompanied by modest improvements for working parents. In contrast, by improving social entitlements for mothers who stayed at home to look after their children, German family policy had already begun to expand in the 1980s. However, conservative governments in both countries were only hesitantly embarking on reconciliation policies and rejected, in part for different reasons (see Chapter 6), an expansion of publicly provided or subsidized child care.

But centre–left parties, too, only began to alter their position explicitly during the 1990s, gradually shifting the emphasis to employment-oriented family policies. Cross-national differences do however remain. For example, employment orientation started earlier and was developed more decisively under the Labour government, linking it to aims of tackling child poverty and social exclusion. By contrast, policies promoting the reconciliation of family life with female employment were explicitly adopted only recently by the red–green German government, alongside an accelerated expansion of family-centred social policy provision. Changing employment patterns and household formations, the impact of unification in Germany, and the growth of labour market inactivity and benefit dependency amongst lone parents in the UK, respectively, were some of the contributing factors.

Comparatively less discrete and expanding, rather than contracting, family support policies were less shaped by institutional factors than pension or unemployment policy. However, as discussed in Chapter 4, the German Constitutional Court played a prominent role. Because of low levels of provision, UK policymaking was influenced by EU directives with respect to maternity leave in the early 1990s. More recently, the EU influenced policymaking regarding parental and paternity leave in both countries (Falkner and Treib 2003; Dienel 2004). However, on the whole, Chapters 4–6 have shown that Europeanization has not been a major influence on welfare state reform. The same applies to globalization, as another force often argued to drive social policy change. There are two main reasons for this. The first one is simply the period of observation. European political integration and economic internationalization became more relevant reference points in public policy only during the 1990s. Economic internationalization became perceived as a threat to Germany as a location for investment only from the mid-1990s. The transfer of German capital to foreign and financial world markets has been considerable but also a relatively recent phenomenon (Ganßmann 2003*a*). The process towards the completion of the European single market accelerated after the Maastricht Treaty in 1992 and the EU's potential for influencing domestic reforms of core social policy domains improved with the adoption of the Open Method of Coordination (OMC). However, involving a system of guidelines, annual reports, benchmarking, recommendations, and peer review processes, this form of governance developed only in the wake of the Amsterdam Treaty from 1997.

A second reason is the analytical interest which guided preceding analyses, that is, investigating reform processes in particular welfare state programmes over time. There is no doubt that economic internationalization, and its perception on the part of relevant actors (Bleses and Seeleib-Kaiser 2004), has limited the menu of policy options regarded (or portayed) as politically desirable or feasible. However, other influences too added fiscal squeeze, such as demographic changes or post-industrial employment trends, economic recessions, and the impact of German unification. Empirical chapters discussed how these factors as a whole influenced political processes, contributing to the erosion of the cross-party pension consensus in Germany, for example. However, conceding that globalization impacted on the conditions within which collective actors make decisions, goes only so far. Dynamic policy preferences, institutional characteristics, and contingent factors play a large part in explaining variations in both the direction and the profile of welfare reform processes unfolding over time.

As for the impact of Europeanization, two different aspects might be distinguished. The broad economic framework within which member states operate has certainly altered since EMU was introduced and the conditions attached to its membership came into being. However, similar to other pressures listed above, it is analytically difficult to trace specific policy decisions to the structural impact of EMU. Within the three policy domains, there have been few examples of a more direct European impact on domestic reforms, at times in a 'negative' way. For example, in the mid 1980s the SPD proposed a non-contributory minimum pension to be introduced within the German pension system. The fact that respective benefit rights would no longer be based on individually earned entitlements and become exportable to other EU countries provided ammunition for those who rejected the idea (Schmähl 2004). Beyond this the EU has not influenced domestic pension reforms in either country during the period of investigation here. However, there are signs that this might change in the medium term.

As for unemployment support policy, the EES has been embedded within the OMC since 1997, but its profile has remained rather weak in British and German public and political reform debates (Ardy and Umbach 2004). The UK has remained reluctant to accept the EES's emphasis on social partnership or training (Büchs 2004). However, on the whole its supply-side agenda makes the EES more congruent with the British than the German political landscape—and is therefore more useful as an instrument for justifying policy change for German governments. Indeed, as discussed, a few years ago the German government made selective use of EU guidelines in order to add legitimacy for the implementation of more prescriptive activation policies (Ostheim and Zohlnhöfer 2004). This seems to have been exceptional, however. Even within the debate on the structurally most far-reaching reform of unemployment support which came into effect in 2005 (see Appendix A), the government failed to capitalize on the potential political leverage provided by the EES. In short, within the past two decades the EU has only had a selective, indirect, and weak influence on national policy reforms in pensions or unemployment protection (Büchs and Friedrich 2005).

By contrast, particularly recent family support policy was more directly affected by the EU. However, this applies only to those components which are linked to the sphere of paid work, such as parental leave and return to work guarantees. Just as European regulations in the field of gender equality can be seen as a 'by-product' of the creation of equal economic conditions in the 1970s, 'parenthood' seems to have become an economic issue in the 1990s for similar reasons. In other words, EU regulations regarding minimum parental leave arrangements are driven by the aim of shaping similar economic conditions across member states (Dienel 2004). This connects family policy with the EES, and the objective of increasing female employment in particular.

In sum, during the 1980s and 1990s there has been little evidence of Europeanization influencing domestic welfare state reform processes in the UK or Germany. Potentially this might change in the medium term due to the adoption of new European governance structures such as the OMC, and a growing alignment between national policy agendas and policy preferences at EU level. Most member countries have begun to create more multi-tiered pension arrangements and the EU has emphasized the aims of 'adequacy' and 'fiscal sustainability' of public schemes within the newly created OMC in the field of pension policy (Nullmeier 2003; Schmähl 2003c). Already congruent with British policies and recent policy change in Germany, the supply-side oriented EES can be expected to play an increasingly relevant role in domestic unemployment support policies. Finally, its employment focus has made the EU a strong ally for advancing a particular 'productivist' notion of family policy which is already dominant in the UK and has been gaining ground also in Germany.

Appendices

Appendix A
Major legislative changes in unemployment support policy, 1980–2004 (Germany)

Year	Measure
1982 SPD and FDP government	• Increase of minimum contributory period (*Arbeitslosengeld*, ALG) from 6 to 12 months. • Exclusion of additional regular earnings (e.g. overtime pay, holiday money) for calculating ALG and *Arbeitslosenhilfe* (ALH) • Increase of benefit suspension period (from 4 to 8 weeks). • Tighter suitability conditions. • Increase of contribution period (from 70 to 150 days) for ALH.
1983 CDU/ CSU and FDP government	• Lower pension insurance contributions for recipients of ALG and ALH (based on level of unemployment support rather than previous gross earnings). • Stricter differentiation of duration of entitlement (ALG) in accordance with contribution record (ratio between former and latter changed from 1:2 to 1:3).
1984	• For recipients without children: decrease in ALG rate (−5 points to 63%) and ALH rate (−2 points to 56%).
1985	• For employees older than 49: increase in ALG entitlement (maximum 18 months; dependent on contribution record).
1986	• For employees older than 43: increase in ALG entitlement (maximum 24 months for those older than 53; dependent on individual contribution record). • Decrease in contribution rate (to 4%).
1987	• For employees older than 42: increase in ALG entitlement (maximum 32 months for those older than 53; dependent on individual contribution record). • Ratio between entitlement and contribution period reverts back to 1:2

(Continues)

Year	Measure
	• Contribution rate up to 4.3%.
1989	• Receipt of ALG/ALH during periods of sickness will count towards max. entitlement period.
1991	• Contribution rate increased to 6.8% (later 6.5%).
1994	• Decrease of ALG and ALH rates by 1 point (−3 points for those without children). • Entitlement to ALH limited to 1 year for those without prior receipt of ALG (indefinite before).
1996	• Decrease of benefit rate for ALH claimants by 3 points per year of claim. • Stricter work test imposed on ALH recipients (from 1998 also for ALG claimants). Employment office can request temporary participation in low paid seasonal jobs.
1998	• New suitability criteria (relevance of previous qualification dropped; suitability of job offers defined merely in monetary terms; after six months any job is deemed suitable with net earnings higher than benefit). Proof of active job search required; benefit for claimants with redundancy money curtailed, stricter benefit sanctions introduced. • Longer ALG duration restricted to over 45-year-olds (previously over 42); maximum of 32 months only for 57-year-olds (previously 54). • Participation in approved training no longer recognized as equivalent to insured employment (i.e. no longer establishes benefit eligibility).
1998	• Eligibility to ALG requires actual contribution period ('equivalent' periods no longer acceptable). • Introduction of 'reintegration contract' stating responsibilities of job seeker and employment office. • Calculation of ALG level based on earnings during a longer period of employment (from 6 to 12 months before unemployment). • Improved entitlement for claimants who accept less well paid job (and then become unemployed within three years) and for those who lose part-time job.
2000 SPD and Green government	• Reversal of legislation from 1982: additional regular earnings (e.g. overtime pay, holiday money) once again included for calculating benefits (but not for ALH). • ALH (for those without prior receipt of ALG) abolished.

Year	Measure
2002	• Stronger activation focus as part of *Job-Aqtiv* legislation (job placement, profiling, job search vouchers, temporary work options, job rotation, training). • Automatic annual deduction (by 3%) of ALH suspended by up to two years if claimant takes part in relevant training course.
2003	• Tighter suitability criteria for younger unemployed; new job placement and counselling instruments; new options for business start-ups; temporary work placements. • In disputed cases, proof for acceptability of job offers transferred from employment office to job seeker.
2004/5	• ALG duration fixed at standard maximum 12 months (from 2006). • Extended entitlement to ALG curtailed from maximum 32 months to maximum 18 months and restricted to claimants aged 55 or older. • Reference period for required contributions shortened from 3 to 2 years before unemployment. • Participation in subsidized employment no longer acceptable as benefit qualification period. • Wage subsidy and pension credits introduced for unemployed above the age of 50 who accept lower paid job. • Introduction of ALG II (2005): ALH and social assistance (for employable claimants) merged into a single scheme (abolition of earnings-related benefits, lower rates for majority of previous ALH claimants). Tighter job suitability criteria for ALG II recipients (any legal work and wage level suitable even if below collective wage agreement or standard wages paid in locality) (from 2005). Young unemployed (under 25) only eligible for ALG II if they accept offers of training, suitable employment, or other job integration measure.

Source: Information derived from Steffen (2003); Reissert, 2005; www.bundesregierung.de.

Appendix B:
Major reforms in unemployment support policy, 1980–2003 (UK)

Year	Measure
1981 Conservative government	• Higher supplementary benefit for unemployed over 60 who chose to retire early. • Decision to make registration at Job Centre becomes voluntary for the unemployed.
1982	• Abolition of Earnings Related Supplement (ERS) to Unemployment Benefit (UB). • UB made subject to income taxation.
1984	• Abolition of child additions (except for claimants over pension age) in UB.
1985	• Exemption from disqualification provisions in UB for those accepting voluntary retirement.
1986	• Increase in maximum disqualification period in UB from 6 to 13 weeks. • Abolition of 1/4 and 1/2 UB rates for those with incomplete contribution records. • With introduction of Income Support, introduction of lower benefit rates for those under 25 (18–25). • Introduction of 'Restart' programme.
1988	• Tighter contribution requirement for UB. • Increase in disqualification period for UB from 13 to 26 weeks. • Exclusion of 16- and 17-year-olds from Income Support, except in special circumstances.
1989	• Introduction of 'Actively Seeking Work' test. • After 13 weeks of unemployment, conditions defining suitable work under Clause 9 (i.e. limitation of possibility to place limitations on 'suitable' or 'acceptable' work) abandoned.

Year	Measure
	• Introduction of 'Employment Trials', allowing people previously unemployed for more than 26 weeks to leave a new job after 4 to 12 weeks without loss of acquired benefit rights.
1990	• Introduction of Employment Service 'back to work plans'. • Reductions in Income Support made possible for unemployed claimants failing to attend Restart interviews.
1992	• Further tightening of disqualification conditions in UB. • Reduction of UB for recipients of occupational pensions over 55.
1996	• Replacement of UB and Income Support for the unemployed with Jobseekers Allowance (JSA), consisting of 'contributory JSA' and 'income-related JSA'. • Reduction of maximum duration of contributory benefit from 1 year to 6 months. • Reduction of benefit rate for claimants aged 18 to 24 (by 20%). • Removal of all remaining dependent additions which existed under UB. • Reduction of contributory benefit rights for unemployed recipients of occupational pensions of all ages. • Introduction of requirement to sign a jobseeker's agreement. • Introduction of obligatory jobseekers' directions, where directions can be given on appearance, etc. to job seekers. • Introduction of a 'permitted period' of 13 weeks for restriction of job search. • Introduction of 'project work' pilots for long-term unemployed, based on 13 weeks compulsory supervised job-search followed by 13 weeks work experience.
1998 Labour government	• Introduction of New Deal programmes for young people under 25 (NDYP) and long-term unemployed (NDLTU) (out of work for 2 years). • New Deal for Lone Parents (NDLP) (voluntary job-related interview).
1999	• New Deal for Partners (NDP); joint claim required for those with partners claiming JSA for over 6 months (for those without children and under 25).
2001	• NDLTU revamped as ND25+ (compulsory after 18 months unemployment within past 21 months).

(Continues)

Year	Measure
	• Introduction of New Deal for disabled people NDDP (voluntary).
2002	• NDLP: introduction of compulsory job-related interview and interview with personal adviser every six months.
	• NDP mandatory for JSA claimants under 45 years of age (if no children).
2004	• Entry into NDYP and ND25+ after 3 months of unemployment (piloted in certain areas).

Source: Journal of Social Policy, 'Social Policy Review'; CPAG 'Welfare Rights Bulletin' (1980–2003).

Appendix C:
Major legislative changes in public pensions,
1980–2004 (Germany)

Year	Measure
1980–2 SPD and FDP	• Tighter condition regarding entitlement to early-retirement pension because of unemployment. • Reduction of pension contributions paid by the federal government on behalf of those engaged in military service. • Gradual introduction of individual health insurance contributions to be paid by pensioners.
1983 CDU/CSU and FPD	• Delayed pension indexation. • Further reduction of pension contributions paid by the federal government on behalf of those engaged in military service. • Reduction of pension contributions paid on behalf of those in receipt of unemployment benefits.
1984	• Reduced waiting period for old-age pension (65 years) from 15 to 5 years. • Tighter eligibility rule for disability pension. • Indexation of pension payments according to development of average wage in previous year (previously 3 years). • Full pension contributions levied on sick pay.
1986	• Increase in contribution paid by pensioners for health insurance (to 4.5% of the pension payment).
1987	• Increase in contribution paid by pensioners for health insurance (to 5.9 % of the pension payment).
1989 (into force in 1992)	• Pension indexation in line with average net wages of previous year (previously gross wages).

(*Continues*)

Year	Measure
	• To start in 2001: gradual increase of retirement age for women and of retirement due to unemployment (to 65 by 2011) and for persons with long contribution records (from 63 to 65; by 2006). Early retirement still possible, but with reduction of 0.3% per month (maximum 3 years = 10.8%).
	• Periods of receipt of unemployment or sickness benefit counted as compulsory contribution periods (after 1995). Pension contributions by unemployment insurance system based on 80% of previous wage (before: level of benefit) from 1995.
	• Crediting for time spent in education or higher education (including polytechnics) reduced to 7 years (previously 13); credits on basis of maximum 75% of average wage of all insured persons (previously 100%).
	• Crediting for first few years in insured employment limited to 4 years (previously 5) at reduced level (90% of average earnings of all insured; previously 100%).
1996	• Retirement pension due to unemployment also possible after part-time work of at least 2 years after 56th birthday (under certain conditions such as employers supplementing wages).
	• Higher age limit (63) for early retirement (for reasons of unemployment or part-time work) to be phased in earlier (between 1997 and 1999). Early retirement at 60 still possible but linked to pension deductions of 0.3% per month.
1997	• Earlier start and faster increase of raising minimum retirement age for women, long-term contributors, and retirement for reasons of unemployment. Age limit for early retirement (for reasons of unemployment or part-time work) to be increased in monthly steps for long-term contributors from 63 to 65 (completed by the end of 2001); for women (and unemployed) from 60 to 65 (completed by the end of 2004); earlier retirement still possible but linked to pension reductions of 3.6% per annum.
	• Students with more than 2 months work per year, and more than insignificant earnings per year, to make pension contributions.
	• Crediting for time spent in education and higher education (including polytechnics) reduced to 3 years (previously 7). Time spent on education before 17 years of age disregarded.
	• Crediting for first few years in insured employment limited to 3 years (previously 4) at reduced level (based on 75% of average earnings of all insured; previously 90%).

Year	Measure
	• Spells of unemployment or sickness (without benefit receipt) discounted from qualifying years can only be used to 'fill gaps' (no negative implications on other periods of non-contributions) and for waiting periods (e.g. 35 years as entitlement to early retirement at 63).
1998 (planned to come into force in 1999)	• Retirement pension for people with long insurance record possible from 63 (previously 64) but deductions of up to 10.8% (previously 7.2%) apply. • Introduction of 'demographic factor' (average life expectancy of cohort built into pension calculation).
1998 SPD–Green government	• Abolition of the above 'demographic factor'. • Some groups of self-employed to make pension contributions. • For employees with insignificant earnings (previously outside social insurance), employers made to pay pension contributions; employees can 'top-up' employer contributions (voluntary).
1999	• Reduction of calculation basis for pension contribution for claimants of unemployment assistance (from 80% of previous wage to benefit level). • Increased tax subsidies to pension insurance based on revenue from environmental tax reform (eco-tax). • Pension payments in 2000 and 2001 to be indexed in line with inflation rather than wages.
2001	• Pension indexation in line with prices reverts to wage indexation. • Cutback in survivor pension.
2002	• Introduction of 'Riester Rente'. • Tax incentive for setting aside eventually (2008) up to 4% of gross wage for voluntary contributions to regulated non-statutory private or occupational pensions (higher incentives for those with children). • As a consequence: increase in contribution rates limited to 22% by 2030 and reduction of formal standard level of public pension to 67%. • New pension indexation formula (linked to changes in gross wages, pension contribution rate, and contribution rate for private 'Riester' pension plan). • Cuts in survivors' pension.

(Continues)

Year	Measure
2003	• Introduction of needs-oriented basic pension payment (no mutual duties to pay maintenance for parents and children if annual income remains below €100,000 per annum; administered at local authority level).
2004	• No increase in pension benefit (zero indexation). • Pensioners to make full contribution (1.7% of pension) to long-term care insurance (previously half). • Occupational pensioners to make full contribution to health and long-term care insurance (previously half). To come into force in 2005: • Abolition of any education period as credits for pension entitlement (except for vocational education which is credited with a maximum of 3 years) (from 2009). • Crediting for first five years of contributions (up to age 25) abolished, unless in conjunction with vocational training (from 2009). • Age of eligibility for early retirement (for reasons of unemployment or part-time work) to be raised from 60 to 63 (phased in between 2006 and 2008). • Introduction of demographic component in pension indexation ('sustainability factor'), taking account of the changing ratio between pensioners and contributors (expected reduction of pension increase between 0.1 and 0.2% per annum until 2010). • Abolition of taxation on pension contributions and introduction of taxation on retirement income (including pension) planned for 2006.

Source: Information derived from Steffen (2003).
Changes in the field of pension crediting for child-raising listed in Appendix E.

Appendix D:
Major legislative changes in public pensions, 1980–2003 (UK)

Year	Measure
1981	• Increases in basic state pension (BSP) linked to prices, rather than the greater of prices or wages as previously. • Standard rate of BSP to rise by 11%, making good earlier shortfall. • Earnings rule relaxed for recipients of state pension.
1983	• Pension rights of unemployed men aged between 60 and 65 to be secured even if they take low paid work.
1986 (into force in 1988)	• Reference years for state earnings related pension (SERPS) to be changed to full lifetime's earnings, rather than best 20 years as previously. • Years without earnings due to incapacity not included in calculation of lifetime earnings. • SERPS to be based on 20% of average earnings (between upper and lower earnings limit) rather than 25% (phased in from 2000–1). • Level of 'inherited' SERPS for surviving spouse reduced from 100% to 50% (after 2000). • Contracting out of SERPS becomes permissible for defined contribution schemes and personal pension plans. Additional rebates for setting up new personal pension plans (restricted until 1993). Membership in company pension schemes becomes voluntary.
1989	• People of pension age will no longer have to retire to receive public pension.If they continue to work beyond state pension age, their pension will be paid in full (previously reduced for earnings over £75 per week).

(Continues)

Year	Measure
1995	• Pensions Act 1995 increases pension age of women from 60 to 65 (phased in between 2010 and 2020). • Stricter regulation of personal pension provision. New regulatory body for occupational pensions. • SERPS benefit calculation method changed (in 1999) with effect of reducing pension entitlements.
1997 Labour government	• Introduction of Winter Fuel Payments for those over 60 and receiving Income Support and income-related JSA, or over pension age (60 for women and 65 for men) for other prescribed benefit.
1999	• Income Support rates for pensioners increased by 3 times the normal amount. • Income Support for those over 60 renamed 'Minimum Income Guarantee' (MIG). • MIG to be raised in line with earnings. • Introduction of 'stakeholder pensions'.
2000	• Increase in the MIG for pensioners, so that lower limit is £6000 and upper limit £12000 from April 2001. • Winter fuel payments increased to £150. • Those earning between the Lower Earning Limit and up to £9500 will be treated as though they had earned £9500 ('shadow lower earnings limit'). • Carers and disabled people be treated as having earned £9500 (even if earned nothing) for years of caring (under specified conditions).
2001 (into force in 2003)	• MIG to be replaced with Pension Credit (PC). PC has 2 parts: the guaranteed income top-up (GITU) which is the same as MIG; and the Savings Credit, which pays an allowance of 60% for any type of income between the BSP and MIG (GITU) threshold. Where total income is above the GITU level, the credit is reduced at 40% of 'excess' income. • Upper savings limit removed.
2002	• Introduction of State Second Pension (S2P) to replace SERPS. • New formula benefiting low income earners without non-statutory pensions (credits top up low earnings and for carers of children under 6 years of age or relatives with a disability; better accrual rates for low earnings). Flat-rate from 2007. • Amount of SERPS which can be inherited by a surviving partner reduced from 100% to 50%.

Source: Journal of Social Policy, 'Social Policy Review'; CPAG 'Welfare Rights Bulletin' (1980–2003); Pensions Policy Institute (2003).

Appendix E
Major reforms in family policy, 1979–2003 (Germany)

Year	Measure
1979 SPD and FDP	• Maternity Leave: Introduction of maternity leave (4 months) and maternity leave allowance (*Mutterschaftsurlaubsgeld*) as contributory wage replacement benefit (restricted to mothers with previous employment covered by social insurance).
1982	• Child benefit cut for second and third child (by 16% and 8% respectively).
1983 CDU/CSU and FDP	• Child benefit: Income test for second and subsequent children introduced (over and above guaranteed minimum for each child which is lower than previous rates). • Child tax allowance: Introduction of child tax allowance (DM432 annually per child) and thus reintroduction of 'dual system' (child benefit as well as child tax allowances). Child benefit supplement (DM48 per month) introduced for parents who cannot make use of tax allowance due to low (or no) earned income. • Maternity leave allowance: Cut in maximum amount (from DM750 to DM510 per month).
1985	• Annual tax allowances for child care costs increased to DM4000 (first child) plus DM2000 (for each subsequent child) per annum for single parents.
1986	• Maternity Leave: Replacement of 'maternity leave' (and allowance) with 'child raising leave' (*Erziehungsurlaub*) and 'child raising benefit' (*Erziehungsgeld*) which becomes applicable also to mothers (or fathers) not in paid employment. Maximal leave entitlement

---

(*Continues*)

Year	Measure
	gradually extended from initially 10 months (1986) to 12 (1988). Return to employment (but not to previous job) is guaranteed. Child raising benefit (DM600 per month) becomes universal and flat-rate for 6 months; income-tested thereafter (with cut-off point at about half average income; cut-off point raised per child). Part-time work of up to 19 hours permitted during leave.
	• Child raising pension credits: Introduction of one year pension credit per child (the so-called 'baby year', equivalent to 75% of average wages of all insured employees), restricted to women not in insured employment during the 'baby year'. Introduction of crediting for child raising (for children up to 10 years of age) and caring for relatives—positive impact on waiting periods (eligibility for a public pension) and filling gaps in 'insurance biography'.
	• Child tax allowance: Increased from DM432 to DM2484 per annum.
1989	• Child raising leave and maximum benefit period increased to 15 months.
1990	• Child raising leave and benefit period increased to 18 months. • Child tax allowance raised to DM3024. • Child benefit: Increase of means-tested element for second child (maximum level up from DM100 to DM130 per month), no change to minimum guarantee (DM50).
1992	• Child tax allowance raised to DM4104 per annum. • Child raising pension credits increased from 1 to 3 years per child (decided in 1989). • Child benefit level increased (guaranteed minimum up from DM50 to DM70 for first child). • Leave entitlement (for sick children) raised to 10 days (previously 5) per year and per child. • Tax allowance for care work provided within families introduced. • Entitlement to a place in kindergarten for all 3-year-olds (from 1997; fully implemented in 1999).
1993	• Child raising leave extended to 3 years and child raising benefit period to 2 years.

Year	Measure
	• Improved benefits for lone parents where absent parent does not make (sufficient) contributions.
1994	• Child raising benefit: Introduction of income testing also for first 6 months for better earners (excluding those with about twice average income).
1996	• Abolition of 'dual system' (child benefit plus child tax allowance). Parents to claim one or the other, whichever is more beneficial (for 80–95% of all parents child benefit is more beneficial). • Child benefit rates raised to DM200 per month (first and second child), DM300 (third), DM350 (each further child). Income testing abolished. • Child tax allowance rates raised to DM6264 (1996; both parents together), DM6912 (1997).
1997	• Child raising pension credit gradually increased from 75% to 100% of average wage (fully implemented in 2000) for current pensioners as well as new entrants. Credits becoming additional to actual contributions made (i.e. not discriminating against working parents).
1999 SPD–Green 2000	• Child benefit increased by DM30 for first and second child (DM250 per month). • Child benefit increased for first and second child to DM270 per month (for children up to age 16). • Child tax allowances: Introduction of child care tax allowance (*Betreuungsfreibetrag*) (DM3024 per annum) which raises the total child tax allowance for each child (up to 16 years of age) to almost DM10,000 per annum.
2001	• Child raising leave and child raising benefit: Cut-off point for receipt of child raising benefit (*Erziehungsgeld*) for the first 6 months increased (to about 250% of average earnings for couple; 200% of average earnings for single parent). Thresholds also raised for subsequent months (to about 80% of average net earnings; previously 50% since 1986). Higher levels for parents with more children (threshold increased by 10% for those with 1 child, by 25% for those with 4 children).

(*Continues*)

Year	Measure
	Choice of receipt of child raising benefit: either 24 months (at maximum €307 per month) or 12 months (at maximum €460 per month).
	The term 'child raising leave' replaced with 'parental time' (*Elternzeit*) with both parents permitted to take parental leave simultaneously and both allowed to work up to 30 hours per week (previously 19). Provided employers agree, up to 12 months of the maximum of 3 years parental time can be used flexibly until the child reaches the age of 8. In companies with at least 15 employees, parents have the right to switch to part-time work during parental leave.
	The receipt of unemployment insurance no longer excludes concurrent receipt of child raising benefit.
	• Tax reform: one outcome of several changes (tax and benefits) is an improvement in parents' average income by the year 2005 (by €2,400 compared with 1998).
2002	• Child benefit: Increase for first, second, and third child (to €154 per child).
	• Child Tax Allowance: Merging of formerly separate child care tax allowance (*Betreuungsfreibetrag*) and educational tax allowance (*Ausbildungsfreibetrag*), contributing to a total child tax allowance of €5,808 per year/child (higher for children in education over 18 who live away from home). Additional child care tax allowance for working parents (for children under the age of 14).
	• Child raising pension credits: Further crediting for child raising for the time when children are aged between 4 and 10 (low contributions due to part-time work or low earnings are upgraded by 50%—up to a maximum which is equivalent to average earnings; also credits for eligibility for early retirement options). Parents not in work and with 2 or more children also receive credits (valued at a level equal to contributions based on a third of average earnings). Cut in survivor pension (from 60% to 55%) more than compensated by child-related credits for widows or widowers.

Source: Bundesregierung (2002); BMFSFJ (2002); Bäcker et al. (2000); Gerlach (1996); Bleses and Rose (1998).

Appendix F:
Major reforms in family policy, 1980–2003 (UK)

Year	Measure
1980	• Child benefit: cut in real value. • Child dependency additions to national insurance benefits, changes in up-rating method results in decline in real value in this and subsequent years. • Family wage subsidies: increase in Family Income Supplement (FIS) above inflation.
1981	• Child benefit: Cut in real value.
1982	• Maternity Grant: instead of contributory condition, eligibility for one-off (£25) • Maternity Grant becomes based on residency only (26 weeks in the year preceding the claim). Any payment of 18-week Maternity Allowance unaffected by this. • Child benefit increases in real value.
1983	• Child benefit increases in real level.
1984	• Child benefit suffers gradual decrease of its level (until 1991) due to insufficient up-rating. • Contributory Maternity Allowance fixed at £27.25 (paid for 18 weeks), with a reduced rate for those with partial contribution records
1985	• Maternity Grant: increases in value (from £25 to £75) but becomes means-tested.
1986	• Maternity Pay: Previous Maternity Allowance and Maternity Pay amalgamated in Statutory Maternity Pay (SMP), administered by employers

(Continues)

Year	Measure
	and reimbursed by the state. SMP payable in two rates: a higher rate of 90% of earnings for 6 weeks, followed by a flat-rate lower benefit, the latter cut back due to making it subject to taxation and removing additions for family dependants. • FIS to be replaced with Family Credit (FC). Switch from gross to net income as the basis for assessment, higher capital savings; minimum qualifying hours dropped to 24 per week; alignment of child additions and threshold above which benefit starts to be withdrawn under FC with those applicable in Income Support. Child care costs to be deducted (from part-time earnings) in the calculation of benefit.
1987–9	• Child benefit frozen.
1991	• £1 per week increase in child benefit and benefit to be indexed in line with inflation.
1992	• FC: definition of full-time work reduced from 24 to 16 hours/week.
1993	• Maternity pay/leave: Following an EU Directive, introduction of 14 weeks minimum maternity leave to all pregnant employees, regardless of length of service or hours of work.
1994	• SMP entitlement for higher rate after 6 months continuous employment (2 years previously). Value of lower rate (12 weeks flat-rate) increased by £3.70 (to correspond to sickness pay). • Maternity Allowance (paid to women who do not qualify for SMP, but earn more than Lower Earnings Limit) increased to same level as lower rate of SMP (increase of £7.95). • Maximum period for which women must have been employed to be eligible for Maternity Pay increased from 52 weeks to 66 weeks. • FC: introduction of child care disregard (for child care costs of up to £40 per week)—known as child care allowance.
1996	• FC: child care disregard increased to £60 per week. Claimants of FC working 30 hours per week or more receive £10 bonus.
1997 Labour	• FC: child care disregard increased to £100 per week (for 2 or more children).
1998	• FC (for a child under 11) increased by £2.50 per week.
1999	• Child Benefit: increase of 26% (20% above inflation). FC replaced by Working Families Tax Credit (WFTC), earnings threshold increased (from £79 to 90), the 'taper' (withdrawal

Year	Measure
	rate) lowered (from 70% to 55%), increased credits for children and child care credit (covering 70% of weekly child care costs up to £100 (later £135) for one child; £150 (£200) for two or more children.
	• Maternity/parental leave: unpaid parental leave introduced (13 weeks per parent and child up to age of 5); 2 weeks unpaid parental leave for fathers.
2000	• Maternity leave increases to minimum of 18 weeks ordinary maternity leave.
	• Maternity Allowance widens coverage to women earning below Lower Earnings Limit but conditional on employment or self-employment for at least 26 weeks (in last 66 weeks) and an earnings test (average earnings of at least £30 a week).
	• Sure Start Maternity Grants replace Maternity Grant. Grant of £200, rising to £300 in Autumn 2000 (conditional on consultation with a health visitor/professional).
2001	• Children's Tax Credits (CTC) replace married couple's allowance and additional pension allowance, taking away a tax break for couples without children and doubling tax break for parents with at least 1 child under 16. CTC includes a tax withdrawal rate of 6.7% for higher rate (40%) tax payers.
	• Basic rates of credit in WFTC increased by £5 per week.
	• Child care limits in tax credits increased to £135 and £200 per week.
	• Children's personal allowances in IS and JSA increased by £1.50 from October 2001.
	• Sure Start Maternity Grant (means-tested) to increase to £500 from April 2002
2002	• Child personal allowances in IS and JSA (income related) increased by £3.50.
	• SMP (lower rate) and Maternity Allowance increase from £60.20 to £75.
2003	• Working Tax Credit to replace WFTC—children no longer basis of eligibility.
	• Introduction of Child Tax Credit amalgamating previous children's tax credit and child credits in WFTC, plus child additions to means-tested and non-means-tested benefits, into a combined single payment.

(*Continues*)

Year	Measure
	• Creation of child trust funds ('baby bonds'). • SMP (lower rate) and Maternity Allowance increases from £75 to £100. • Statutory Maternity Pay and Maternity Allowance period extended from 18 to 26 weeks. • Introduction of Statutory Paternity Pay (SPP)—same work conditions as SMP (26 weeks employment; earning above Lower Earnings Limit), payable to fathers at lower rate of SMP for 2 weeks.

Source: Journal of Social Policy, 'Social Policy Review'; CPAG 'Welfare Rights Bulletin' (1980–2003); Daly and Clavero (2002); Gauthier (1996); Leicester and Shaw (2003).

REFERENCES

ABRAMOVICI, G. (2003). Social Protection: Cash Family Benefits in Europe, Eurostat, Statistics in Focus, Population and Social Conditions, Theme 3, 19, Luxembourg: Eurostat.

ADAM, S. and BREWER, M. (2004). Supporting Families: The Financial Costs and Benefits of Children since 1975, Joseph Rowntree Foundation. Bristol: Policy Press.

ADLER, M. (1988). 'Lending a Deaf Ear: The Government's Response to Consultation on the Reform of Social Security', in R. Davidson and P. White (eds.), *Information and Government: Studies in the Dynamics of Policy-Making*. Edinburgh: Edinburgh University Press.

—— (2004). 'Combining Welfare-to-Work Measures with Tax Credits: A New Hybrid Approach to Social Security in the United Kingdom', *International Social Security Review*, 57(2): 87–106.

ALBER, J. (1989). *Der Sozialstaat in der Bundesrepublik 1950–1983*. Frankfurt: Campus.

—— (1996). Selectivity, Universalism, and the Politics of Welfare Retrenchment in Germany and the United States, University of Konstanz, mimeo.

—— (1998). 'Der deutsche Sozialstaat im Licht international vergleichender Daten', *Leviathan*, 26(2): 199–227.

—— (2003). 'Recent Developments in the German Welfare State: Basic Continuity or a Paradigm Shift?', in N. Gilbert and R. A. van Voorhis (eds.), Changing patterns of social protection, *International Social Security Series*, vol. 9, New Brunswick: Transaction 9–73.

ALCOCK, P., BEATTY, C., FOTHERGILL, S., MACMILLAN, R., and YEANDLE, S. (2003). *Work to Welfare: How Men Become Detached from the Labour Market*. Cambridge: Cambridge University Press.

ALLMENDINGER, J. and LEIBFRIED, S. (2003). 'Bildungsarmut', *Aus Politik und Zeitgeschichte*, B21–2: 12–18.

AMENTA, E. (2003). 'What We Know about the Development of Social Policy: Comparative and Historical Research in Comparative and Historical Perspective', in J. Mahoney and D. Rueschemeyer (eds.), *Comparative Historical Analysis in the Social Sciences*. Cambridge: Cambridge University Press, pp. 91–130.

ANDERSON, K. and MEYER, T. (2003). 'Social Democracy, Unions, and Pension Politics in Germany and Sweden', *Journal of Public Policy*, 23(1): 23–54.

ANTHES, J. (1984). *Die sogenannte 'Neue Soziale Frage' im Licht der Haushaltsoperationen 1983 und 1984.* Cologne: Hans Böckler Stiftung.

ARDY, B. and UMBACH, G. (2004). Employment Policies in Germany and the United Kingdom: The Impact of Europeanisation, AGF report. London: Anglo-German Foundation.

ARMINGEON, K. and BONOLI, G. (eds.), (2005). *The Politics of the Post-industrial Welfare State.* (forthcoming) Routledge.

ATKINSON, A. (1989). *Poverty and Social Security.* New York: Harvester Wheatsheaf.

ATTANASIO, O., BANKS, J., BLUNDELL, R., CHOTE, R., and EMMERSON, C. (2004). 'Pensions, Pensioners and Pension Policy: Financial Security in UK Retirement Savings?', ESRC Seminar Series, Mapping the Public Policy Landscape, ESRC and IFS.

AUTH, D. (2002). *Wandel im Schneckentempo: Arbeitszeitpolitik und Geschlechtergleichheit im deutschen Wohlfahrtsstaat.* Opladen: Leske und Budrich.

BÄCKER, G. BISPINK, R., HOFEMANN, K., and NAEGELE, G. (2000). *Sozialpolitik und Soziale Lage in Deutschland.* Wiesbaden: Westdeutscher Verlag.

—— —— —— —— (2003). *Sozialpolitik und Soziale Lage in Deutschland.* Various tables and data available at www.sozialpolitik-aktuell.de.

—— (2003). 'Child and Family Poverty in Germany', in P. Krause, G. Bäcker, and W. Hanesch (eds.), *Combating Poverty in Europe: the German Welfare Regime in Practice.* Aldershot: Ashgate, pp. 289–304.

BAHLE, T. (1995). *Familienpolitik in Westeuropa.* Frankfurt: Campus.

BANKS, J. and EMMERSON, C. (2000). 'Public and Private Pension Spending: Principles, Practise and the Need for Reform', *Fiscal Studies.* 21(1): 1–63.

BARBIER, J.-C. (1990). 'Comparing Family Policies in Europe: Methodological Problems', *International Social Security Review*, 3: 326–41.

BARR, N. (1998). *The Economics of the Welfare State*, 3rd edn. Oxford: Oxford University Press.

BBF (Bundesministerium für Bildung und Forschung) (2004). 'Größtes deutsches Schulprogramm bundesweit ein Erfolg', press release, 11 May 2004. Berlin: BBF.

BDA (Bundesvereinigung der Deutschen Arbeitgeberverbände) (1994). *Sozialstaat vor dem Umbau.* Cologne: BDA.

BECKER, U. (1989). 'Frauenerwerbstätigkeit—eine vergleichende Bestandsaufnahme', *Aus Politik und Zeitgeschichte*, B 28–9: 22–33.

BECKMANN, P. (2003). 'EU—Beschäftigungsquote. Auch richtige Zahlen können in die Irre führen', *IAB Kurzbericht*, 11. Nürnberg: Bundesanstalt für Arbeit.

BENNETT, F. (1987). 'What Future for Social Security?', in A. Walker and C. Walker (eds.), *The Growing Divide.* London: Child Poverty Action Group, pp. 120–8.

—— (1992). *Poverty and the Parties: An Analysis of the Main Parties' Manifestos.* London: CPAG.

—— (2004). 'Developments in Social Security', in N. Ellison, L. Bauld, and M. Powell (eds.), *Social Policy Review*, 16. Bristol: Policy Press, pp. 45–60.

BERTHOUD, R. (1987). 'New Means Tests for Old: the Fowler Plan for Social Security', in M. Brenton and C. Ungerson (eds.), *Year Book of Social Policy 1986–7*. London: Longman.

BIRD, K. and GOTTSCHALL, K. (2004). 'Erosion of the Male-Breadwinner Model? Female Labor-Market Participation and Family-Leave Policies in Germany', in H. Gottfried and L. Reese (eds.), *Equity in the Workplace: Gendering Workplace Policy Analysis*. Lanham, MD: Lexington Books, pp. 281–304.

BLAKE, D. (2003). 'Contracting Out of the State Pension System: The British Experience of Carrots and Sticks', in M. Rein and W. Schmähl (eds.), *Rethinking the Welfare State*. Aldershot: Edward Elgar, pp. 19–55.

BLANCKE, S. and SCHMID, J. (2003). 'Bilanz der Bundesregierung im Bereich der Arbeitsmarktpolitik 1998–2002: Ansätze zu einer doppelten Wende', in C. Egle, T. Ostheim, and R. Zohlnhöfer (eds.), *Das rot-grüne Projekt: Eine Bilanz der Regierung Schröder 1998–2002*. Wiesbaden: Westdeutscher Verlag.

BLESES, P. (2003*a*). 'Wenig Neues in der Familienpolitik', in A. Gohr and M. Seeleib-Kaiser (eds.), *Sozial- und Wirtschafispolitik unter Rot-Grün*. Wiesbaden: Westdeutscher Verlag, pp. 189–209.

—— (2003*b*). 'Der Umbau geht weiter—Lohnarbeit und Familie in der rot-grünen Sozialpolitik', *Zeitschrift für Sozialreform*, 49(4): 557–83.

—— and ROSE, E. (1998). *Deutungswandel der Sozialpolitik*. Frankfurt: Campus.

—— and SEELEIB-KAISER, M. (2004). *The Dual Transformation of the German Welfare State*. London: Palgrave.

BMAS (2001). *Materialband zum Sozialbudget 2001*. Berlin: BMAS.

BMFSFJ (Bundesministerium für Familie, Senioren, Frauen und Jugend) (1998). *Zehnter Kinder- und Jugendbericht*. Berlin: Deutscher Bundestag.

—— (2002). *Chronologie der familienpolitischen Entscheidungen seit Beginn der Legislaturperiode*. Berlin: BMFSFJ (www.bmfsfj.de).

—— (2003). *Die Familie im Spiegel der amtlichen Statistik.* (revised edition). Berlin: BMFSFJ.

—— (2004). Bericht zur Elternzeit 16 June 2004. Berlin: BMFSFJ.

BMGS (Bundesministerium für Gesundheit und Soziale Sicherung) (2003). *Statistisches Taschenbuch 2003: Arbeits- und Sozialstatistik*. Bonn: BMGS.

—— (2004). *Statistisches Taschenbuch 2004*. Bonn: BMGS.

BOLDERSON, H. (1982). 'Ambiguity and Obscurity in Policy-Making for Social Security', *Policy and Politics*, 10: 298–30.

BÖNKER, F. and WOLLMANN, H. (1999). 'Sozialstaatlichkeit im Übergang: Entwicklungslinien der bundesdeutschen Sozialpolitik in den Neunzigerjahren', in R. Czada and H. Wollmann (eds.), Von der Bonner zur Berliner Republik, *Leviathan* (special issue 19). Wiesbaden: Westdeutscher Verlag, pp. 514–38.

BÖNKER, F. and WOLLMANN, H. (2001). 'Stumbling Towards Reform: The German Welfare State in the 1990s', in P. Taylor-Gooby (ed.), *Welfare States under Pressure*. London: Sage, pp. 75–99.

BONOLI, G. (2000). *The Politics of Pension Reform: Institutions and Policy Change in Western Europe*. Cambridge: Cambridge University Press.

BONOLI, G. (2003*a*). 'Two worlds of pension reform in Western Europe', *Comparative Politics*, July: 399–416.

—— (2003*b*). 'Social policy through labor markets. Understanding national differences in the provision of economic security to wage earners', *Comparative Political Studies*, 36(9): 1007–30.

—— (2005). The Politics of the New Social Policies. Providing Coverage against New Social Risks in Mature Welfare States, Policy and Politics (forthcoming)

BÖRSCH-SUPAN, A., REIL-HELD, A., and SCHNABEL, R. (2002). 'Pension Provision in Germany', in R. Disney and P. Johnson (eds.), *Pension Systems and Retirement Incomes Across OECD Countries*. Aldershot: Edward Elgar, pp. 160–96.

BRADSHAW, J., DITCH, J., HOLMES, H., and WHITEFORD, P. (1993). 'Support For Children: A Comparison of Arrangements in Fifteen Countries', *DSS Research Series*. London: HMSO.

—— and FINCH, N. (2002). 'A Comparison of Child Benefit Packages in 22 Countries', *DWP Research Report* No. 174. Leeds: DWP.

BREWER, M. and GREGG, P. (2003). 'Eradicating Child Poverty in Britain: Welfare Reform and Children since 1997', in R. Walker and M. Wiseman (eds.), *The Welfare We Want? The British challenge for American reform*. Bristol: Policy Press, pp. 81–115.

——, CLARK, T., and WAKEFIELD, M. (2002). 'Five Years of Social Security Reform in the UK', *Working Paper* 02/12. London: Institute for Fiscal Studies.

——, GOODMAN, A., MYCK, M., SHAW, J., and SHEPHARD, A. (2004). 'Poverty and Inequality in Britain: 2004', *Commentary 96*. London: Institute for Fiscal Studies.

BRÜDERL, J. (2004). 'Die Pluraliinerung patnerschaftlicher Lebensformen in Westdeutschland und Europa, *Aus Politik und Zeitgeschichte*, B19: 3–18.

BÜCHEL, F. and SPIEß, C.K. (2002). 'Form der Kinderbetreuung und Arbeitsmarktverhalten von Müttern in West und Ostdeutschland', *Schriftenreihe des BMFSFJ*, vol. 220. Stuttgart: Kohlhammer.

BÜCHS, M. (2004). 'Asymmetries of policy learning? The European Employment Strategy and its role in labour market policy reform in Germany and the UK', paper presented at ESPAnet Annual Conference, University of Oxford, 10 September.

—— and FRIEDRICH, D. (2005). 'Surface Integration—the National Action Plan for Employment and Social-Policy Co-ordination', in J. Zeitlin, P. Pochet, and E. Magnusson (eds.), *The Open Method of Co-ordination in Action*. Brussels: Peter Lang pp. 249–85.

BUHR, P. (2003). 'Wege aus der Armut durch Wege in eine neue Armutspolitik?', in A. Gohr and M. and Seeleib-Kaiser (eds.), *Sozial- und Wirtschaftspolitik unter Rot-Grün*. Wiesbaden: Westdeutscher Verlag, pp. 147–66.

BUNDESREGIERRUNG (2001). 'Lebenslagen in Deutschland—Erster Armuts- und Reichtumsbericht', *Bundestags-Drucksache* 14/5990. Berlin: Deutscher Bundestag.

—— (2002). *Sozialbericht 2001*. Berlin Bundesregierrung.

—— (2004). *Jahreswirtschaftsbericht 2004*. Berlin: Bundesministerium der Finanzen.

—— (2004). Schwerpunkt Agenda 2010—Familienpolitik; in *e.balance. Das Magazin für Arbeit und soziales*, 20, 06/2004 (www.bundesregierung.de).

BUSCH, A. and MANOW, P. (2001). 'The SPD and the Neue Mitte in Germany', in S. White (ed.), *New Labour: The progressive future?* Houndmills: Palgrave, pp. 175–89.

BUTTERWEGE, C. (ed.) (2000). *Kinderarmut in Deutschland*, 2nd edition. Frankfurt: Campus.

BYRNE, D. (2003). 'The new politics of the welfare state', *Work, Employment and Society*, 17(1): 197–205.

CARD, D., BLUNDELL, R., and FREEMAN, R. B. (eds.) (2004). *Seeking a Premiere Economy: the economic effects of British economic reforms, 1980–2000*. Chicago: Chicago University Press.

CARMEL, E. and PAPADOPOULOS, T. (2003). 'The new governance of social security in Britain', in J. Millar (ed.), *Understanding social security*. Bristol: Policy Press, pp. 31–52.

CASEY, B and WOOD, S. (1994). 'Great Britain: Firm Policy, State Policy and the Employment of Older Workers', in F. Naschold and B. de Vroom (eds.), *Regulating Employment and Welfare: Company and National Policies of Labour Force Participation at the End of Worklife in Industrial Countries*. Berlin: de Gruyter.

Castles, F. G. (1998). *Comparative Public Policy: Patterns of Post-War Transformation* Cheltenham: Edward Elgar.

—— (2002). 'Developing Measures of Welfare State Change and Reform', *European Journal of Political Research*, 41(5): 613–41.

—— (2004). *The Future of the Welfare State: Crisis Myths and Crisis Realities*. Oxford: Oxford University Press.

CEBULLA, A., HEINELT, H., and WALKER, R. (2000). *Unemployment and the Insurance Compensation Principle in Britain and Germany*. London: Anglo-German Foundation.

—— and REYES DE-BEAMAN, S. (2004). 'Employers' Pension Provision Survey', *DWP Research Report no. 207*. Leeds: Corporate Document Services.

CLARK, T., and EMMERSON, C. (2003). 'Privatising Provision and Attacking Poverty? The Direction of UK Pension Policy Under New Labour', *Journal of Pension Economics and Finance*, 2(1): 67–89.

CLASEN, J. (1992). 'Unemployment Insurance in Two Countries: A Comparative Analysis of Great Britain and West Germany in the 1980s', *Journal of European Social Policy*, 2(4): 279–300.

—— (1994). *Paying the Jobless: A Comparison of Unemployment Benefit Policies in Great Britain and Germany*. Aldershot: Avebury.

CLASEN, J. (1997). 'Social Insurance in Germany—Dismantling or Reconstruction?', in J. Clasen (ed.), *Social Insurance in Europe*. Bristol: Policy Press, pp. 60–83.

—— (2000). 'Motives, Means and Opportunities: Reforming Unemployment Compensation in the 1990s', *West European Politics*, 23(2): 89–112.

—— (2001). 'Social Insurance and the Contributory Principle: A Paradox in Contemporary British Social Policy', *Social Policy and Administration*, 35(6): 641–57.

CLASEN, J. (2002). 'Unemployment and Unemployment Policy in Britain: Increasing Employability and Re-defining Citizenship', in J. Goul-Andersen, J. Clasen, K. Halversen, and W. van Oorschot (eds.), *Europe's new state of welfare: Unemployment, employment policies and citizenship*. Bristol: Policy Press, pp. 59–74.

—— GOULD, A., and VINCENT, J. (1998). *Voices within and without: Responses to long-term unemployment in Germany, Sweden and Britain*. Bristol: Policy Press.

—— KVIST, J., and VAN OORSCHOT, W. (2001). 'On Condition of Work: Increasing Work Requirements in Unemployment Compensation Schemes', in M. Kautto, J. Fritzell, B. Hvinden, J. Kvist, and H. Uusitalo (eds.), *Nordic Welfare States in the European Context*. London: Routledge, pp. 198–231.

—— and VAN OORSCHOT, W. (2002). 'Changing Principles in European Social Security', *European Journal of Social Security*, 4(2): 89–115.

—— and CLEGG, D. (2004). 'Does the Third Way Work? The Left and Labour Market Policy Reform in Britain, France and Germany', in J. Lewis and R. Surender (eds.), *Comparative Perspectives on the Third Way*. Oxford: Oxford University Press, pp. 89–109.

—— DAVIDSON, J., GANSSMANN, H., and MAUER, A. (2004). *Non-employment and the Welfare State: The UK and Germany Compared*. London: Anglo-German Foundation (www.agf.org.uk/pubs/pdfs/1401web.pdf).

CLEGG and CLASEN, J. (2003). 'Conceptualising and Measuring the Changing Principles of Social Security in Europe: Reflections from a Five-country Study'. Paper presented at ESPAnet conference on Changing European Societies—the role of social policy, Copenhagen, 15 November.

COX, R. H. (1998). 'From Safety Net to Trampoline, Labor Market Activation in the Netherlands and Denmark', *Governance*, 11(4): 397–414.

—— (2001). 'The Social Construction of an Imperative: Why Welfare Reform Has Happened in Denmark and the Netherlands but not in Germany', *World Politics*, 53, April, 463–98.

CROUCH, C. (1999). 'Employment, Industrial Relations and Social Policy: New Life in an Old Connection', *Social Policy and Administration*, 33(4): 437–57.

—— (2003). 'Institutions within which Real Actors Innovate', in R. Mayntz and W. Streek (eds.), *Die Reformierbarkeit der Demokratie. Innovationen und Blockaden*. Frankfurt: Campus, pp. 71–98.

—— and FARRELL, H. (2002). 'Breaking the Path of Institutional Development? Alternatives to the New Determinism', discussion paper 02/5, Max-Planck-Institut für Gesellschaftsforschung, Cologne.

CZADA, R. (1998). 'Vereinigungskrise und Standortdebatte', *Leviathan*, 26(1): 24–59.

DALY, M. (2000). *The Gender Division of Welfare: The impact of the British and German Welfare States*. Cambridge: Cambridge University Press.

—— and CLAVERO, S. (2002). *Contemporary Family Policy: A Comparative Review of Ireland, France, Germany, Sweden and the UK*. Dublin: Institute of Public Administration.

Daycare Trust (2004). 'Two Steps Forward, One Step Back', 27 February. London: Daycare Trust.

DEACON, A. (1997). ' "Welfare to Work". Options and Issues', in E. Brunsdon, H. Dean, and R. Woods (eds.), *Social Policy Review*, 9. London: Social Policy Association, 34–49.

—— (2000). 'Learning from the US? The influence of American ideas upon "new labour" thinking on welfare reform', *Policy and Politics*, 28(1): 5–18.

DEAKIN, N. (1994). *The Politics of Welfare*. London: Methuen.

—— and PARRY, R. (1993). 'Does the treasury have a social policy?', in R. Page and N. Deakin (eds.), *The Costs of Welfare*. Aldershot: Avebury.

—— and PARRY, R. (2000). *The Treasury and Social Policy*. Basingstoke: Macmillan.

DEAKIN, S. and WILKINSON, F. (1989). *Labour Law, Social Security and Economic Inequality*. London: Institute of Employment Rights.

DHSS (Department of Health and Social Security) (1980). *A Fresh Look at Maternity Benefits*. London: HMSO.

DIENEL, C. (2002). *Familienpolitik: Eine praxisorientierte Gesamtdarstellung der Handlungsfelder und Probleme*. Weinheim and Munich: Juventa.

DIENEL, C. (2004). 'Eltern, Kinder und Erwerbsarbeit: Die EU als familienpolitischer Akteur', in S. Leitner, I. Ostner, and M. Schratzenstaller (eds.), *Wohlfahrtsstaat und Geschlechterverhältnis im Umbruch, Jahrbuch für Europa- und Nordamerika-Studien*. Wiesbaden: VS Verlag für Sozialwissenschaften, pp. 285–307.

DILNOT, A. and WEBB, S. (1988). 'The 1988 Social Security Reforms', *Fiscal Studies*, 9(3): 26–53.

DINGELDEY, I. (2001a). 'European tax systems and their impact on family employment patterns', *Journal of Social Policy*, 30(4): 653–72.

—— (2001b). 'Familienbesteuerung in Deutschland', in A. Truger (ed.), *Rot-grüne Steuerreform in Deutschland*. Marburg: Metropolis-Verlag, pp. 201–27.

—— (2002). 'Das deutsche System der Ehegattenbesteuerung im europäischen Vergleich', *WSI Mitteilungen*, 3: 154–60.

DISNEY, R., EMMERSON, C. and SMITH, S. (2004). 'Pension reform and economic performance in the 1980s and 1990s', in D. Card, R. Blundell, and R., B. Freeman (eds.), *Seeking a Premiere Economy: The Economic Effects of British Economic Reforms 1980–2000*. Chicago: University of Chicago Press.

—— and WAKEFIELD, M. (2001). 'Pension Reform and Saving in Britain', *Oxford Review of Economic Policy*, 17(1): 70–94.

DONNISON, D. (1982). *The Politics of Poverty*. Oxford: Martin Robertson.

DSS (Department of Social Security) (1985). *Reform of Social Security*, Vol. 1, Cmnd 9517, HMSO.

—— (1994). *Households Below Average Income: A Statistical Analysis 1979–1991/ 92*. London: HMSO.

—— (1998a). *New ambitions for our country: a new contract for welfare*, Cm 3805, London: Stationery Office.

DONNISON, D. (1998*b*). *A new contract for welfare: partnerships in pensions*, Cm 4179, London: Stationery Office.

—— (1999). Memorandum submitted by the Department of Social Security (CP24); Select Committee on Social Security, Minutes of Evidence, House of Commons, 13 December.

—— (2000). Households below average income: a statistical analysis 1994/5 to 1998/9. Leeds: Corporate Document Services.

DTI (Department of Trade and Industry) (1998). *Fairness at Work*. London: HMSO.

DWP (Department for Work and Pensions) (2003). The Pensioners' Incomes Series 2001/2, Pensions Analysts Division, DWP.

—— (2004*a*). Benefit Expenditure Tables, updated 9/1/2004.

—— (2004*b*). The abstract of statistics: 2003 edn., IAD Information Centre, London.

—— (2004*c*). The Pensioners' Incomes Series 2002/3, Pensions Analysts Division, DWP.

EBBINGHAUS, B. (2001). 'When Labour and Capital Collude', in B. Ebbinghaus and P. Manow (eds.), *Comparing Welfare Capitalism: Social Policy and Political Economy in Europe, Japan and the USA*. London: Routledge, pp. 76–101.

—— and MANOW, P. (eds.) (2001). *Comparing Welfare Capitalism*. London: Routledge.

EGLE, C. and HENKES, C. (2003). 'Später Sieg der Modernisierer über Traditionalisten? Die Programmdebatte in der SPD', in C. Egle, T. Ostheim, and R. Zohlnhöfer (eds.), *Das rot-grüne Projekt*. Wiesbaden: Westdeutscher Verlag, pp. 67–92.

—— OSTHEIM, T., and R. ZOHLNHÖFER (eds.) (2003). *Das rot-grüne Projekt*. Wiesbaden: Westdeutscher Verlag.

EMMERSON, C. (2002). 'Pension Reform in the United Kingdom. Increasing the Role of Private Provision?', working paper WP 402. London: Institute for Fiscal Studies.

—— and JOHNSON, P. (2002). 'Pension provision in the United Kingdom', in R. Disney and P. Johnson (eds.). *Pension Systems and Retirement Incomes Across OECD Countries*. Aldershot: Edward Elgar, pp. 296–333.

—— and WAKEFILED, M. (2003). 'Achieving simplicity, security and choice in retirement? An assessment of the government's proposed pension reforms', Briefing note 36. London: Institute for Fiscal Studies.

ENGELBRECH, G. (2002). 'Transferzahlungen an Familien—demographische Entwicklung und Chancengleichheit', *WSI Mitteilungen*, 3: 139–46.

—— and JUNGKUNST, M. (2001). 'Erwerbsbeteiligung von Frauen', *IAB Kurzbericht* no. 7, Nürnberg: Bundesanstalt für Arbeit.

ESPING-ANDERSEN, G. (1990). *The Three Worlds of Welfare Capitalism*. Cambridge: Polity Press.

—— (ed.) (1996*a*). *Welfare States in Transition. National Adaptations in Global Economies*. London: Sage.

—— (1996*b*). 'Welfare States without Work: The Impasse of Labour Shedding and Familism in Continental European Social Policy', in G. Esping-Andersen (ed.), *Welfare States in Transition. National Adaptations in Global Economies*. London: Sage, pp. 66–87.

ESTEVEZ-ABE, M., IVERSEN, T., and SOSKICE, D. (2001). 'Social protection and the formation of skills: a reinterpretation of the welfare state', in P. A. Hall and D. Soskice (eds.), *Varieties of Capitalism. The Institutional Foundations of Comparative Advantage*. Oxford: Oxford University Press, pp. 145–83.

Euromonitor (2004). Global Market Information Database (www.euromonitor .com/GMID).

European Commission (1997). *Employment in Europe 1997*. Luxembourg: Statistical Office of the European Communities.

—— (1998). *Social protection in Europe 1997*. DG Employment and Social Affairs, Luxembourg: Office for Official Publications of the European Communities.

Eurostat (2004). *Living conditions in Europe*. Statistical Pocketbook, 2003 edition. Luxembourg: Office for Official Publications of the European Communities.

EVANS, M. (1998). 'Social Security: dismantling the pyramids?', in H. Glennerster and J. Hills (eds.), *The State of Welfare*. Oxford: Oxford University Press, pp. 257–303.

FAGGIO, G. and NICKEL, S. (2003). 'The Rise of Inactivity Among Adult Men', in R. Dickens, P. Gregg, and J. Wadsworth (eds.), *The Labour Market under New Labour*. Houndmills: Palgrave, pp. 40–52.

FALKNER, G. and TREIB, O. (2003). 'The EU and New Social Risks: The Case of the Parental Leave Directive'. Paper presented at the conference 'The Politics of New Social Risks', University of Bern, Lugano, 25–7 September.

FERRERA, M. and RHODES, M. (eds.) (2000). *Recasting European Welfare States*. London: Frank Cass.

FIELD, F. (2002). 'Making Welfare Work: The Politics of Reform', *Scottish Journal of Political Economy*, 49(1): 91–103.

FINN, D. (2000). 'From Full Employment to Employability: A New Deal for Britain's Unemployed?', *International Journal of Manpower*, 21(5): 384–99.

FIORETOS, O. (2001). 'The Domestic Sources of Multilateral Preferences: Varieties of Capitalism in the European Community', in P.A. Hall and D. Soskice (eds.), *Varieties of Capitalism. The Institutional Foundations of Comparative Advantage*. Oxford: Oxford University Press, pp. 213–44.

FLORA, P. (ed.) (1986). *Growth to Limits*, 3 vols. Berlin: de Gruyter.

—— and HEIDENHEIMER, A. (eds.) (1981). *The Development of Welfare States in Europe and America*. London: Transaction.

FORD, R. and MILLAR, J. (1998). *Private Lives and Public Responses: Lone Parenthood and Future Policy in the UK*. London: Policy Studies Institute.

FÖRSTER, M. (2000). 'Trends and Driving Factors in Income Distribution and Poverty in the OECD Area, Labour Market and Social Policy'. Occasional Paper 42, OECD: Paris.

FRANCO, A. and WINQVIST, K. (2002). Women and Men Reconciling Work and Family Life, Eurostat: Statistics in Focus, Population and Social Conditions, Theme 3, 9–2002. Luxembourg: Eurostat.

FRASER, D. (2002). *The Evolution of the British Welfare State*. London: Macmillan.

FREEMAN, R. (2000). *The Politics of Health in Europe*. Manchester: Manchester University Press.

FRICK, J. and GRABKA, M.M. (2003). 'Imputed Rent and Income Inequality: A Decomposition Analysis for Great Britain, West Germany and the US', *Review of Income and Wealth*, 49(9): 513–37.

FUCHS, J. and WEBER, B. (2004). 'Frauen in Ostdeutschland. Erwerbsbeteiligung weiterhin hoch', *IAB Kurzbericht* 4. Nürnberg: Bundesanstalt für Arbeit.

FUNK, L. (2004). 'Mehr Beschäftigung für Ältere—Lehren aus dem Ausland', *IW-Positionen* Nr. 8. Cologne: Institut der deutschen Wirtschaft.

GALLIE, D. and PAUGAM, S. (2000). 'Replacement rates in Europe', in D. Gallie and S. Paugam (eds.), *Welfare Regimes and the Experience of Unemployment in Europe*. Oxford: Oxford University Press.

GAMBLE, A. (1988). *The Free Economy and the Strong State. The Politics of Thatcherism*, London: Macmillan.

GANßMANN, H. (1991). 'Pull-down Effects, Unemployment and Interests in the Welfare State', in Adler, M., Bell, C., Clasen, J., and Sinfield, A. (eds.), *The Sociology of Social Security*. Edinburgh: Edinburgh University Press, pp. 128–44.

—— (2000). 'Labor Market Flexibility, Social Protection and Unemployment', *European Societies*, 2(3): 243–69.

—— (2003*a*). Globalization and the German labour market, in DPAP-Analyse, 23, November. Berlin: Forschungsinstitut der deutschen Gesellschaft für Auswärtige Politik, pp.1–15.

—— (2003*b*). 'Labor Force Mobilization and the Feasibility of Comprehensive Welfare States', paper presented at ESPAnet annual conference, Danish National Institute for Social Research, Copenhagen.

—— (2004). '30 Jahre Massenarbeitslosigkeit in der Bundesrepublik—ein deutscher Sonderweg', *Leviathan*, 32(2): 164–84.

GAUTHIER, A. (1996). *The State and the Family*. Oxford: Clarendon.

GEISSLER, H. (1976). *Die neue soziale Frage*. Freiburg: Herde.

GERLACH, I. (1996). *Familie und staatliches Handeln. Ideologie und politische Praxis in Deutschland*. Frankfurt: Campus.

—— (2000). 'Politikgestaltung durch das Bundesverfassungsgericht am Beispiel der Familienpolitik', *Aus Politik und Zeitgeschichte*, B3–4, 21–31.

—— (2004). *Familienpolitik*. Wiesbaden: VS Verlag für Sozialwissenschaften.

—— (2005). Familien- und Altenpolitik, in Bundesministerium für Gesundheit und Soziale Sicherung und Bundsarchiv (eds.), *Geschichte der Sozialpolitik in Deutschland seit 1945*, vol. 11 (1989–94). Baden-Baden: Nomos Verlag.

GILBERT, N. and VAN VOORHIS, R. (eds.) (2001). *Activating the Unemployed: A Comparative Appraisal of Work-Oriented Policies*. New Brunswick: Transaction.

GLENNERSTER, H. (2003). *Understanding the Finance of Welfare*. Bristol: Policy Press.

GOHR, A. (2001). 'Eine Sozialstaatspartei in der Opposition: Die Sozialpolitik der SPD in den 80er Jahren', in M.G. Schmidt (ed.), *Wohlfahrtsstaatliche Politik. Institutionen politischer Prozess und Leistungsprofil*. Opladen: Leske und Budrich, pp. 262–93.

—— (2003). 'Auf dem "dritten Weg" in den "aktivierenden Sozialstaat"? Programmatische Ziele von Rot-Grün', in A. Gohr and M. Seeleib-Kaiser (eds.), *Sozial- und Wirtschaftspolitik unter Rot-Grün*. Wiesbaden: Westdeutscher Verlag, pp. 37–60.

—— and SEELEIB-KAISER, M. (eds.) (2003). *Sozial- und Wirtschaftspolitik unter Rot-Grün*. Wiesbaden: Westdeutscher Verlag.

GOLDING, P. and MIDDLETON, S. (1982). *Images of Welfare. Press and Public Attitudes to Poverty*. Oxford: Martin Robertson.

GÖTTING, U., HAUG, K., and HINRICHS, K. (1994). 'The Long Road to Long-term Care Insurance in Germany', *Journal of Public Policy*, 14: 285–309.

GOUL ANDERSEN, J. (2002). 'Change without Challenge? Welfare States, Social Construction of Challenge and Dynamics of Path Dependency', in J. Clasen (ed.), *What Future for Social Security? Debates and Reforms in National and Cross-national Perspective*. Bristol: Policy Press, pp. 121–38.

GRAHAM, A. (1997). 'The UK 1979–95: Myths, and Realities of Conservative Capitalism', in C. Crouch and W. Streek (eds.), *Political Economy of Modern Capitalism*. London: Sage, pp. 117–32.

GREEN-PEDERSEN, C. (2002). *The Politics of Justification. Party Competition and Welfare State Retrenchment in Denmark and the Netherlands from 1982 to 1998*. Amsterdam: Amsterdam University Press.

—— (2004). 'The Dependent Variable Problem within the Study of Welfare-State Retrenchment: Defining the problem and looking for solutions', *Journal of Comparative Policy Analysis*, Vol. 6, No. 1: 3–14.

GREGG, P. and HARKNESS, S. (2003). 'Welfare Reform and the Employment of Lone Parents', in R. Dickens, P. Gregg, and J. Wadsworth (eds.), *The Labour Market under New Labour*. Houndmills: Palgrave, pp. 86–97.

—— and WADSWORTH, J. (2003). 'Workless Households and the Recovery', in R. Dickens, P. Gregg, and J. Wadsworth (eds.), *The Labour Market under New Labour*. Houndmills: Palgrave, pp. 32–9.

GREGG, P., HARKNESS, S., GUTIÉRREZ-DOMÈNECH, M., and WALDFOGEL, J. (2003). 'The employment of married mothers in Great Britain: 1974–2000', discussion paper, Centre for Economic Performance, London.

HALL, P. A. (2002). 'The comparative political economy of the "third way" ', in O. Schmidtke (ed.), *The Third Way Transformation of Social Democracy*. Aldershot: Ashgate, pp. 31–58.

—— and SOSKICE, D. (eds.) (2001*a*). *Varieties of Capitalism. The Institutional Foundations of Comparative Advantage*. Oxford: Oxford University Press.

—— and SOSKICE, D. (2001*b*). 'An Introduction to Varieties of Capitalism', in P. A. Hall and D. Soskice (eds.), *Varieties of Capitalism. The Institutional Foundations of Comparative Advantage*. Oxford: Oxford University Press, pp. 1–68.

HALL, P. A. and TAYLOR, R. (1996). 'Political Science and the Three New Institutionalisms', *Political Studies*, 44(5): 936–57.

Hank, K, Kreyenfeld, M, and Spieß, C. K. (2004). 'Kinderbetreuung und Fertilität in Deutschland: Zeitschrift für Soziologie, 33, 3, 228–44.

HANTRAIS, L. (1994). 'Comparing Family Policy in Britain, France and Germany', *Journal of Social Policy*, 23(2): 135–60

HARRIS, B. (2003). *Origins of the British Welfare State*. London: Macmillan.

HASSEL, A. and WILLIAMSON, H. (2004). 'The Evolution of the German model: How to Judge Reforms in Europe's Largest Economy', discussion paper, London: Anglo-German Foundation for the Study of Industrial Society.

HAY, C. (1999). *The Political Economy of New Labour*. Manchester: Manchester University Press.

HEINELT, H. (2003). 'Abeitsmarktpolitik—von "versorgenden" wohlfahrtsstaatlichen Interventionen zur "aktivierenden" Beschäftigungsförderung', in A. Gohr and M. Seeleib-Kaiser (eds.), *Sozial- und Witschaftspolitik unter Rot-Grün*. Wiesbaden: Westdeutscher Verlag, pp. 125–46.

—— und WECK, M. (1998). *Arbeitsmarktpolitik. Vom Vereinigungskonsens zur Standortdebatte*. Opladen: Leske und Budrich.

HEMERIJCK, A., MANOW, P., and VAN KERSBERGEN, K. (2000). 'Welfare without work? Divergent Experiences of Reform in Germany and the Netherlands', in S. Kuhnle (ed.), *Survival of the European Welfare State*. London: Routledge, pp. 106–27.

HERDEN, R.-E. and Münch, R. (2000). 'Die Bevölkerungsentwicklung in Deutschland 1950–1998/99', mimeo, Institut für Sozialwissenschaften, Lehrbereich Bevölkerungswissenschft, Humboldt University, Berlin.

HEWITT, M. (1999). 'New Labour and Social Security', in M. Powell (ed.), *New Labour, New Welfare State?* Bristol: Policy Press, pp. 149–70.

—— (2002). 'New Labour and the Redefinition of Social Security', in M. Powell (ed.), *Evaluating New Labour's Welfare Reforms*. Bristol: Policy Press, pp. 189–209.

HILLS, J. (1998). 'Thatcherism, New Labour and the Welfare State', CASE paper no. 13. London: CASE, London School of Economics.

—— (2001). 'Poverty and Social Security: What Rights? Whose responsibilities?', in A. Park et al. (eds.), *British Social Attitudes. The 18th Report*. London: Sage.

—— (2002). 'Following or Leading Public Opinion? Social Security Policy and Public Attitudes Since 1997', *Fiscal Studies*, 23(4): 539–58.

—— (2003). 'Inclusion or Insurance? National Insurance and the Future of the Contributory Principle', *Centre for Analysis of Social Exclusion*, CASE paper 68. London: London School of Economics.

—— (2004). *Inequality and the State*. Oxford: Oxford University Press.

HINRICHS, K. (1997). 'Social Insurances and the Culture of Solidarity: The Moral Infrastructure of Interpersonal Redistributions—with special reference to the German Health Care System', ZeS working paper 3/97. University of Bremen: Centre for Social Policy Research.

—— (1998). 'Reforming the Public Pension Scheme in Germany: The End of the Traditional Consensus?', ZeS working paper 10, University of Bremen, Centre for Social Policy Research.

—— (2000). 'Auf dem Weg zur Alterssicherungspolitik—Reformperspektiven in der gesetzlichen Rentenversicherung', in S. Leibfried und U. Wagschal (eds.), *Der deutsche Sozialstaat. Bilanzen—Reformen—Perspektiven.* Frankfurt: Campus, pp. 276–305.

—— (2002). 'Ageing and Public Pension Reforms in Western Europe and North America: Patterns and Politics', in J. Clasen (ed.) *What Future for Social Security?* Bristol: Policy Press, pp. 157–77.

—— (2003). 'Altersicherungspolitik in Deutschland: Zwischen Kontinuität und Paradigmenwechsel', in J. Beyer and P. Stykow (eds.), *Gesellschaft mit beschränkter Hoffnung. Reformfähigkeit und die Möglichkeit rationaler Politik.* Wiesbaden: Westdeutscher Verlag, pp. 266–86.

—— and KANGAS, O. (2003). 'When is a Change Big Enough to be a System Shift? Small System-shifting Changes in German and Finnish Pension Policies', *Social Policy and Administration,* 37(6): 573–91.

H. M. TREASURY (1999). *'Supporting Children Through the Tax and Benefit System.* London: HMSO.

—— (2002). 'The Modernisation of Britain's Tax and Benefit System: the Child and Working Tax Credit', No 10. London: Stationery Office.

—— and DTI (Department of Trade and Industry) (2003). Balancing work and family life: enhancing choice and support for parents. London: HM Treasury and DTI.

—— and DWP (2001). The Changing Welfare State: Employment Opportunity for All. London: HM Treasury and DWP.

HMSO (1985). Lifting the Burden, Cmnd 9571. London.

HOBSON, B., LEWIS, J., and SIIM, B. (eds.) (2002). *Contested Concepts in Gender and Social Politics.* Cheltenham: Edward Elgar.

HOFÄCKER, D. (2004). 'Typen europäischer Familienpolitik—Vehikel oder Hemmnis für das "adult worker model" ', in S. Leitner, I. Ostner, I., and M. Schratzenstaller (eds.), *Wohlfahrtsstaat und Geschlechterverhältnis im Umbruch, Jahrbuch für Europa- und Nordamerika-Studien.* Wiesbaden: VS Verlag für Sozialwissenschaften, pp. 257–84.

HOLMWOOD, J. (2000). 'Europe and the "Americanization" of British Social Policy', *European Societies,* 2(4): 453–82.

HOLLINGSWORTH, J.R. and BOYER, R. (1998). 'Coordination of Economic Actors and Social Systems of Production', in J.R. Hollingsworth and R. Boyer (eds.), *Contemporary Capitalism. The Embeddedness of Institutions.* Cambridge: Cambridge University Press, pp. 1–47.

Home Office (1998). *Supporting Families.* London: HMSO.

HUBER, E. and STEPHENS, J. D. (2001). *Development and Crisis of the Welfare State.* Chicago: University of Chicago Press.

HUSTER, E.-U. (2003). 'Kinderarmut in Deutschland—zentrale Ergebnisse der AWO/ISS-Studie, gute Kindheit—schlechte Kindheit', *Sozialer Fortschritt,* 1: 10–16.

HUTTON, W. (1995). *The State We're In*. London: Jonathan Cape.

IMMERGUT, E.M. (1992). 'The Rules of the Game: the Logic of Health Policy-making in France, Switzerland, and Sweden', in S. Steinmo, K. Thelen, and F. Longstreth (eds.), *Structuring Politics. Historical Institutionalism in Comaparive Perspective*. Cambridge: Cambridge University Press, pp. 90–113.

Inland Revenue (2003). Working Families' Tax Credit Statistics, Summary Statistics. February 2003. London: Inland Revenue, Analysis and Research.

International Monetary Fund (2004). *International Financial Statistics and World Economic Outlook Database*. Washington, DC: IMF.

JEFFERY, C. and HANDL, V. (1999). 'Blair, Schröder and the third way', in L. Funk (ed.), *The Economics and Politics of the Third Way. Essays in Honour of Eric Owen Smith*. Münster: Lit Verlag.

JENKINS, S.P., SCHLUTER, C., and WAGNER, G.G. (2002). 'Einkommensarmut von Kindern—ein deutsch-britischer Vergleich für die 90er Jahre', *DIW Wochenbericht*, 5, 2002.

JOCHEM, S. (2001). 'Reformpolitik im deutschen Sozialversicherungsstaat', in M. G. Schmidt (ed.), *Wohlfahrtsstaatliche Politik*. Opladen: Leske und Budrich, pp. 193–226.

JOCHEM, S. (2003). 'Veto Players or Veto Points? The Politics of Welfare State Reforms in Europe', paper presented at annual meeting of the American Political Science Association, Philadelphia.

Joseph Rowntree Foundation (1995). 'Inquiry into Income and Wealth', vol. 1. York: Joseph Rowntree Foundation.

KAUFMANN, F.-X. (1993). 'Familienpolitik in Europa', in Bundesministerium für Familie und Senioren (ed.), *Vierzig Jahre Familienpolitik in der Bundesrepublik Deutschland*. Berlin: Luchterhand, pp. 141–67.

—— (2002) 'Politics and Policies Towards the Family in Europe: A Framework and an Inquiry into their Differences and Convergences', in F.-X. Kaufmann, A, Kuijsten, H.-J. Schulze, and K. P. Strohmeier (eds.), *Family Life and Family Politics in Europe*, vol. 2. Oxford: Oxford University Press, pp. 419–90.

—— (2003) *Variationen des Wohlfahrtsstaats*. Frankfurt: Suhrkamp.

KAUTTO, M. (2001). 'Moving Closer? Diversity and Convergence in Financing of Welfare States', in M. Kautto, J. Fritzell, B. Hvinden, J. Kvist, and H. Uusitalo (eds.), *Nordic Welfare States in the European Context*. London: Routledge, pp. 232–61.

—— FRITZELL, J., HVINDEN, B., KVIST. J., and UUSITALO, H. (eds.) (2001). *Nordic Welfare States in the European Context*. London: Routledge.

KING, D. (1993). 'The Conservatives and Training Policy 1979–1992: From Tripartite to a Neoliberal Regime', *Political Studies*, XLI: 214–35.

—— (1995). *Actively seeking work? The politics of unemployment and welfare policy in the United States and Great Britain*. London: University of Chicago Press.

—— and WICKHAM-JONES (1999). 'From Clinton to Blair: the Democratic (Party) Origins of Welfare to Work', *Political Quarterly*, 70(1): 62–74.

—— and WOOD, S. (1999). 'The Political Economy of Neo-liberalism: Britain and the United States in the 1980s', in H. Kitschelt, P. Lange, G. Marks, and

J.D. Stephens (eds.), *Continuity and Change in Contemporary Capitalism*. Cambridge: Cambridge University Press, pp. 371–97.

KINGDON, J. W. (1995). *Agendas, Alternatives and Public Policies* (2nd edn.). New York: HarperCollins.

KITSCHELT, H. (2001). 'Partisan Competition and Welfare State Retrenchment: When do Politicians Choose Unpopular Policies?', in P. Pierson (ed.), *The New Politics of the Welfare State*. Oxford: Oxford University Press, pp. 265–302.

—— and STREEK, W. (2003). 'From Stability to Stagnation: Germany at the Beginning of the Twenty-First Century', *West European Politics*, 26(4): 1–36.

KITTEL, B. and OBINGER, H. (2003). 'Political parties, institutions, and the dynamics of social expenditure in times of austerity', *Journal of European Public Policy*, 10(1): 20–45.

KLAMMER, U. and KLENNER, C. (2004). 'Geteilte Erwerbstätigkeit–gemeinsame Fürsorge. Strategie und Perspektiven der Kombination von Erwerbs- und Familienleben in Deutschland', in S. Leitner et al. (eds.), *Wohlfahrtsstaat und Geschlechterverhältnis im Umbruch, Jahrbuch für Europa- und Nordamerika-Studien*. Wiesbaden: VS Verlag für Sozialwissenschaften, pp. 177–207.

KNIJN, T. and OSTNER, I. (2002). 'Commodification and De-commodification', in B. Hobson, J. Lewis, and B. Siim (eds.), *Contested concepts in gender and social politics*. Cheltenham: Edward Elgar, pp. 141–69.

KOLBE, W. (2002). *Elternschaft im Wohlfahrtsstaat. Schweden und die Bundesrepublik im Vergleich 1945–2000*. Frankfurt: Campus.

KOLLER, M. (2003). 'Die stillen Kosten der Einigung', *IAB Kurzbericht*, 13, 14 August. Nürnberg: Bundesanstalt für Arbeit.

KORPI, W. and PALME, J. (2003). 'New Politics and Class Politics in the Context of Austerity and Globalization: Welfare State Regress in 18 Countries, 1975–95', *American Political Science Review*, 97(3): 425–46.

KVIST, J. (1998). 'Complexities in Assessing Unemployment Benefits and Policies', *International Social Security Review*, 51/4: 33–55.

LAMPERT, H. (1996). 'Zur Lage der Familien und den Aufgaben in der Familienpolitik der neuen Bundesländern', in R. Hauser (ed.), *Sozialpolitik im vereinten Deutschland*, vol. 3. Berlin: Duncker and Humbolt, pp. 11–52.

LAMPING, W. and RÜB, F.W. (2004). 'From the Conservative Welfare State to an "Uncertain Something Else": German Pension Politics in Comparative Perspective', *Policy and Politics*, 32(2): 169–91.

LAND, H. and LEWIS, J. (1998). 'Gender, Care and the Changing Role of the State in the UK', in J. Lewis (ed.), *Gender, Social Care and Welfare State Restructuring in Europe*. Ashgate: Aldershot, pp. 51–84.

LAYARD, R. (2000). 'Welfare-to-work and the New Deal', *World Economics*, 1(2): 29–39.

LE GRAND, J. and BARTLETT, W. (eds.) (1993). *Quasi-markets and Social Policy*. Basingstoke: Macmillan.

LEIBFRIED, S. and TENNSTEDT, F. (eds.) (1985). *Politik der Armut und die Spaltung des Sozialstaats*. Frankfurt: Suhrkamp.

LEICESTER, A. and SHAW, J. (2003). 'A survey of the UK benefit system', *IFS briefing note no. 13*. London: Institute for Fiscal Studies.

LEISERING, L. (2000). 'Kontinuitätssemantiken: Die Evolutionäre Transformation des Sozialstaates im Nachkriegsdeutschland', in S. Leibfried and U. Wagschal (eds.), *Der deutsche Sozialstaat. Bilanzen—Reformen—Perspektiven*. Frankfurt: Campus, pp. 91–114.

—— and HILKERT, B. (2000). *Von Grossbritannien lernen? Wohlfahrtsstaatreform im Zeichen des dritten Weges—das Beispiel aktivierender Sozialhilfepolitik unter Blair.* London: Anglo-German Foundation.

LEITNER, S. and LESSENICH, S. (2003). 'Assessing Welfare State Change: the German Social Insurance State between Reciprocity and Solidarity', *Journal of Public Policy*, 23(3): 419–41.

—— OSTNER, I., and SCHRATZENSTALLER, M. (2004). 'Was kommt nach dem Ernährermodell? Sozialpolitik zwischen Re-Kommodifizierung und Re-Familisierung', in S. Leitner, I. Ostner, and M. Schratzenstaller (eds.), *Wohlfahrtsstaat und Geschlechterverhältnis im Umbruch, Jahrbuch für Europa- und Nordamerika-Studien*. Wiesbaden: VS Verlag für Sozialwissenschaften, pp. 9–27.

LEITNER, S., OSTNER, I., and SCHRATZENSTALLER, M. (eds.) (2004). *Wohlfahrtsstaat und Geschlechterverhältnis im Umbruch, Jahrbuch für Europa- und Nordamerika-Studien*. Wiesbaden: VS Verlag für Sozialwissenschaften.

LESSENICH, S. (1999). 'Lohnarbeit, Familie und die Grenzen konstruktivistischer Sozialpolitikanalyse', *Zeitschrift für Soziologie*, 28(3): 235–40.

LEVIN, P. (1997). *Making Social Policy*. Buckingham: Open University Press.

LEWIS, J. (1992). 'Gender and the Development of Welfare Regimes', *Journal of European Social Policy*, 2(3): 131–52.

—— (1999). 'The 'problem' of Lone Motherhood in Comparative Perspective', in J. Clasen (ed.), *Comparative Social Policy*. Oxford: Blackwell, pp. 181–99.

—— (2002). 'Gender and Welfare State Change', *European Societies*, 4(4): 331–57.

—— (2003). 'Developing Early Years Childcare in England, 1997–2002: The Choices for (working) Mothers', *Social Policy and Administration*, 37(3): 219–38.

—— and OSTNER, I. (1994). 'Gender and the Evolution of European Social Policies', ZeS working paper 4/94. Bremen: Centre for Social Policy Research.

—— and SURENDER, R. (eds.) (2004). *Welfare State change. Towards a Third Way?*. Oxford: Oxford University Press.

LISTER, R. (1989a). 'Social Security', in M. McCarthy (ed.), *The New Politics of Welfare*. London: Macmillan, pp. 104–31.

—— (1989b). 'The politics of Social Security: an Assessment of the Fowler Review', in A. Dilnot and I. Walker (eds.), *The Economics of Social Security*. Oxford: Oxford University Press, pp. 200–23.

—— (1994). ' "She Has Other Duties"—Women, Citizenship and Social Security', in S. Baldwin and J. Falkingham (eds.), *Social Security and Social Change*. Hemel Hempstead: Harvester.

—— (1997). 'Back to the Family: Family Policies and Politics under the Major government', in H. Jones and J. Millar (eds.), *The Politics of the Family*. Aldershot: Avebury, pp. 11–31.

—— (2000). 'The Politics of Child Poverty in Britain from 1965 to 1990', *Revue Française de Civilisation Britannique*, 11(1): 67–80.

LØDEMEL, I. and TRICKEY, H. (eds.) (2001). *An Offer You Can't Refuse. Workfare in International Perspective*. Bristol: Policy Press.

LONSDALE, S. and BYRNE, D. (1988). 'Social Security: From State Insurance to Private Uncertainty', in M. Brentson and C. Ungerson (eds.), *Year Book of Social Policy 1987–8*. Harlow: Longman, pp. 142–65

LUDWIG, I. and SCHLEVOGT, V. (2002). 'Bessere Zeiten für erwerbstätige Mütter?', *WSI Mitteilungen*, 3: 133–8.

MACKROTH, P. and RISTAU, M. (2002). 'Die Rückkehr der Familie', *Berliner Republik*, 6 (Internet version).

MACLEAN, M. (2002). 'The Green Paper Supporting Families, 1998'; in A. Carling, S. Duncan, and R. Edwards (eds.), *Analysing families*. London: Routledge, pp. 64–8.

MAHONEY, J. and RUESCHEMEYER, D. (2003). 'Comparative Historical Analysis: Achievements and Agendas', in J. Mahoney and D. Rueschemeyer (eds.), *Comparative Historical Analysis in the Social Sciences*. Cambridge: Cambridge University Press, pp. 3–38.

MANOW, P. (1997). 'Social Insurance and the German Political Economy', discussion paper 97/2. Cologne: Max-Planck-Institut für Gesellschaftsforschung.

—— and SEILS, E. (2000). 'Adjusting Badly: the German Welfare State, Structural Change, and the Open Economy', in F.W. Scharpf and V.A. Schmidt (eds.), *Welfare and Work in the Open Economy*, vol. 2. Oxford: Oxford University Press, pp. 264–307.

MARES, I. (2003). *The Politics of Social Risk. Business and Welfare State Development*. Cambridge: Cambridge University Press.

MAU, S. (2003). *The Moral Economy of the Welfare State. Britain and Germany compared*. London: Routledge.

MCGREGOR, S. (1985). 'Making Sense of Social Security? Initiatives and Implementation 1979–83', in Jackson, P. (ed.), *Implementing Government Policy Initiatives. The Thatcher Administration 1979–83*. London: Royal.

MCKAY, S. and Rowlingson, K. (1999). *Social Security in Britain*. Houndmills: Palgrave.

MCLAUGHLIN, E. and GLENDINNING, C. (1994). 'Paying for Care in Europe: Is There a Feminist Approach?', in L. Hantrais and S. Mangen (eds.), *Family policy and the welfare of women*. Cross-National Research Papers, third series. Loughborough: Loughborough University.

MCLAUGHLIN, E., TREWSDALE, J., and McCAY, N. (2001). 'The Rise and Fall of the UK's First Tax Credit: The Working Families Tax Credit 1998–2000', *Social Policy and Administration*, 35(2): 163–80.

MEAGER, N. (1997). United Kingdom. Active and Passive Labour Market Policies in the United Kingdom, Employment Observatory, SYSDEM Trends, No.28, European Commission, DG Employment and Social Affairs. Berlin: IAS, 69–75.

MEYER, T. (2003*a*). 'Politik der Einsichtigen für die Schwachen? Ursachen für die Expansion der Familienpolitik am Beispiel Grossbritanniens', *Zeitschrift für Sozialreform*, 48(4): 596–612.

MEYER, T. (2003*b*). 'Reasonable Measures for a Sustainable Future? An Analysis of the Expansion of Familiy Policies in Strong Breadwinner Models. Britain and Germany Compared', paper presented at the 2003 ESPAnet Annual Conference. Copenhagen: Danish National Institute of Social Research.

MICHALSKY, H. (1985). 'The politics of social policy', in K. von Beyme and M.G. Schmidt (eds.), *Policy and Politics in the Federal Republic of Germany*. Aldershot: Gower, pp. 56–81.

MICKLEWRIGHT, J. (1989). 'The Strange Case of British Earnings-Related Un-employment Benefit', *Journal of Social Policy*, 18(4).

MILLAR, J. (2003*a*). 'The Art of Persuasion? The British New Deal for Lone Parents', in R. Walker and M. Wiseman (eds.), *The Welfare We Want: The British Challenge for American Reform*. Bristol: Policy Press, pp. 115–42.

—— (2003*b*). 'From Wage Replacement to Wage Supplement: Benefits and Tax Credits', in J. Millar (ed.), *Understanding Social Security*. Bristol: Policy Press, pp. 123–43.

—— and RIDGE, T. (2002). 'Parents, Children, Families and New Labour: Devel-oping Family Policy?', in M. Powell (ed.), *Evaluating New Labour's welfare reforms*. Bristol: Policy Press, pp. 85–106.

MOHR, K. (2004). 'Pfadabhängige Restrukturierung oder Konvergenz? Reformen in der Arbeitslosensicherung und der Sozialhilfe in Groabritannien und Deutschland', *Zeitschrift für Sozialreform*, 50(3): 283–311.

MÜNCH. U. (2005). 'Familien- und Altenpolitik', in Bundesministerium für Gesundheit und Soziale Sicherung und Bundesarchiv (eds.) *Geschichte der Sozialpolitik in Deutschland seit 1945*, vol. 7 (1982–89). Baden-Baden: Nomos Verlag (forthcoming).

MYLES, J. and PIERSON, P. (2001). 'The Comparative Political Economy of Pension Reform', in P. Pierson (ed.), *The New Politics of the Welfare State*. Oxford: Oxford University Press, pp. 305–33.

—— and QUADAGNO, J. (2002). 'Political Theories of the Welfare State', *Social Service Review*, March: 34–57.

National Pensioners Convention (2004). 'Pensioner facts and figures', briefing no. 32. London: NPC.

NESBITT, S. (1995). *British pension policy making in the 1980s*. Aldershot: Avebury.

NICKELL, S. (1997). 'Unemployment and Labour Market Rigidities: Europe versus North America', *Journal of Economic Perspectives*, 11(3): 53–74.

—— (2003). 'A picture of European Unemployment: Success and Failure', dis-cussion paper 579, Centre for Economic Performance. London: LSE.

—— and QUINTINI, G. (2002). 'The Recent Performance of the UK Labour Market', *Oxford Review of Economic Policy*, 18(2): 202–20.

NOTZ, G. (2004). 'Impulse für eine Gesellschaft von morgen geben', *Das Parla-ment*, 54 (33/34): 1.

NULLMEIER, F. (2003). 'Alterssicherungspolitik im Zeichen der "Riester Rente" ', in A. Gohr and M. Seeleib-Kaiser (eds.), *Sozial- und Wirtschaftspolitik unter Rot-Grün*. Wiesbaden: Westdeutscher Verlag, pp. 167–87.

—— UND RÜB, F.W. (1993). *Die Transformation der Sozialpolitik. Vom Sozialstaat zum Sicherungsstaat*. Frankfurt: Campus.

O'CONNELL, A. (2003). *A guide to pension reform*. London: Pensions Policy Institute.

OECD (1994). The OECD Jobs Study: Evidence and Explanations; Part 1: Labour Market trends and underlying forces of change; Part 2: The adjustment potential of the labour market. Paris: OECD.

—— (1998). *Employment Outlook*. Paris: OECD.

—— (1999*a*). *Benefit systems and work incentives*. Paris: OECD.

—— (1999*b*). *Historical Statistics 1960–97*. Paris: OECD.

—— (2000). The OECD Programme for International Student Assessment (PISA) (www.pisa.oecd.org).

—— (2001*a*). SOCX (CD-ROM), *Social Expenditure Database*. Paris: OECD.

—— (2001*b*). *Employment Outlook*. Paris: OECD.

—— (2002*a*). *Benefit and Wages*. Paris: OECD.

—— (2002*b*). *Society at a glance, social indicators*. Paris: OECD.

—— (2003). *Employment Outlook*. Paris: OECD.

—— (2004*a*). *Labour Force Statistics*. Internet version, Paris: OECD.

—— (2004*b*). *Employment Outlook*. Paris: OECD.

—— (2004*c*). *Benefits and Wages*. Paris: OECD.

OFFE, C. (1991). 'Smooth Consolidation in the West German Welfare State: Structural Change, Fiscal Policies, and Populist Politics', in Piven, F. F. (ed.), *Labor Parties in Postindustrial Societies*. Cambridge: Polity Press, pp. 124–46.

OGUS, A. and WIKELEY, N. (eds.) (1995). *The Law of Social Security*. London: Butterworths.

OPIELKA, M. (2002). 'Familie und Beruf. Eine deutsche Geschichte', *Aus Politik und Zeitgeschichte*, B22–3: 20–30.

OPPEN, M. (1997). 'Concerted Cooperation and Immobilism: Labour Policy in Germany and the Regulation of Early Exit', in M. Muramatsu and F. Naschold (eds.), *State and Administration in Japan and Germany*. Berlin: Walter de Gruyter, pp. 247–80.

OSTHEIM, T. and ZOHLNHÖFER, R. (2004). 'Europäisierung der Arbeitsmarkt- und Beschäftigungspolitik? Der Einfluss des Luxemburg-Prozesses auf die deutsche Arbeitsmarktpolitik', in S. Lütz and R. Czada (eds.), *Der Wohlfahrtsstaat. Transformation und Perspektiven*. Wiesbaden: VS-Verlag.

OSTNER, I. (1993). 'Slow Motion: Women, Work and the Family in Germany', in J. Lewis (ed.), *Women and social policy in Europe: work, family and the state*. Aldershot: Ashgate, pp. 92–115.

—— (1995). 'Arm ohne Ehemann? Sozialpolitische Regulierung von Lebenschancen für Frauen im internationalen Vergleich', *Aus Politik und Zeitgeschichte*, B36–7/95: 3–12.

OSTNER, I. (1998). 'The Politics of Care Policies in Germany', in J. Lewis (ed.) *Gender, social care and welfare state restructuring in Europe*. Ashgate: Aldershot, pp. 111–37.

—— (2002). 'Am Kind vorbei—Ideen und Interessen in der jüngeren Familienpolitik', *Zeitschrift für Soziologie der Erziehung und Sozialisation*, 22: 247–66.

—— (2003). ' "Individualisation"—the Origins of the Concept and its Impact on German Social Policies', *Social Policy and Society*, 3(1): 47–56.

PALIER, B. (2000). ' "Defrosting" the French Welfare State', in Ferrera, M. and Rhodes, M. (eds.), *Recasting European Welfare States*. London: Frank Cass, pp. 113–36.

—— (2002). 'Beyond Retrenchment: Four Problems in Current Welfare State Research and One Suggestion How to Overcome Them', in J. Clasen (ed.), *What Future for Social Security? Debates and reforms in national and cross-national perspective*. Bristol: Policy Press, pp. 105–20.

PARRY, R. (2000). 'Exploring the Sustainable Limits of Public Expenditure in the British Welfare State', in S. Kuhnle (ed.), *Survival of the European Welfare State*. London: Routledge.

PASCALL, G. (1997). 'Women and the Family in the British Welfare State: The Thatcher/Major Legacy', *Social Policy and Administration*, 31(3): 290–304.

PECK, J. and THEODORE, N. (2000). 'Beyond "employability" ', *Cambridge Journal of Economics*, Vol. 24: 729–49.

PEDERSEN, A.W. (2003). 'Der Mix aus privaten und staatlichen Quellen der Einkommenssicherung im Alter im internationalen Vergleich', *Zeitschrift für Sozialreform*, 49(1): 109–33.

Pensions Commission (2004). *Pensions: Challenges and Choices*. The first report of the Pensions Commission. Norwich: HMSO.

Pensions Policy Institute (2003). *The Pensions Primer*. London: Pensions Policy Institute.

PHILPOTT, J. (1999). *Behind the Buzzword: 'Employability'*. London: Employment Policy Institute.

PIERSON, P. (1993). 'When Effect Becomes Cause: Policy Feedback and Political Change', *World Politics*, 45: 595–628.

—— (1994). *Dismantling the Welfare State? Reagan, Thatcher, and the Politics of Retrenchment*. Cambridge: Cambridge University Press.

—— (1996). 'The New Politics of the Welfare State', *World Politics*, 48: 143–79.

—— (1998). 'Irresistible Forces, Immovable Objects: Post-industrial Welfare States Confront Permanent Austerity', *Journal of European Public Policy*, 5(4): 539–60.

—— (2000). 'Increasing Returns, Path Dependence, and the Study of Politics', *American Political Science Review*, 94(2): 251–67.

—— (ed.) (2001a). *The New Politics of the Welfare State*. Oxford: Oxford University Press.

—— (2001b). 'Coping with Permanent Austerity: Welfare State Restructuring in Affluent Democracies', in P. Pierson (ed.) *The New Politics of the Welfare State*. Oxford: Oxford University Press, pp. 410–56.

PLANT, R. (2003). 'Citizenship and Social Security', *Fiscal Studies*, 24(2): 153–66.

POWELL, M. (2004). 'In Search of the Dependent Variable: Welfare Change in Europe', paper presented at COST A15 conference, 21/2 May, Nantes.

—— (ed.) (1999). *New Labour, New Welfare State?* Bristol: Policy Press.

RAINWATER, L., REIN, M., and SCHWARZ, J. (1986). *Income Packaging in the Welfare State. A Comparison of Family Income.* Oxford: Clarendon.

RAKE, K. (2001). 'Gender and New Labour's Social Policies', *Journal of Social Policy*, 30(2): 209–31.

RANDALL, V. (2002). 'Child Care in Britain, or, How Do You Restructure Nothing?', in S. Michel and R. Mahon (eds.), *Child Care Policy at the Crossroads.* London: Routledge, pp. 219–38.

REISSERT, B. (1998). 'Arbeitslosigkeit, Arbeitslosenversicherung und Sozialhilfebelastung der Kommunen', in H. Mäding and R. Voigt (eds.), *Kommunalfinanzen im Umbrunch.* Opladen: Leske and Budrich. pp. 201–14.

—— (2005). 'Germany: a Late Reformer', in J. Clasen, M. Ferrera, and M. Rhodes (eds.), *Welfare States and the Challenge of Unemployment: Reform Policies and Institutions in the European Union.* London: Routledge (forthcoming).

RHODES, M. (2000*a*). 'Restructuring the British Welfare State: Between Domestic Constraints and Global Imperatives', in F. W. Scharpf and V. A. Schmidt (eds.), *Welfare and Work in the Open Economy*, vol. 2. Oxford: Oxford University Press, pp. 19–68.

—— (2000*b*). 'Desperately Seeking a Solution: Social Democracy, Thatcherism and the "Third Way" in British Welfare', *West European Politics*, 23(2): 159–86.

RIDGE. T. (2003). 'Benefiting Children? The Challenge of Social Security Support for Children', in J. Millar (ed.), *Understanding social security*. Bristol: Policy Press, pp. 167–88.

RINGEN, S. (1997). 'Family Change and Family Policies: Great Britain', in S.B. Kamerman and A.J. Kahn (eds.), *Family Change and Family Policies in Great Britain, Canada, New Zealand, and the United States.* Oxford: Clarendon Press, pp. 25–101.

RISTAU, M. (2003). ' "Gedöns" als Chefsache. Wie Familienfreundlichkeit zum rot-grünen Überraschungsthema wurde', *Neue Gesellschaft/ Frankfurter Hefte*, 50(3): 38–40.

ROBINSON, H. (2003). 'Gender and Labour Market Performance in the Recovery', in R. Dickens, P. Gregg, and J. Wadsworth (eds.), *The Labour Market under New Labour*. Houndmills: Palgrave, pp. 232–47.

ROBINSON, R. (1986). 'Restructuring the Welfare State: An Analysis of Public Expenditure 1979/80–1984/5', *Journal of Social Policy*, 15(1): 1–22.

RODER, K. (2003). *Social Democracy and Labour Market Policy. Developments in Britain and Germany.* London: Routledge.

ROLL, J. (1988). Young People at the Crossroads: Education, Jobs, Social Security and Training. Family Policy Studies Centre, London.

ROLLER, E. (1996). 'Kürzungen von Sozialleistungen aus der Sicht der Bundes-bürger', *Zeitschrift für Sozialreform*, 42(11/12): 777–88.

ROLOFF, J. (1993). 'Erwerbsbeteiligung und Familienstand von Frauen—ein deutsch-deutscher Vergleich', *Zeitschrift für Bevölkerungswissenschaft*, 1: 105–12.

ROSS, F. (2000). 'Interests and choice in the "not quite so new" 'politics of welfare', in M. Ferrera and M. Rhodes (eds), Recasting European Welfare States, *West European Politics*, special issue, 23(2): 11–34.

ROTH, D. and JUNG, M. (2002). 'Ablösung der Regierung vertagt. Eine Analyse der Bundestagswahl 2002', *Aus Politik und Zeitgeschichte*, B 49–50: 3–17.

RÜB, F.W. and NULLMEIER, F. (1991). 'Alterssicherungspolitik in der Bundesre-publik Deutschland', in B. Blanke und H. Wiesenthal (eds.), Die alte Bundes-republik, *Leviathan* Sonderheft 12. Wiesbaden: Westdeutscher Verlag, pp. 437–62.

SABATIER, P. (1993). 'Advocacy-Koalitionen, Policy Wandel und Policy-Lernen. Eine Alternative zur Phasenheuristik', in A. Héritier (ed.) *Policy Analyse. Kritik und Neuorientierung*, PVS special issue 24: 116–48.

SAINSBURY, D. (2001). 'Welfare State Challenges and Responses: Institutional and Ideological Resilience or Restructuring?', *Acta Sociologica*, 44(3): 257–65.

SCARBOROUGH, E. (2000). 'West European Welfare States: The Old Politics of Retrenchment', *European Journal of Political Research*, 38(2): 225–59.

SCHARPF, F.W. (2000). 'Institutions in Comparative Policy Research', *Comparative Political Studies*, 33(6/7): 762–90.

—— and SCHMIDT, V.A. (eds.) (2000). *Welfare and Work in the Open Economy*, vols. 1 and 2. Oxford: Oxford University Press.

SCHERER, P. (2001). 'Age of withdrawal from the labour market in OECD coun-tries', Labour Market and Social Policy, Occasional Papers 49. Paris: OECD.

SCHLUDI, M. (2001). 'The Politics of Pensions in European Social Insurance Countries', discussion paper 01/11. Cologne: Max-Planck-Institut für Gesellschaftsforschung.

—— (2002). The Reform of Bismarckian Pension Systems. A Comparison of Pension Politics in Austria, France, Germany, Italy and Sweden, unpublished Ph.D., Humboldt University Berlin.

SCHMÄHL, W. (1999). 'Rentenversicherung in der Bewährung: Von der Nachk-riegszeit bis an die Schwelle zum neuen Jahrhundert', in M. Kaase and G. Schmid (eds.), *Eine lernende Demokratie: 50 Jahre Bundesrepublik Deutschland*. Berlin: Edition Sigma, 357–96.

—— (2003a). 'Paradigm Shift in German Pension Policy: Measures Aiming at a New Public–Private Mix and their Effects', in M. Rein and W. Schmähl (eds.), *Rethinking the Welfare State*. Edward Elgar, pp. 153–204.

—— (2003b). 'Dismantling the Earnings-related Social Pension Scheme. Germany beyond the Crossroad', ZeS working paper 9/03. University of Bremen: Centre for Social Policy Research.

—— (2003c). 'Erste Erfahrungen mit der "Offenen Methode der Koordinier-ung": Offene Fragen zur "fiskalischen Nachhaltigkeit" und "Angemessenheit"' von Renten in einer erweiterten Europäischen Union', ZeS working paper 11/03. University of Bremen: Centre for Social Policy Research.

—— (2004). 'Sicherung bei Alter, Invalidität und für Hinterbliebene', in Bundesministerium für Gesundheit und Soziale Sicherung und Bundesarchiv (ed.), *Geschichte der Sozialpolitik in Deutschland seit 1945*, vol. 7 (1982–9).

SCHMID, A. (1997). Sozialpolitische Kürzungsmaßnahmen in Deutschland und Großbritannien seit Anfang der 80er Jahre, unpublished Diplomarbeit, University of Konstanz, Fakultät für Verwaltungswissenschaft.

SCHMID, G. (1998). 'Das Nadelöhr der Wirklichkeit verfehlt: Eine beschäftigungspolitische Bilanz der Ära Kohl', in G. Wewer (ed.), *Bilanz der Ära Kohl*. Opladen: Leske und Budrich.

—— (2003). 'Moderne Dienstleistungen am Arbeitsmarkt: Strategie und Vorschläge der Hartz-Kommission', *Aus Politik und Zeitgeschichte*, B6–7: 3–6.

—— REISSERT, B., and BRUCHE, G. (1987). *Arbeitslosenversicherung und aktive Arbeitsmarktpolitik. Finanzierungssysteme im internationalen Vergleich*. Berlin: Edition Sigma.

SCHMID, J. (1990). *Die CDU*. Opladen: Westdeutscher Verlag.

SCHMIDT, M. G. (1998). 'Sozialstaatliche Politik in der Ära Kohl', in G. Wewer (ed.), *Bilanz der Ära Kohl*. Opladen: Leske und Budrich, pp. 59–87.

—— (2003*a*). 'Ausgaben für Bildung im internationalen Bereich', *Aus Politik und Zeitgeschichte*, B21–2: 6–11.

—— (2003*b*) *Political Institutions in the Federal Republic of Germany*. Oxford: Oxford University Press.

—— (2003*c*). 'Rot-grüne Sozialpolitik (1998–2002)', in, C. Egle, T. Ostheim, and R. Zohlhöfer (eds.), *Das rot-grüne Projekt*. Wiesbaden: Westdeutscher Verlag, 239–58.

SCHMIDT, V. A. (2002). 'Does Discourse Matter in the Politics of Welfare State Adjustment?', *Comparative Political Studies*, 35(2): 168–93.

SCHRATZENSTALLER, M. (2002). 'Familienpolitik—wozu und für wen? Die aktuelle familienpolitische Reformdebatte', *WSI Mitteilungen*, 3: 127–33.

SCHWARTZ, H. M. (2003). 'Globalisation/welfare: what's the preposition? And, or, versus, with?', in C. Bochel, N. Ellison, and M. Powell (eds.), *Social Policy Review*, 15. Bristol: Policy Press.

SEELEIB-KAISER, M. (2001). *Globalisierung und Sozialpolitik. Ein Vergleich der Diskurse und Wohlfahrtssysteme in Deutschland, Japan und den USA*. Frankfurt: Campus.

—— (2003). 'Politikwechsel nach Machtwechsel?', in Gohr, A., and Seeleib-Kaiser, M. (eds.) *Sozial- und Witschaftspolitik unter Rot-Grün*. Wiesbaden: Westdeutscher Verlag, pp. 11–28.

Sell, S. (2002). 'Bedarfsorientierte', Modernisierung der Kinderbetreuungsinfrastruktur in Deutschland, *WSI-Mittielungen*, 3: 147–53.

SHAW, E. (2003). 'The Blair Government, Labour Market Flexibility and the Social Democratic Project in Britain', paper presented at the conference 'Social Governance in a Global Era', Sapporo Sessions, Hokkaido University, 14/15 October.

SIEGEL, N. A. (2002). *Baustelle Sozialpolitik. Konsolidierung und Rückbau im internationalen Vergleich*. Frankfurt: Campus.

—— (2003). 'Worlds of Comparative Welfare State Analysis: Some Suggestions for Potential Bridge-Over Strategies', paper presented at the ESPAnet Annual Conference, Copenhagen: Eigtveds Pakhus, 13–15 November.

SILVIA, S. (1999). 'Reform gridlock and the Role of the Bundesrat in German Politics', *West European Politics*, 22(2): 167–81.

SIMS-SCHOUTEN, W. (2000). 'Child care services and parents' attitudes in England, Finland, and Greece', in A. Pfenning and T. Bahle (eds.), *Families and Family Policies in Europe. Comparative Perspectives*. Frankfurt: Peter Land, pp. 270–88.

SINFIELD, A. (1993). 'Unemployment Benefit—An Active right For Citizens', in European Institute of Social Security (ed.), *EISS Yearbook 1992. Reforms in East and Central Europe*. Leuven: Acco.

—— (1997). 'Blaming the Benefit: The Costs of the Distinction Between Active and Passive Programmes', in J. Holmer and J. C. Karlsson (eds.), *Work—Quo Vadis? Re-thinking the Question of Work*. Aldershot: Ashgate.

SOSKICE, D. (1991). 'The Institutional Infrastructure for International Competitiveness: A Comparative Analysis of the UK and Germany', in A. B. Atkinson and R. Brunetta (eds.), *Economics for the new Europe*. New York: New York University Press, pp. 45–66.

SPIEß, C.K. (2003). 'Vereinbarkeit von Familie und Beruf—Fakten, Mängel und Reformen', *Sozialer Fortschritt*, 1: 17–23.

—— and FRICK, J. R. (2002). 'Kinderbetreuung in West und Ostdeutschland. Sozioökonomischer Hintergrund entscheidend', *DIW Wochenbericht*, 31/02 (Internet version).

Stafford, B. (2003). 'Beyond lond parents: extening welfare-to work to disabled people and the young unemployed', in R. Walker and M. Wiseman (eds.). *The welfare we want? The British challenge for American reform*. Briston: Policy Press, 143–74.

Statistisches Bundesamt (various years) Fachserie 13. Wiesbaden: Kohlhammer.

—— (2004*a*) *Volkswirtschaftliche Gesamtrechnungen*, Fachserie 18/Reihe S.21. Wiesbaden: Statistisches Bundesamt.

—— (2004*b*) *Kindertagesbetreuung in Deutschland. Einrichtungen, Plätze, Personal und Kosten*. Wiesbaden: Statistisches Bundesamt.

STEFFEN, J. (2003). Sozialpolitische Chronik. Die wesentlichen Veränderungen in der Arbeitslosen-, Renten-, Kranken- und Pflegeversicherung sowie bei der Sozialhilfe (HLU)—von den siebziger Jahren bis heute. Bremen: Arbeitnehmerkammer Bremen (www.arbeitnehmerkammer.de/sozialpolitik).

STEINMO, S., THELEN, K., and LONGSTRETH, F. (eds.) (1992). *Structuring Politics. Historical Institutionalism in Comaparive Perspective*. Cambridge: Cambridge University Press.

STRANGE, S. (1997). 'The Future of Global Capitalism; or, Will Divergence Persist Forever?', in C. Crouch and W. Streek (eds.), *Political Economy of Modern Capitalism. Mapping convergence and diversity*. London: Sage, pp. 182–91.

STREEK, W. (2003). 'From State Weakness as Strength to State Weakness as Weakness: Welfare Corporatism and the Private Use of Public Interest', MPIfG working paper 03/2. Cologne: Max-Planck-Institut für Gesellschafts-forschung.

—— and HASSEL, A. (2003). 'The Crumbling Pillars of Social Partnership', *West European Politics*, 26(4): 101–24.

TAYLOR-GOOBY, P. (1987). 'Citizenship and Welfare', in R. Jowell, S. Wither-spoon, and C. Brook (eds.), *British Social Attitudes—The 1987 Report*. London: Gower.

—— (1988). 'The Future of the British Welfare State: Public Attitudes, Citizen-ship and Social Policy under Conservative Governments of the 1980s', *European Sociological Review*, 4(1): 1–19.

—— (1989). 'Welfare, Hierarchy and the 'New Right': the Impact of Social Policy Changes in Britain, 1979–1989', *International Sociology*, 4(4): 431–46.

—— (1996). 'The United Kingdom: Radical Departures and Political Consensus', in V. George and P. Taylor-Gooby (eds.), *European Welfare Futures. Squaring the Welfare Circle*. London: Macmillan, pp. 95–116.

—— (2001a). 'Welfare Reform in the UK: The Construction of a Liberal Con-sensus', in P. Taylor-Gooby (ed.), *Welfare States under Pressure*. London: Sage, pp. 147–70.

—— (ed.) (2001b). *Welfare States under Pressure*. London: Sage.

—— (ed.) (2004). *New Risks, New Welfare?* Oxford: Oxford University Press.

THELEN, K. and STEINMO, S. (1992). 'Historical Institutionalism in Comparative Politics', in S. Steinmo, K. Thelen, and F. Longstreth (eds.), *Structuring Politics. Historical Institutionalism in Comaparive Perspective*. Cambridge: Cam-bridge University Press, pp. 1–32.

TIMMINS, N. (2001). *The Five Giants. A Biography of the Welfare State*. London: HarperCollins.

TITMUSS, R. (1958). *Essays on the Welfare State*. London: Allen and Unwin.

TRICKEY, H. and WALKER, R. (2001). 'Steps to Compulsion within British Labour Market Policies', in I. Lødemel and H. Trickey (eds.), *An offer you can't refuse. Workfare in international perspective*. Bristol: Policy Press, pp. 181–214.

TSEBELIS, G. (2002). *Veto players: How Political Institutions Work*. Princeton, NJ: Princeton University Press.

Unemployment Unit (1995). Working Brief, Issue 66. June.

Unicef (2000). A League Table of Child Poverty in Rich Nations, United Nations Children's Fund, Innocenti Report Card 1. Florence: Innocenti Research Centre.

VAN BASTELAER, A., and VAGUER, C. (2004). Working Times. Eurostat: Statistics in Focus, Population and Social Conditions, Theme 3, 7–2004. Luxembourg: Eurostat.

VAN KERSBERGEN, K. (1995). *Social Capitalism*. London: Routledge.

VdR (Verband deutscher Rentenversicherungsträger) (2004). *Rentenversicherung in Zeitreihen*. Frankfurt: VdR.

VEIL, M. (2004). Eigenständige Alterssicherung von Frauen in Deutschland—Handlungsbedarf und Perspektiven, unpublished paper, Cologne, 7/8 June.

VOBRUBA, G. (1990). 'Lohnarbeitszentrierte Sozialpolitik in der Krise der Lohnarbeit', in G. Vobruba (ed.), *Strukturwandel der Sozialpolitik*. Frankfurt: Suhrkamp.

WALKER, A. (1999). 'The Third Way for Pensions (by way of Thatcherism and Avoiding Today's Pensioners)', *Critical Social Policy*, 19(4): 511–27.

WALKER, R. (1999). 'The Americanization of British Welfare: A Case Study of Policy Transfer', *International Journal of Health Services*, 29(4): 679–97.

—— and Howard, M. (2000). *The Making of a Welfare Class?* Bristol: Policy Press, pp. 45–106.

—— and WISEMAN, M. (eds.) (2003). *The Welfare We Want? The British challenge for American reform*. Bristol: Policy Press.

WALTERS, W. (1997). 'The "active" society: new designs for social policy', *Policy and Politics*, 25(3): 221–34.

WARTH, L. (2004). 'The State as 'Enabler' of Enhanced Work—Family Reconciliation in Germany and the UK', paper presented at CCSW/ESPAnet conference, European welfare states: legitimacy and institutional change, Aalborg University, 1–3 October.

WEAVER, R. K. (1986). 'The politics of blame avoidance', *Journal of Public Policy*, 6: 371–89.

WEBBER, D. (1984). German Social Democracy in the Economic Crisis. Unemployment and Politics of Labour Market Policy in the Federal Republic of Germany from 1974 to 1982, Ph.D. thesis, University of Essex.

WENDT, C. (2003). *Krankenversicherung oder Gesundheitsversorgung? Gesundheitssysteme im Vergleich*. Wiesbaden: Westdeutscher Verlag.

WHITE, S. (ed.) (2001). *New Labour. The progressive future?* Houndmills: Palgrave

WHITESIDE, N. (1995). 'Employment Policy: A Chronicle of Decline?', in D. Gladstone (ed.), *British Social Welfare. Past, present and future*. London: University College London.

WICKS, M. (1995). 'New Deal for Families', *Guardian*, 21 June.

WIESENTHAL, H. (2003). 'German Unification and "Model Germany": An Adventure in Institutional Conservatism', *West European Politics*, 26(4): 37–58.

WIKELEY, N. J., OGUS, A. I., and BARENDT, E. (2002). *The Law of Social Security* (5th edition). London, Butterworths.

WILKINSON, M. (1993). 'British tax policy 1979–90: equity and efficiency', *Policy and Politics*, 21(3): 207–17.

WILLETS, D. (1989). 'The Family', in D. Kavanagh (ed.), *The Thatcher Effect*. Oxford: Clarendon, pp. 262–73.

WINTER, T. VON (1990). 'Die Sozialausschüsse der CDU. Sammelbecken für christdemokratische Arbeitnehmerinteressen oder linker Flügel einer Partei?', *Leviathan*, 18: 390–416.

WOOD, S. (2001a). 'Labour Market Regimes under Threat? Sources of Continuity in Germany, Britain, and Sweden', in P. Pierson (ed.) *The New Politics of the Welfare State*. Oxford: Oxford University Press, pp. 368–409.

—— (2001*b*). 'Business, Government, and Patterns of Labor Market Policy in Britain and the Federal Republic of Germany', in P. A. Hall and D. Soskice (eds.), *Varieties of Capitalism. The institutional foundations of comparative advantage*. Oxford: Oxford University Press, pp. 247–74.

ZOHLNHÖFER, R. (2001). 'Parteien, Vetospieler und der Wettbewerb um Wählerstimmen. Die Arbeitsmarkt- und Beschäftigungspolitik der Ära Kohl', *Politische Vierteljahresschrift*, 42(4): 655–82.

INDEX